AN IRISH

ATLANTIC

RAINFOREST

A Personal Journey into
the Magic of Rewilding

EOGHAN DALTUN

HACHETTE
BOOKS
IRELAND

First published in Ireland in 2022 by HACHETTE BOOKS IRELAND

A CIP catalogue record for this book is
available from the British Library.

ISBN 978 1 39970 527 1

Typeset in Sabon LT Std by Bookends Publishing Services, Dublin
Printed and bound in Great Britain by Clays Ltd, Elcograf, S.p.A.

With thanks to Cló Iar-Chonnacht for permission to use an
excerpt from 'Iascairí an Chladaigh' by Máirtín Ó Direáin.

Hachette Books Ireland policy is to use papers that are natural,
renewable and recyclable products and made from wood
grown in sustainable forests. The logging and manufacturing
processes are expected to conform to the environmental
regulations of the country of origin.

Hachette Books Ireland
8 Castlecourt Centre
Castleknock
Dublin 15, Ireland

A division of Hachette UK Ltd
Carmelite House, 50 Victoria Embankment, EC4Y 0DZ

www.hachettebooksireland.ie

To my two brilliant sons, Liam and Seán:
May your lives be filled with the beauty,
wonder and joy of all this, our living world.

Contents

1

Rainforest in the City

Sometimes I would wake in the morning to the very distinctive sound of monkeys whooping crazily in the distance. Not the sort of thing you expect close to the centre of a city like Dublin. This used to happen mostly early on Sundays, when there was little traffic about, and especially if conditions were misty and still, the semi-liquid air seeming to make the sound travel better. The roof light window of my upstairs bedroom had a distant but extensive view out over the Phoenix Park (where the monkeys lived in the city's zoo), and on such occasions I'd open it and spend some time looking out, the bottom of the window just the right height to place my arms on comfortably and rest the chin.

With the canopy of trees shrouded in mist to the visible horizon, and no sound other than the monkeys whooping it up, in those moments there was the very surreal feeling of being in a tropical rainforest, rather than a capital city.

Speaking of moments, there are some in life that afterwards stand out in the mind as having been pivotal, and one of those for me was – at my request – sitting by myself in a room in

the offices of Matheson Ormsby Prentice solicitors in Dublin
in 1993. I was fully kitted out in cycling gear, including black
skin-tight Lycra shorts and almost unwalkable cycle-racing
shoes. Strapped around my chest was a heavy Motorola two-
way radio, and a large black bag with the words 'Cyclone
Couriers' emblazoned across the front.

The reason I had asked for some time alone was because
my solicitor had just told me that he'd found out that the
vendor – a property developer – of a small plot of land I was
in the process of buying in the Kilmainham area had accrued
some very serious debts. The solicitor had further informed
me that, if I went ahead with the deal, there was a serious
risk the creditors could take the site, which would still be
registered in the seller's name for some time afterwards. So I
would end up with nothing, despite having paid for the land.
Therefore, should I still want to proceed, the solicitor would
need me to sign a typed statement saying that I had been fully
advised of the risks, and had decided to chance it regardless,
although those were probably not the precise words used.

The money to buy the piece of land was on loan from my
mother, and was pretty much everything she had, an inheritance
from her father. This was definitely *not* a decision to be taken
lightly: it would need a great many years on my wages as a
bicycle courier to pay her back if it all went wrong. So I had
asked the solicitor for some time by myself to weigh it all up
in my mind. As I sat there for what seemed much longer than
the half an hour or so the clock registered, I reflected carefully
on the possible disastrous consequences of such a reckless act
as buying under these circumstances.

But I also considered the potential I saw in the site in
question, the fact that the available funds wouldn't stretch

to much else, and that this would be the first time since I was born that there would be a fixed physical space on which rent wouldn't have to be continually paid. So I signed the solicitor's statement and the sale went ahead. A trainee in the law firm was given the task of registering the deeds in my name as urgently as possible, and after a very anxious ten days or so I was told it had all gone through without mishap.

The site I had bought contained the ruins of an old stone cottage, dating back to at least the middle of the eighteenth century, when Kilmainham was still open countryside (the cottage features on John Roque's map of 1756, the first detailed map ever made of Dublin). The area was only swallowed up by the city in the 1950s and '60s, but is now quite central. It sat at the top of a steep hill – the steepest in Dublin, I afterwards came to learn – overlooking the Royal Hospital, historic Kilmainham gaol, and the Phoenix Park, the largest in any European capital. It was close enough to the Guinness brewery over in James's Street to be often within range of the distinctively pungent, but reassuringly familiar, smell of fermented barley, wafting on the breeze.

My plan was to dismantle the stones from the cottage and then reuse them to build a new one, but in the same spot, of the same dimensions, and in a similar vernacular style to the original. The new house would, however, have a modern damp-proof course and high levels of insulation, creating a space that retained the aesthetics of traditional architecture without being damp or cold to live in, as so many old stone buildings are in Ireland.

But the land had also been used for decades as a dumping ground for builders' earth, rubble and assorted rubbish. This material came mainly from excavating foundations for extensions built onto a terrace of 1940s ex-council houses along the rear boundary. The result was that, behind the front wall of the ruined cottage – which ran right along the public footpath – most of the site was buried under a huge mound several metres deep. So the first task was to hand-dig and wheelbarrow away all that material into a succession of builders' skips in the street, hired for the purpose.

At the bottom of the hill was a pub named Carrigan's, and on one occasion two old codgers passing by on their way home after a few pints stopped to ask what I was doing. Upon hearing my explanation, with a mixture of amusement and disbelief one of them dramatically threw his head back, slapped his hand to his forehead and cried out, 'Oh, to be young again!'

After a couple of months of intense weekend digging, often helped by friends, a holiday seemed in order. So I took myself off to Prague for six months, hoping to teach English, drink a share of the excellent Czech *pivo* (beer), and generally have a good time as a means of gathering strength for the house-building trials and privations to come. Arriving in the city with just an old canvas rucksack I had picked up several years before in a Paris flea market, and the phone number of a friend of a friend, I quickly landed a teaching job at a language school in the city centre. I found good accomplices in seeking fun and adventure there among the other teachers, who mostly hailed from various other parts of the English-speaking world.

We had some great times, with numerous blissfully languorous picnics in a hillside orchard overlooking the Vltava River, the spires of St Vitus's Cathedral, and the red-tiled rooftops of the old town. There was a memorable camping trip in Bohemia's Český ráj, to the northeast of the city, a protected area of forests interspersed with naturally carved volcanic rock pillars. Sleeping tentless around a stick fire, I remember the flames flickering in warming solidarity with the stars above the silhouetted treetops all around.

Sometimes I used to go exploring in an area of ancient ruined cottages covering a couple of acres in the historic area of Prague where I was living, Vršovice. Although relatively centrally located, just like the Kilmainham cottage they had evidently been built when the area was still rural. I was motivated by curiosity about traditional building styles and techniques, the recesses of my brain being still deeply engaged with the building project to come once I returned to Dublin.

But while doing so one day, I became aware of a phenomenon that had never entered my consciousness before. Trees were growing everywhere throughout the ruins, and clearly hadn't been planted by human hands, but had instead sprouted spontaneously of their own volition. I remember talking to a friend about it later, saying that to create a natural forest, all it would take would be to leave land alone and it would happen all by itself. That thought was to stay put for the time being, but a seed had been sown in the back of my mind.

The idyllic Prague interlude over, I returned to Dublin and threw myself once again into clearing the site in Kilmainham, continuing to teach English as a foreign language to cover costs. Digging out the great mass of earth, which filled a dozen or more six-ton skips, I retained any pieces of the original building stone I came across, stacking them at the back of the site for use in the new house I'd be constructing. The whole process was fascinating in an almost archaeological sense, and, as I got down to the remains of the old back wall and floor, I found pieces of unburned turf still in the fireplace, and all manner of other objects from the cottage.

Older residents of the area told me that the last inhabitant had been a petite elderly woman with wispy white hair by the name of Molly Maughan, who still wore the traditional black shawl over her shoulders and a long skirt that reached to the ground. For years, every morning the neighbours living in the terrace to the rear would witness the same ritual at Molly's place. Her arm would appear out of the one very narrow slit window in the back of the cottage with a teapot in hand, turn it upside down dumping the used tea leaves onto the ground below, and withdraw back inside. Many people still remembered Molly in her shawl at the half-door of her whitewashed cottage, a smell of turf smoke hanging over the whole scene. The repeated refrain was that it was more like a vision from west Donegal, or somewhere else along the Atlantic, rather than Dublin city.

One half of the roof collapsed in the 1970s, and for a time Molly continued to live in the remaining one of the cottage's original two rooms. She was eventually moved into an old folks' home (very reluctantly, by all accounts), after which the rest of the roof fell in, and the earth mountain began to accumulate. Molly passed away some time in the 1980s. The land at the back of the house, which was to become my garden, was previously part of a long sloping field where, through the 1950s and '60s, vegetables were grown for sale in a grocer's shop on the street running along the bottom, Old Kilmainham. From what I was able to gather, the field and shop were a one-man operation, run by a character who coincidentally bore the colourfully distinctive moniker of 'Duckser' Dalton.

Dismantling the existing walls of the cottage was a continuation of the archaeological exercise. As is usual in old stone walls, the construction technique had involved creating two walls in one: an outer face and an inner one, tied together with occasional long 'through stones', which extended from one face to the other. Everywhere else, there was a void between the two faces, into which the builders had thrown all types of unwanted material as filling, creating a kind of 250-year-old time capsule. Even if there was no treasure in the contents, there was still a thrill in the knowledge that I was the first person to lay eyes on them after so long. I also pictured the people who would have been building the house, at a time when Irish was still likely to have been spoken locally, and in my mind the work I was doing established a certain bond of sorts over the centuries.

The objects I found in the cavities included numerous fragments of rough pottery and centimetre-thick green bottle glass. Sometimes I'd find the long twisted horns of cattle that must have resembled what we would now recognise as the Highland breed. Tantalisingly, they would look perfectly intact, but when picked up would practically disintegrate in the hand, their structure weakened by the passage of time. The masonry was of the local rubble – i.e. not dressed with a chisel – limestone called 'calp', and it was clear from their irregularly eroded forms that most of the stones had been picked from the surrounding fields, rather than quarried. The mortar between them was simply clay, without lime, animal hair, or any other apparent binding agent.

Pieces of the long, delicate, traditional clay smoking pipes of past centuries – known as *dúidíns*, resembling fibulae in their whiteness and frailty – were liberally scattered through the surrounding earth. Their bowls, with insides still blackened from use, often had emblems such as crowns or shamrocks decorating the front, seemingly a common way of demonstrating political outlook back then. Among a plethora of other objects that turned up was an iron cannonball of about 10 centimetres in diameter.

Reading up on the local history, I learned that Kilmainham had had an extremely rich and motley past down through the ages. There were connections to Vikings, Brian Boru (a high king of Ireland in the early eleventh century) and the Order of Knights Hospitallers, which had a priory on the present site of the Royal Hospital. The area also featured prominently in the 1916 Rising – both the actual fighting itself, some of which took place on my very street, and its aftermath, with sixteen of the leaders subsequently executed by firing squad in Kilmainham gaol.

The road is now a side street to a major artery, the South Circular Road, wide at that end and narrowing greatly as it drops down to meet Old Kilmainham. But it predates all the surrounding streets by a thousand years or more, and was once part of the principal route from Dublin to the west of the country, going right back to medieval times and probably beyond. When I was there, many of the older people living in the area still called the street by its original name, Watery Lane, which came from a natural spring that continues to seep out of the retaining wall on the other side of the road, down the hill a little from the cottage. They did so despite its name being officially changed around 1900 to the more genteel-sounding Brookfield Road, as it's presently known.

Other locals, perhaps with a different focus in life, preferred to call it 'Carrigan's Hill' after the pub.

Building the house was a labour of love, but also entailed living the life of a penitential hermit for several years. While all my friends were dedicating their lives to more normal pursuits like girls, travelling, careers, and partying (we were in our mid-twenties), my existence had taken on one purpose only: either teaching to make money for house materials, or working on the house. Most of them – probably rightly – thought I had lost the plot altogether.

It was all done on an absolute shoestring, with much of the material scavenged from skips or salvage yards, which were still very cheap. The skips, which I came across while cycling around the city, provided especially rich pickings in the form of old doors with hand-forged iron hinges and thumb latches, which I prised off and carried home in a rucksack-turned-swagbag. All the house's internal doors were made from old tongue-and-groove floorboards a neighbour was throwing away, and fitted entirely with this liberated antique ironmongery.

The central supporting element of the spiral staircase was a thick, undulating tree trunk I managed to source from a tree surgeon, the idea inspired by a similar arrangement I had seen in a centuries-old farmhouse outside Prague. I cut the stair treads that jointed into it from the scaffolding planks I used while building the walls, which in turn had previously been old floor joists, salvaged somewhere or other. The light switches and sockets were 1960s Bakelite units I managed to pick up, arousing incredulity on the part of the Electricity Supply Board representative, and greatly complicating efforts to get connected to the mains. All the many presses were made from free wooden pallets passed over the wall to me on a forklift from the printing press next door. The entire house was built in that same spirit, rough and rounded, trying to recapture the organic essence of vernacular architecture.

In those years, my daily routine was a strict combination of teaching at Portobello College, Rathmines, and working on the house. After teaching all morning, I'd cycle back down the Grand Canal from the language school straight to the site and change, Clark Kent style, out of my jacket, shirt and tie into scruffy work clothes in an old caravan I had placed at the rear of the site. I would then work for the rest of the day until it began to get dark, which might be nearing 10 o'clock during the long summer evenings.

While teaching, I'd sometimes catch my students staring with shock at the ingrained dirt under the nails of their otherwise fairly presentable teacher. On non-teaching days I was on site from morning to night, and was very fortunate throughout that time to have help from a bunch of friends of fairly 'eclectic' appearance. The resulting scenes were watched with great amusement and curiosity by the people living in the street and wider area, who seemed to view the whole thing as pure spectacle, laid on especially for their entertainment.

Such investments of time, energy, creativity and love, while mostly single-handedly building the house, couldn't but give rise to a very powerful sense of attachment to this small plot of ground. They produced an equally strong feeling of connection to its past, not just that of the site itself, but of the surrounding area. When we picture how things might once have been, we generally tend to think in mostly human terms. And so I'd often imagine what the place and its people would have been like 50 years previously, or a hundred, two hundred, and so on, going right back to St Maighneann, who established a church there in the early seventh century. (The name Kilmainham originated as an Anglicisation of *Cill Mhaighneann*, or 'Chapel of Maighneann'.)

But my mind would also frequently go back even further in time, to how the steep valley below must have looked before people ever settled it at all. The land running down to the Camac River, and the Liffey valley beyond, would once have been covered in thick forest, with massive old oaks, elms, ash and a great variety of other native trees, inhabited by a complex weave of native wildlife. Once people arrived, the picture would have slowly started to change, as our ancestors hunted out the animals and began clearing the trees for farms. That process of change would have continued at an ever-accelerating pace down through the ages, as expanding technologies gave us increased power to shape the environment according to a human vision.

While hand-digging foundations into the undisturbed boulder clay beneath (with a fractured finger, the result of a bicycle accident – 'Oh, to be young again!'), I had plenty of time to ponder the fact that this layer of material had been deposited by glacial action during the Pleistocene era. Mountainous sheets of ice, as much as a kilometre thick, had scraped, crushed, ground, scoured, scooped, pushed, carried, and finally dumped a mineral blanket over the living limestone bedrock, perhaps three or four metres below.

By accessing these strata, I was more than just digging a hole. I was reaching into another time capsule, this one untouched for tens or even hundreds of thousands of years. On occasion I reflected on what lay below the lithospheric upper crust of the land: the liquid magma of the Earth's interior. I was beginning to perceive the landscape around me and under me in ecological and geological terms and time frames, rather than just those structured around the narrow window of time that is a human life.

At the back of the house I was building, there was space for a small raised garden, and it seemed a good idea to plant it during construction, so that everything would have more time to mature. Large old fuchsia and lilac bushes were already present, and I wanted to add a few trees. It occurred to me that putting in native species would be best, so I spent a little time looking into which ones would be small enough for my city garden. I ended up planting a mixture of bare-root whitethorn (hawthorn), hazel, blackthorn, spindle and bird cherry saplings. I hoped this choice would be good for wildlife, while at the same time providing some privacy, and also strengthening with their roots a steep bank sloping down to the car park of the printing press next door, which had partially collapsed the previous winter during heavy rain.

As soon as I had the roof, with a covering of salvaged natural slates, on the house, I moved in, sleeping upstairs in a beat-up old army sleeping bag on unfixed floorboards among bags of plaster, tins of paint, and a hodge-podge of other materials and tools. It may have been rough, but it was *my* rough, and for the first time in my life. During that time living in and working on the house, there were many enduring moments, like looking out over the Dublin 'rainforest' with monkey calls echoing through the mist. Or lying in my sleeping bag at night and overhearing snippets of drunken conversation and laughter only yards away through the as yet unsealed roof, as people passed by on their way home from Carrigan's.

To heat the place, I picked up a second-hand Jøtul cast-iron stove. I later discovered that the particular model had been designed in collaboration with the Norwegian writer, anti-Nazi resistance member, adventurer and ethnographer Thor Heyerdahl (best known for his fantastic book *Kon-Tiki*). Amazingly, it had been designed to imitate the enormous monolithic Easter Island statues, the moai, which were carved from volcanic rock and erected around the island's coasts by the Polynesian inhabitants. Once installed, the stove was a dominating presence, its chiselled countenance throwing stern looks out over the sitting room area, and warming the whole house through the winter.

Towards the end of working on the house, on a few occasions I found myself having a verging-on-heated discussion with passers-by in the street. Many of them believed it was the original centuries-old house I was working on, and adamantly refused to accept that it was a complete reconstruction from the ground up. In the end I decided not to waste any more time trying to convince anyone, and instead to see it as a compliment of sorts that I had at least got something right with regard to authenticity. One of my more erudite friends described the house as 'idiosyncratic', and being only vaguely familiar with the word at the time, I again took it as praise, but of a more classy form.

At the time of writing, the cottage features on the online National Inventory of Architectural Heritage, which lists it as dating from 1760 to 1800. The profile description, which is complete with recent photos, reads:

This modest vernacular house is significant as an example of a traditional style of architecture which is increasingly rare in an urban context. It retains much of its original form and fabric, its small windows and high roof-pitch more characteristic of its rural counterparts than urban dwellings. Its painted rubble stone walls would originally have been whitewashed and provide a pleasing contrast to the predominant use of red brick on the street, making this a focal point on the streetscape.

It's hard not to smile looking at that now.

Working with the old stone on the house brought about a realisation that all my life there had been a love of stone as a material. My mother told me of trips to the sea when I was four or five, where I'd run up and down the beach shoving pebbles into the pockets of my duffel coat, excitedly repeating the mantra 'Stone! Stone!', and she would end up having to carry me and the laden-down duffel coat home. When travelling in my teens and early twenties, I had often humped home largish stones eroded into especially striking forms from the places I visited, a habit I have never managed to shake.

Among the dozens of stones in the house where I live now is a saucer-sized fragment of pink-red sandstone, shotblasted into a pitted Klingon battle cruiser by the sand-laden winds of the Sinai Desert; a globulous shrapnel mass of purplish lava, cooled on the slopes of Mount Vesuvius; a natural limestone Henry Moore, its chiaroscuro volumes and voids weathered by millennia of Burren sea-rain; a limestone oblong dug from the Kilmainham subsoil, peppered with a standing-proud-of-the-surface mishmash of the fossils of ancient tropical sea creatures; a meteoritic-looking fragment of the Westmeath cottage my father's family lived in; a chunk of smoothly rounded, and deeply gryked, black basalt, resembling a segment of giant iron walnut; and so on, ad infinitum. Collectively, they have always symbolised for me the raw stuff from which our planet is hewn, and by extension the wondrous living whole into which it has developed over billions of years.

I spent several years handling the rough Dublin 'calp' of the cottage, lifting, appraising and rejecting many of the thousands of pieces perhaps a dozen times or more before finding the right resting place. Again, there was a profoundly satisfying temporal symmetry in reusing the same stones with which the original cottage had been built centuries before. Working gloveless, throughout that time I was without fingerprints, their micro-ridges completely abraded away to leave featureless smooth pads.

The allure of stone as a material, reawoken by prolonged physical contact, now coalesced with an earlier passion for making sculpture in metal into a keen desire to learn the art of carving sculpture in stone. On looking into it, I discovered that probably the best place in the world to do that was a small town in Tuscany named Carrara. My intention had always been to head abroad for an extended period once the house was finished, and rent it out as a means of paying off the money I had borrowed from my mum to buy the site. And, after the monkish existence I had been leading for the previous few years, a dose of Italy was hugely appealing.

Long before leaving, though, I already knew I'd be selling the Kilmainham cottage to move to the country at some point. I didn't yet know where, only that it would be in Ireland, and somewhere I could continue to enjoy a strong attachment to place, but on a much heightened scale in the extent of land, its content and surroundings. As an aid to 'research' into just where I might eventually end up, I bought myself a copy of *Atlas of the Irish Rural Landscape*, a very comprehensive work recently published by Cork University Press, covering just about every aspect of rural Ireland. On only page four was a prominent image of a spectacularly sculptural rocky eminence, with the unforgettable name of Hungry Hill.

It's the highest point of a mountainous southwestern peninsula called Beara, which protrudes finger-like from west Cork and Kerry into the Atlantic.

2

Soggiorno italiano

Carrara is a small town in the foothills of the Apuan Alps in the northwestern corner of Tuscany, looking out over the Mediterranean. The landscape, history, dialect and accent of the area are unique, being quite distinct from the rest of Tuscany, or anywhere else in Italy.

Right back to Roman times, the town has attracted sculptors on account of the quality of the white marble in the surrounding quarries. Michelangelo, Bernini, Canova and many others frequented the place over the centuries, often living and working in what remains a Mecca for sculptors from all over the world. Other than an awareness that it was *the* place to learn to carve in stone and marble, I knew nothing about it when I arrived in September 1998 with just the usual old rucksack on my back. Nor did I speak a word of Italian, or have any contacts there.

But the people of the town were open and friendly, and I very soon fell in with an international bunch of other wannabe sculptors. Most of us were enrolled at the town's *Scuola del Marmo* (Marble School), which trained local artisans to work in the many sculpture studios dotted around the area. We led a pretty bohemian life that, apart from learning how to carve sculpture, involved cooking lots of big dinners together, drinking plenty of red wine and long discussions into the early hours about art, culture, history, philosophy and life in general. We spoke a very rudimentary Italian among ourselves, despite the fact that none of us was Italian, thereby passing on our many grammatical errors to everyone else in the group. But none of that mattered: we were there doing what we wanted to, and with much passion and *joie de vivre*.

One of the most memorable first impressions of Carrara was the sight, visible throughout the zone, of what initially looked like snow covering some of the higher points of the surrounding mountains, even in summer. In reality, this was the discarded rubble spoils from the marble quarries, which were simply bulldozed down the mountainsides. In the evening, the setting sun would reflect off these white tracts, lighting the mountains up in deep, glowing hues of tangerine or rose.

The apartment where I lived at first was in Via Caffaggio, an old, fairly rough part of town, and outside my bedroom was a balcony overlooking the bell tower of the eleventh-century Romanesque *duomo* (cathedral). Countless happy hours were spent there sitting in the sun, reading and listening to the sounds of life emanating from the jumble of dwellings all around and the streets below. There was a sense of living cheek by jowl with the neighbours here, and in the warmer months when everyone's windows stayed open day and night it often felt like communal living, with everybody able to hear everyone else's conversations, rows and everything else.

This became my life for the following seven years, punctuated with summers spent back in Ireland. At the start of my second year in Carrara, I got a place in the most famous sculpture studio in the town, Nicoli's, not as an employee but by paying a nominal monthly fee for a space in which to carve my own sculptures. There I was able to learn continually from the experienced artisans and artists working around me. The previous year's apartment had been let to someone else while I was away, so I found a house in Viale Potrignano on the outskirts, where I lived for the next few years. It was high on the side of town that rose up towards the mountains, and looked down on the rooftops of the old town below.

Built in the seventeenth century, it was essentially a tall and narrow freestanding stone tower, with just one big open space on each floor. The house was surrounded by a very large, old and semi-wild garden, with a profusion of fruit trees and all manner of other greenery. My bedroom consisted of the top floor, and from the biggest, west-facing window I could see the sea, while those on the southern and eastern sides looked down respectively on the old town and up at the mountains. A Mexican friend who was studying sculpture in the town's academy of fine arts moved into the floor downstairs, and we shared the ground floor where there was a kitchen and eating area that opened out onto a terrazzo in the surrounding garden.

What I liked most about that house was its easy access to the countryside nearby. Within only a minute's walk from the front door through the garden was an old cobbled mule path that zigzagged steeply up through abandoned olive groves on the slopes of the hill of Monte d'Armi, beyond which were the mountains. Through decades of disuse, the land under and around the twisted and wrinkled old olive trees, each one a sculpture in its own right, had gone wild. It was sheer bliss to regularly head up there with a blanket, a good book, some *focaccina* bread, maybe olives and tomatoes and a bottle of water (or wine, occasionally), and spend the day sprawled in the sun among a profusion of wild flowers and plants.

Nobody else ever seemed to go there, and I would find myself immersed in a private world full of the buzzing of myriad funky-looking insects, the rich perfumes of the *erbette* (the wild herbs that grew all around), and exotically coloured birds such as green woodpeckers. It was like stepping into the magic realism of an Henri Rousseau nature painting, minus the big cats. In late spring, my favourite time of the year there, as night fell the *lucciole* (fireflies) would make their appearance, like dozens of glowing embers dancing in the darkness. It was during this time that I also met and fell in love with Giuliana, the woman who would become my wife and the mother of my two sons.

Over the course of seven years in Carrara, I got to know the surrounding Alpi Apuane. Sometimes I would simply walk out the door and up Monte d'Armi, over 'la Rocchetta' beyond, and carry on all day without stopping until reaching the high ridge of Campocecina, at about 1,350 metres above sea level. From there on a clear day the island of Corsica is visible, floating distantly in the sparkling Mediterranean. Other days myself and friends would drive farther afield into the mountains and spend the day hiking.

In contrast to the more ancient, and thus mostly lower and much more round-topped, mountains of Ireland, these were truly alpine in form, towering straight up from the generally flattish land near the sea. Also in contrast to Irish mountains, which are (now) almost all devoid of trees, apart from quadrangular blocks of lifeless non-native conifer plantations, the mountains near Carrara were clothed in thick deciduous forest, right up to the natural treeline, not far below the peaks.

As I became more familiar with the mountains, I began to perceive the hundreds of marble quarries dotted around, and their associated infrastructure, in a very different, and much less romantic, light. At first, like most visitors to the region, I had been enthralled by the spectacularly unique landscapes created by the excavations. The quarries follow the veins of better-quality marble, and might plunge hundreds of metres below ground level, carving out deep underground chasms. Others have hollowed out the insides of entire mountains, leaving only an outer shell. Venturing inside one of these husks reveals a cathedral of glistening wet stone, scores of metres high, the roof supported by remaining pillars of 'living' marble. Elsewhere whole mountaintops have just been cut away, leaving only stumps, alternately roasted in the hot sun or frozen by thick mountain mists.

The more time I passed in the wilder, more pristine parts of the mountains, the more I came to see the many quarries as open wounds on the landscape. The native *carrarini* I knew spoke to me of seeing whole mountains, in whose shadow they had grown up, vanish over the course of only a few decades, in exchange for a detritus of rusting machinery and toxic chemicals in the drinking water. Until the 1960s, the extraction of marble blocks was a slow and hugely laborious process, but accelerated exponentially after that with the introduction of new technologies, particularly the diamond cutting wire. Five million tons are now removed annually, and more marble has been taken out in just the last two decades than in the previous 2,000 years.

Enormous areas of one of the most stunningly beautiful mountain ranges in Europe have been, and continue to be, rapidly transformed into industrial wastelands by the quarrying. Only an infinitesimally tiny proportion of the marble extracted is used for the artistic purposes that had drawn me to Italy. The vast bulk is sawn into thin slabs for use as cladding in buildings all around the world, or ground into powder as an additive to a wide range of consumer products, from ceramics to toothpaste. After a few years in Carrara, it became quite bizarre to recall just how enchanted I had once been by the quarried landscape and its history.

The richness and diversity of the area's flora and fauna, as well as its natural beauty, led to the designation in 1979 of much of the Apuan Alps as one of Italy's regional parks. Numerous factors have created a natural mosaic of fascinating and contrasting microhabitats: variations in altitude, an orientation towards or away from the sea, or sun, differences in the underlying geology, and so on. Inhabiting them are many rare, and even endemic (not found anywhere else), species, along with a range of wild mammals, such as boar, squirrels, pine marten, foxes, badgers and mouflon. In the last decade or so, both wolves and red deer have begun to spread in naturally from other zones, while at least 300 different species of birds inhabit the region, including golden eagles. Away from the quarries and roads, there is a feeling of real expansive wilderness, in which you can walk all day and encounter little that isn't natural.

Throughout my life I had always loved spending time in nature whenever the opportunity presented itself. In the area where I lived most as a child, Rathmines in Dublin, there seemed to be no shortage of the old ruined mansions and grounds of a departed gentry. They were essentially pieces of waste ground, but retained what had by then become incongruously regal-sounding names like 'Lady Longford's'. Filled with broken sculpture, exotic trees and bamboo plantations gone wild, they were the favoured and most constant playgrounds of myself and friends for years, places free of any adult supervision where there were no limits to our imagination.

But those many exquisite days on Monte d'Armi, or walking in the surrounding Apuan Alps, were an introduction to an altogether new level of intensity in the deep sense of well-being and joy that can come from being in a wild or even semi-natural environment. That time aroused in me a visceral need for regular personal contact with nature in as raw a state as possible that has never left, and never will.

After the year at Nicoli Studios, I began a four-year course in the conservation and restoration of sculpture at the *Accademia di Belle Arti di Carrara* – the Academy of Fine Arts, housed in buildings some of which date back to the twelfth century. The course was run in collaboration with the *Opificio delle Pietre Dure*, a Florentine institution with a world-famous reputation in art conservation, and I was very lucky to get a place. Myself and other students had the opportunity to observe at first hand pieces by Michelangelo, Donatello, Jacopo della Quercia and other master sculptors being conserved and restored during regular visits to the *Opificio* workshops in Florence. A Dublin Corporation mature student grant paid my fees throughout the four years of the course, and gave me a little extra to live on. A few evenings per week teaching English at a local language school made up the rest.

Every summer would take me back to Ireland, and after the first few years I was able to spend them back in the cottage in Kilmainham, as the teacher who was renting had no need of it during the school holidays. Most of the native trees I had planted were growing away vigorously, turning into a mini-forest and attracting plenty of wild songbirds. Only ever seeing the trees over a single season made their development seem much more dramatic year on year, and checking on how they had come on became one of the absolute highlights of coming home.

Often I would be asked by a Dublin-based sculpture conservator and friend, Jason Ellis, to help out on projects in various parts of the country. Doing so suited me perfectly for a range of reasons, not least that I still had in mind to move out of Dublin eventually, and this was as good a way as any of getting to know some of the places where I might want to live. But the more I thought about it, the more it became clear to me that what I was really looking for was somewhere very wild and near the sea, and to my mind that meant just one thing: the Atlantic coast.

The garden in Kilmainham had brought a realisation that trees would figure very prominently in the future I had in mind. While in Italy, I read for the first time, and was deeply affected by, *The Man Who Planted Trees* by Jean Giono, a classic work of fiction published in 1953. The book tells the story of a man who spends most of his life seeding oak and other native species into a lifeless and no longer inhabited valley, returning its lost forests, which in turn allows communities of people to come back. My own plan back then was to buy some land, plant lots of native saplings, and watch them grow into a forest over the years, just as in my Dublin garden but on a much larger scale.

Around that time I came across a feature in a magazine about an artist couple named Ian and Lynn Wright, who had been doing just that on their 80 acres near Skibbereen in west Cork. Some weeks later I was working with Jason and another colleague and friend, Miriam Hennessy, to restore the wonderfully ornate twelfth-century Romanesque portal at Clonfert, County Galway. And by the sort of coincidence that is so common in Ireland, it turned out that Miriam knew Lynn and Ian well. She got permission for me to visit, and they very kindly spent most of a day showing Giuliana and me what they had been doing with their land.

I was utterly astonished by what I saw there. In addition to the many thousands of native trees they had planted, Lynn and Ian had created wildflower meadows, three lakes and six smaller ponds. Otters, ducks, herons and an assortment of other wildlife had, over time, moved in of their own accord. To see a living, working example showing that it was actually possible to give land back to nature in this way was an incredible inspiration to me at the time.

Returning to the southwest the following year, again with Giuliana, I visited the Beara Peninsula for the first time. With its epic landscape, I had never seen anywhere in Ireland so stunningly beautiful, despite, for example, spending many childhood summers not far away on the Dingle Peninsula. The natural rock formations were sheer sculpture to my eyes, and, owing to several factors I was unaware of at the time, the area was far less spoiled than many others of comparable scenery in the west.

And for me there was another special appeal to this section of the coast: pockets of wild native trees seemed more common in the less exposed parts of the peninsula than anywhere else I had seen in Ireland. The friendliness of the people (and the creamy pints of Guinness in MacCarthy's bar in Castletownbere – surprisingly much better than in Dublin) clinched it, and the search for a future place to live narrowed to the Beara.

When the conservation course at the Carrara academy of fine arts ended, I leaped straight into an MLitt research degree in art history with Trinity College Dublin, again funded by the 'corpo'. The particular types of medieval sculpture my research was focused on are found mainly in Romanesque *pievi* (parish churches) in isolated and often mountainous rural parts of Tuscany and beyond. And so I spent most of my seventh and final year in Italy driving my little battered old Fiat Panda around remote country lanes, photographing thousands of pieces of architectural sculpture and filling writing pads with copious scribbled notes.

Many of these places had been largely abandoned by their younger inhabitants, who had been leaving in droves since the 1960s to seek 'better' lives in the big towns and cities. There was something very sad in seeing dozens of villages that had clearly once been centres of thriving communities right back to medieval times, now reduced to just a handful of elderly residents. Most of the beautiful old stone houses were either lying empty or were used only fitfully as holiday homes by affluent owners from northern Italy and elsewhere.

But one of the side-effects of the big drop in the number of people working the land was that it had enabled nature to come flooding back. Wild native forests had sprung up naturally where previously they had been absent, echoing what I had seen in Prague. And those forests in turn had attracted a great wealth and variety of wildlife, including boar, deer, wolves and a host of other species, which were able to migrate in from other regions. Just as in the Wrights' place in west Cork, once the natural habitat was there, everything else followed. It seemed a terrible pity that the people had had to leave to allow this to happen, and I wondered if it might not be possible to make the return of nature instead actually play a contributing role in revitalising declining rural communities.

Only ten days after the birth of our first son Liam, Giuliana and I moved with him and her teenage son by a previous marriage, Andri, from Italy to the cottage in Kilmainham. There was a mixture of some tough and very wonderful times ahead.

3

The Heist

Moving back to Dublin in September 2005 was a system shock for us all, on so many levels. After seven years in Italy, to me it felt like the city had transformed from the relaxed, provincially atmosphered town I was familiar with into a frantic metropolis. The boom economy that was in full swing at the time had driven up property prices to the extent that most people I knew were no longer able to live centrally as before, but had had to move out to distant suburbs or far beyond to be able to afford a place to live. Rather than being able to hop on my bicycle and be at a friend's door in five or ten minutes as I used to, catching up now generally required getting in the car and driving on jam-packed roads for an hour or more each way.

Even the mood on my street had shifted, for many of the mainly elderly residents had passed away or been moved into old folks' homes, their houses now occupied by younger professionals in a remarkably fast generational turnover. Although by and large fine people, the latter were all extremely busy with their lives and careers, and there was rarely time for the sort of relaxed banter I had been accustomed to enjoying with neighbours while building the house.

The printing press next door to the cottage had upped and moved to a less central location, and the 0.7-acre site sold to developers. Just before our return from Italy, the new owners had put in a planning application for a large, high-density apartment complex. Under the proposal, where our windows looked out over the trees of the Royal Hospital and the Phoenix Park – the city rainforest – they would now be hemmed in by an unbroken blank wall only a couple of metres away, and towering up two storeys. This wall was to run right along the full extent of the boundary, blocking any western afternoon or evening light from reaching either the cottage or the garden. As if that wasn't enough, at the top of this block would be a roof garden, so we'd have the added pleasure of our new neighbours looking almost directly down on us from a great height above.

Incredibly, Dublin City Council ignored our written objections and those of neighbours and granted permission for the development to go ahead. I spent weeks working on an appeal to An Bord Pleanála – the 'high court' in the planning process. Against all the odds, it succeeded and the council's decision was overturned, with the application refused outright (seemingly a rare occurrence). But I knew it was only a matter of time before another application went in and the battle would resume. What we were up against was just another phase in the relentless passage that had taken the landscape from thick wild forest to fields, to semi-rural, and was now heading rapidly towards concrete jungle. Dublin's skyline at this time had become another 'forest': of construction cranes, each one indicating a major new building project.

I was also trying to juggle the pressures of a family life that included a young baby and a teenage stepson with little

English, writing my thesis, working to earn a living for my new family, and building a wooden conservatory onto the house to gain much-needed space. So to say that those were stressful times would be putting it mildly. Practically every aspect of life was in total contrast to the far more relaxed pace we had been used to in Italy. Unsurprisingly, Andri quickly decided that none of this was for him, and at the end of the school year he returned to Carrara to live with his dad.

Over that first winter and spring I was engaged on a large project in Cork as assistant to Jason, restoring the ogham stone collection at the university there, and was home only at weekends. I would often then spend an hour or more sitting in the new conservatory with Liam on my knee, looking out at the trees I had planted in the garden years before. Watching the wild birds flitting between them, I dreamed of living somewhere more tranquil, with a closer relationship to the natural world.

There were of course still (and always will be) plenty of wonderful things about Dublin: the proximity of the sea, the Wicklow Mountains, the Phoenix Park, for example, as well as good friends and all the familiar faces and places of the city itself. But there were now no doubts remaining in our minds about moving out, and Beara was still the preferred destination if we could only find the right place. We began making occasional trips to the peninsula and exploring its various localities, often driving around checking out properties the local auctioneers had up for sale.

I was looking for a piece of land of at least several acres, preferably near the sea, which had the right feel to it. Whether there was a house, or what condition that might be in, was of far lesser concern as this could be altered over time, while the underlying characteristics of the land and its setting could not. For Giuliana, the most essential criteria were not to be too far from a village, shops and schools.

It quickly became clear that the places we saw for sale that were most appealing held one thing in common: they were all pieces of land that had been left unfarmed for a longish period, during which time they'd gone wild. In most of them, native trees had naturally popped up all around, just as I had seen in Prague and Tuscany. I was beginning to realise that it might not be necessary to plant any trees after all, and that, with luck, I'd be able to find somewhere with ready-made wild forest. But after briefly and unsuccessfully pursuing one or two such spots, I decided to temporarily park the search, since I had begun extending the cottage in Kilmainham again, and we had a second baby son, Seán.

This extension was a much more intense project than the conservatory had been, not least because it involved digging out a large section of the raised garden even before foundations could be excavated. As there was no access for a machine, this again all had to be done by hand, and the spoils barrowed out through the side gate to another series of skips in the street. There was more than a slight feeling of déjà vu about it all, and I was starting to seriously wonder whether swinging a pick and shovel in hard Kilmainham clay was to be my eternal destiny.

Another requirement was demolishing one wall of the kitchen, as well as taking off its roof, and so for a time we had no kitchen area at all. Giuliana sensibly took herself and the boys off to Italy for about six weeks to escape the very worst of it. When they returned, the roof was back on, but the place was still up in a heap, with dust everywhere and only a mini camping gas stove for cooking.

It was July 2008, and we decided to have a holiday in Beara, with the agreed intention of avoiding looking at any places on the market this time, given the state of the house in Dublin. But during the long drive down, a farm that had been up for sale for some time near Eyeries on the north side of the peninsula came into my mind, and refused to leave. The auctioneer, J.J. O'Sullivan, had posted me the details, my having left word about the type of thing we were looking for. There were over 33 acres of ground, plus almost another 40 of mountain commonage, an old ruined farmhouse and what looked from J.J.'s brochure like a decent view out to sea.

I had spoken to J.J. on the phone about the place a couple of times over the preceding months, but it seemed that several parties had been bidding against one another and pushing the price up quite high. And since I was also in the middle of tearing asunder the house in Kilmainham, I had let it slide. The thought must have remained in the back of my mind though, and I realised now that I was curious enough to want to at least take a look. So we agreed to make this one exception.

Calling into J.J.'s premises on Castletownbere's main square, he told us that the farm had been temporarily taken off the market. It had come to light that there were probate issues with the property title, and a sale would be impossible until these were resolved. He nonetheless gave me location and boundary maps, and I said we would check it out and perhaps come back to him. We made the quick drive out to the farm, which was divided by a stream between two townlands named 'Bofickil' and 'Faunkill and The Woods', parked the car on the main road and climbed over an old stone wall onto part of the land.

Within seconds, I knew with absolute clarity that this was where I wanted to spend the rest of my life, if at all possible, and said out loud the words, 'This is it.' That might sound a bit of a stretch, but for me it really was a case of love at first sight. The land was extremely wild, with native trees and enormous rocky outcrops of all shapes everywhere, and ran down to within 350 metres of the sea. On the landward side it rose up, very steeply in places, before giving way to the mountain commonages in which the farm had shares. The views were simply heart-stopping, with the nearby Atlantic and seven islands – including the Skelligs – glittering and glowing in the sunshine. Carrauntoohil, the highest mountain in Ireland, and the rest of the MacGillycuddy's Reeks range were also visible to the northeast.

For somewhere so untamed, it was also amazingly well located, bounding both sides of the main road between Castletownbere and Kenmare. The village of Eyeries, with its primary school, shops, post office and pubs, was only about two minutes' drive away, and Castletownbere – the 'capital' of Beara – another five more, so Giuliana was happy with it too. The old farmhouse and outbuildings, which were about 125 metres off the road down towards the sea, were total ruins, most of the roofs having caved in many years before. Mature trees were growing both within the house and from the walls of rubble sandstone.

Nevertheless, the place as a whole seemed ideal in every way, almost too much so to be real. The following day I returned alone to spend a few hours walking the land and making sure there was nothing seriously negative we needed to know about before expressing an interest to J.J. While doing so, I had great difficulty containing my emotions; everything I saw had my heart thumping with excitement and a fixed lump in my throat.

Essentially, most of the farm was a wild forest of oak, birch, holly and a great variety of other native trees, including evidently very old behemoths. Underneath, a network of streams flowed through a terrain that was incredibly varied topographically, with rocky bluffs, valleys, high precipices, deep gorges, ravines and vertical escarpment faces a good 10 metres high. Ancient weathered sandstone boulders, crags and wedges, some the size of trucks, were strewn all around, as if randomly tossed about by rampaging mythical ogres.

Knife-edge slabs stood on edge, pointing skyward at all angles. In several spots there were large cavities running into the sides of cliffs, with walls and roofs of enormous sheets of rock, cleaved and fractured into jumbled heaps like megalithic Jenga blocks. Much of the rock was living bedrock – exposed undetached sections of the underlying geological crust, in a multitude of forms.

The trees were growing from, through, around, into and over this dramatic setting, their roots organically flowing across rock where it was naked, as though semi-liquid lava. But every available surface of tree or rock exposed to rain was clad in thick, lush, spongy layers of mosses up to 12 centimetres deep, as well as a profusion of ferns and lichens.

As a result, often it was difficult to determine where mineral gave way to vegetal, as rock, root and trunk merged into one, mantled underneath a mini-forest of micro fronds. Some of the lower parts of the land were extremely wet underfoot – swampy even, with patches of strangely Jurassic-looking horsetails here and there.

The many streams varied greatly in mood, according to the type of ground being traversed: in some places gently meandering, in others, where there was a steep fall or sheer drop over sculpted bedrock, they became mini whitewater rapids or even Niagaras. They were everywhere surrounded by the same bewildering variety of mosses and ferns, all revelling in the raised aerial humidity. I had never before laid eyes on anything remotely like this wild, verdant and primeval landscape, and had no idea that such places existed anywhere in Europe, never mind Ireland. It looked as though it belonged more in the tropical jungles of Costa Rica or Papua New Guinea, than our wind-blasted island in the Atlantic. I was in complete awe of the place.

But I did my very best to stay as detached as I could from what I was seeing and feeling, because I knew there were more than just a few obstacles in the way of ever being able to actually live in this magical place. So having made sure there was nothing obviously untoward there, I made a mental note never to go back unless I somehow managed to actually conclude a deal. We did, however, make a point of introducing ourselves to the people living in the two farmhouses nearby – the Harringtons and Houlihans – and were warmly received in both. Our holiday over, we headed back to Dublin, and a few days later I told J.J. over the phone that I was seriously interested. We agreed that he'd let me know as soon as the legal issues were sorted out, which he thought was likely to take another six months or so.

In between sculpture jobs, I threw myself into finishing the extension to the house in Kilmainham, and then bringing the rest of the place as close to perfection as I could in readiness for selling. During this time I also made an appointment at the local county council office in Castletownbere for a 'pre-planning meeting': knowing whether or not we would be able to get planning permission to build a new house on the farm was crucial.

At the meeting, it was explained to me that the main difficulty wouldn't be so much permission for a house itself, because the old ruin established what is called 'precedence'. The big problem was creating an access road down to it, since the old entrance gate – dating from a time when cars didn't exist – was on the wrong side of a bad bend in the main road, with limited visibility in either direction. Nevertheless, it seemed likely that, with some imagination, a solution could be found, and I felt happy enough to proceed on that basis. After a quick visit to the lovely primary school in nearby Eyeries, where I was very kindly given a tour by the head teacher and assured that two more kids would be welcomed with open arms, I drove back to Dublin.

Nine months after first seeing the land in Beara, I finally reached a point with work on the house in Kilmainham where I felt satisfied that it was as ready to sell as it would ever be. Unbelievably, and as if by prearrangement, only a few days later J.J. telephoned from Castletownbere to tell me that the probate issue had been dealt with, and the farm was now properly on the market. Within just a few more days our house was up for sale, and I was making an offer on the farm.

Negotiating with the sellers was a complicated affair, as J.J. had to pass on any offer I made to a solicitor in Bantry, who then relayed it to the executor of the will – a priest in Florida named Father Kevin Brassil. He in turn had to telephone all the other heirs, of whom there were apparently quite a few, located in different time zones across the United States. Once they had agreed on a response, the whole process would happen in reverse, until I'd get a message back from J.J. after a couple of weeks to say, for example, 'They feel your offer is too low, and want to know if you'll better it?' And it would all have to start over.

This was April 2009, right in the aftermath of the economic crash. The recession was making life difficult in many ways, but it did mean that there now appeared to be little other interest in the farm, and after a few circuitous rounds of back and forth between Kilmainham and the US, a deal was struck. Luckily, our house sold very quickly too and, in mid-May, the time came for us to move out.

For more than a decade I had known this moment would eventually come, and had often wondered how it would feel to walk out the door of the house I had poured so much of myself into for the last time. But when it actually happened, close to midnight on the last day in which we were allowed to be in the house, I surprised even myself by just leaving with scarcely a backwards glance. The reason was very simple: I had the feeling that the swap, if all went well, seemed almost criminally disproportionate – as if pulling a heist. A wild native forest and a share of a mountain, all overlooking the most beautiful stretch of Atlantic imaginable, plus enough funds left over to build a new place to live, all in exchange for quite a small house and garden in the city.

But the conveyancing on the farm in Beara wasn't yet complete. And so, just as when buying the site in Kilmainham sixteen years before, a very anxious ten days or so were spent in a state of limbo, this time waiting to know for sure that we weren't going to be left with nowhere to go.

4

A New Life Down South

We drove down overnight from the Kilmainham cottage in mid-May, arriving at the house we had rented in Eyeries village in a fairly groggy state early the next morning. All our things were packed into a large van loaned by a good friend, Owen Kelly, who also kindly came along to help out. 'The pink house', as it was called, had the most spectacular views out to sea, and it didn't seem real to be actually living in such a place, rather than just on holiday. I did my best not to dwell on the fact that the legal process involved in buying the farm hadn't been finalised, and that, if anything went wrong with that, we would be left very seriously out on a limb.

But after about a week and a half we finally received word that everything was done, and that evening we celebrated with a bottle of Italian red wine, looking out at an orange ball of sun melting into the shimmering Atlantic.

The next day I went out to the land and spent much of the day there. I also called in to the neighbours to tell them the news, which was received with obvious pleasure. For as long as I live,

I will never forget the way Michael Harrington (Caupey) gave me his great big hand and warm smile, looked me straight in the eye and said: 'You're very, very welcome here.'

Michael, who grew up in the area in the 1940s and '50s, had led an interesting and varied life that included a long spell working in Britain, all of which had helped give him a broad and thoughtful perspective on the world, as well as a powerful sense of humour. You could not have wished for better neighbours than the Caupeys. Over the years, Michael and his son Finbarr were to play a huge role in helping me find my feet in Bofickil, in so many ways. This included much practical advice, as there were many aspects of rural life about which I had a lot to learn.

No less important for me was the fact that Michael had known very well the Crowleys – the family who had lived on our farm in the past – and was able to fill me in on them and myriad other aspects of local history and folklore. The family had come to Bofickil in 1863, when a Mick Crowley from nearby Urhan went *cliamhain isteach* (meaning 'son-in-law', and used when a man married into a farm or household) to local girl Catherine Houlihan, and half of the family farm was given to the couple.

The main part of the existing old farmhouse was likely built at that time, with an extension and outhouse added in subsequent decades, along with other outbuildings now gone. Through Michael, I learned such details as the fact that the house had been very roughly searched from top to bottom for guns by the infamous Black and Tans during the 1919–21 War of Independence, and that four of the five children from the last generation of Bofickil Crowleys had emigrated to the United States in the 1930s.

One of them, Eileen (Father Brassil's aunt), was the last inhabitant of the old house. Just like Molly Maughan in Kilmainham, she too passed away at a good old age in the 1980s, after which her cottage started to fall apart. From Michael's telling, as well as everyone else who had known Eileen, she was a great character, but had a sharp tongue and you crossed her at your peril, for she was well known for tearing long strips off people in public. She had lived for decades in New York where she had a restaurant, and seemingly never lost her American twang. Eileen came home to Bofickil to live in the old farmhouse with her sister Margaret at some point after their mother, Ellen, died in the late 1950s. Ellen used to often call up to Michael's parents on visits, and would as a rule arrive complaining of weakness and fierce pains to her heart. Amazingly though, these were always instantly and miraculously cured with a large brandy, following which she could 'talk for Ireland'.

After Margaret died, Eileen lived alone, apart from what has invariably been described to me as a 'pack' of a dozen or more dogs of all shapes and sizes. By all accounts, several of these you were wise to be highly wary of, for, given half a chance, they would remove a large lump from the back of your leg, especially one still locally notorious individual named 'Tiger'. The whole gang would apparently sit in a long line up the stairs, intently watching through the banisters any visitors nervously taking tea in the kitchen alongside. Eileen also had a few semi-wild cattle, which were famous throughout Beara and beyond for their long twisting horns and roving habits. Seemingly they did as, and went where, they pleased, and were regularly to be seen grazing 'the long acre': i.e. wandering the roads of the locality, 'thieving' the 'free' grass growing at the verges.

More than any other person, Michael opened up an awareness of a rich tapestry of local life and lore in the past, of which I would otherwise have remained largely ignorant. For example, he told how, up to the 1960s or '70s, neighbours exchanged days of work on a constant basis without money ever changing hands. Known as *meitheal*, such locally cooperative systems are thought to have been practised for millennia in Beara, and other similarly far-flung places that dictated a high degree of mutual dependency.

Michael also spoke of 'nightwalking', in which people would regularly call to each other's homes for several hours in the evening for cups of tea, long chats by the fire, and maybe a few stories or songs. That age-old practice sadly died away with the arrival of television, taking a great wealth of the oral tradition with it. I was thrilled to learn that both Seán Ó Riada and Seán Ó Sé had spent time in the Caupey house recording songs, as well as singing a few themselves, in the late 1960s. My dad used to play his record of *Ó Riada sa Gaiety* so constantly when I was small that I wouldn't be at all surprised if it was the only one he had at the time. Every last track is still ingrained in my mind, and even now hearing it again never fails to move me deeply: both the undiminished raw power of the music itself, and its capacity to stir my own earliest memories.

Michael knew the old Irish place-names for many parts of the Crowley farm and commonage – Gleann, Crowley's Currachán, Cappaughleen, Béal, Glann, Conoceeneasc and Goulagh for example. He also told me others in the immediate locality, like Fíleacha, Illaunameanla, Íonrais and Cnuicín. Although Irish died out in Beara about a century ago, many people in the area still sprinkle their speech with words and expressions in the language, such as the names of wild plants or land features. Its linguistic ghosts sometimes also reveal themselves in a particular turn of phrase in English, such as 'There's no hunger/thirst *on me*': on the face of it, direct translations of *Níl aon ocras/tart orm*.

Sadly, Irish was seen as a handicap to emigration to the United States, as so many Beara people have been forced to do down the centuries (switching to Britain from the Second World War), and as a barrier to generally getting on in life. The Great Famine of 1845–52, which decimated the population of the peninsula, undoubtedly also played a major role in its demise. With the passing of Irish, unique expressions of whole forms of consciousness and understanding would have been lost from the area. In the words of anthropologist and ethnobotanist Wade Davis, 'Every language is an old-growth forest of the mind, a watershed of thought, an entire ecosystem of spiritual possibilities.'

Michael also remembered very well the Crowley farm from when he was young, having spent plenty of time there while growing up. So he was able to describe in considerable detail how most corners of it had been back then, giving me much valued insight into the ecological transformation that had taken place over the course of the many decades since.

The *fear an tí* (man of the house), Phillip Crowley (Mick's son and Eileen's father), had gone to work in the copper mines of Butte, Montana, around 1909. Previously he had been a copper miner in the Allihies mines farther west in Beara, and it's likely that his leaving was a result of their closure around that time, less than a decade after reopening. Whatever happened over in Montana, Phil Crowley never came home. Essentially, very little was done with the farmland from the time of his departure, allowing wild nature to return. The

Bofickil woods came into being through neglect, rather than by human design or agency.

The six-inch Ordnance Survey maps of 1842 and 1901 don't indicate any woodland or scrub on the Crowley land, but there would have been pockets here and there in rougher spots, as well as hedgerows and older trees on field boundaries, similar to neighbouring farms now. In the absence of any serious grazing by livestock, germinating seeds from these trees were able to grow in the surrounding open ground, creating new woodland. There were plenty of trees there by the time Michael was a boy in the 1950s – showing that the process had been in train for many decades by then – but not as many as when we arrived.

All this correlated with what is visible in an image I came across in a book of old photographs published by the Beara Historical Society, which shows a stretch of road several hundred yards to the east of the Crowley land, but still in Faunkill. The image is undated, but the pony and trap, and the clothes of the people on board, probably place it somewhere in the 1940s. In the background are some trees and scrub, but nothing like the dense native forest that exists on the same piece of ground today.

However, while the process of returning to wild woodland seems to have commenced with Phil Crowley's leaving, coincidentally a century before our arrival in 2009, it had ceased entirely for the previous decade or two, as I was soon to realise.

Exploring the land and woods properly was, emotionally, a close to overwhelming experience. After my first visits the previous July, I had made a conscious decision not to allow myself to think of the place in any way other than as a sort of dreamlike abstraction, existing only in another dimension of the universe. My fear was that too strong an engagement might compromise my ability to remain cool while trying to negotiate its purchase.

But now I was able to let go of that restraint and appreciate the land fully, and over the next weeks and months I began to discover an ecological and aesthetic wonderland of simply aching beauty and diversity. It was possible to stand still in any one spot for a half hour or more, as I sometimes did, and still feel I hadn't had time to take everything in properly from just that single vantage point. And no one part resembled another: with every few steps the specifics of the rocks and other features of the land, as well as the species composition and growth patterns of the trees, were all so different as to make it seem another place entirely.

A great variety of native tree species were present: sessile oak, downy birch, holly, eared and grey willows (and a range of hybrids), whitethorn, blackthorn, rowan, hazel, ash, alder and wild crab apple. Guelder-rose and dog-rose, more large shrubs than trees, were also there. But unlike the native trees I had planted in the garden in Kilmainham, these trees were *wild*. That is to say, they had all self-seeded, and were in all probability descendants of a genetic lineage specific to this area stretching back thousands of years, to the first trees to colonise after the end of the last Ice Age.

The difference between planted and wild native trees is far from merely an academic one. While planted trees tend to be quite uniform genetically, and hence all look fairly similar in terms of overall shape, leaf size, colour and other characteristics, the very opposite is true of their wild equivalents. The oaks and other trees in the Bofickil (and Faunkill) woods are all distinct individuals in every way: no two of them are alike.

By contrast, for example, many of the oaks in some less remote parts of Killarney National Park are remarkably similar to one another, indicating that they were likely planted. While magnificent – much taller in stature than the often scraggly storm-blasted oaks of Beara – they are the result of centuries of selection of the characteristics *people* desire in trees. They are tamed, cultivated, de-natured versions of their wild ancestors, something like poodles or shih-tzus are of wolves.

Another arresting aspect of the Bofickil woods was the highly opulent assortment of ferns, which, along with the mosses and lichens, covered much of the available surfaces, from the ground to otherwise bare rock, tree trunks and branches. Hard fern, polypody, scaly male fern, hart's tongue, lady fern, bracken, hay-scented and broad buckler ferns, maidenhair spleenwort, royal fern, Tunbridge filmy, Wilson's filmy, and the rare and protected Killarney fern were all there. (Although it was a year or more before I came across the last; since then I have discovered several more colonies.)

At a micro level, there were even more layers to perceive in the woods, with a mind-boggling diversity of intricate mosses and liverworts (collectively known as bryophytes), as well as other plant forms. These and the leaf litter on the forest floor were inhabited by a multitude of insects, spiders and other invertebrates, all going about their business. Many of them, up close, looked like creatures from another planet.

On one of those first captivating exploratory visits to the woods, I looked up at one point to see a female sparrowhawk perched on a branch about six metres above. I found myself transfixed through and through by her piercing raptor's stare and take-no-prisoners poise. After eyeballing each other intensely for what seemed an eternity, but was in reality only seconds, she swooped off acrobatically through the trees. The encounter left me literally 'enraptored', and close to tears. It felt like a very personal welcome from another world, and in a sense perhaps it was.

Village life in Eyeries was very different from Dublin, and the pace pleasantly slower and more easy-going. But Liam, who was about three and a half at the time, and who still had a strong Dublin accent picked up at his playschool in Ballyfermot, adamantly refused to go to the village playschool, clearly feeling this was all just too much change, too fast. Seán, or Seánie as we all called him, being a couple of years younger, seemed to accept our radically altered environment as perfectly normal.

For me, one of the most immediately striking differences was in the night sky. The absence of the light pollution that is so overwhelming in large cities, along with pure ocean air, means that on a clear night, the stars, moon, planets, Milky Way and, occasionally, shooting stars can seem impossibly vivid. The only skies I have ever seen to surpass it are those of the deserts of North Africa and the Middle East, the sheer desiccation making the air crystal clear. When dark clouds sweep across that richly animated celestial backdrop in Beara, momentarily obscuring, diffusing and revealing infinite points of light, the effect can be hauntingly dramatic.

The pink house was only a few doors away from Causkey's

pub, but the roughly two score steps home after a couple of pints might easily be interrupted by a long spell of skyward gawping. At times I'd waken at night to see a rising moon, close to the horizon of the sea, casting a long, gently rippling wedge of reflected silvery light towards me across the water, and wonder whether I was still dreaming. More than twelve years on, I still do.

A few months after arriving, there was an almighty storm – our first real taste of just how demented the weather can get along the Atlantic seaboard. The whole house was shaking violently, and I remember lying wide awake in bed half the night quite terrified, convinced that either the roof was about to be ripped off, or the windows come crashing in. It felt as if there was an enraged giant going berserk outside, intent on tearing the building apart. But we survived, and with time I came to love the intense exhilaration of these tempestuous eruptions, a love well tempered with healthy respect, however.

They are always humbling experiences, and periodic reminders of the unbounded power of the raw elements. When feeling brave, walks near the sea on such occasions are to behold awe-inspiring displays of ferocity, with breakers crashing 20 metres high or more into the sky, launching salt-laden spray and even large boulders far inland. Looking at the coast from a distance over the days following a storm's abating, a bright haze of wave-slammed moisture hangs visibly in the air, slowly drifting away in clouds from the still-heaving, seething, conflict zone below. Outdoors on such days, the background roar of the ocean is so palpable it attains an inescapable, physical presence.

Living with the Atlantic as a next-door neighbour means

accepting an often high degree of volatility in the weather. Within minutes, it can go from sunny and calm to dark, with howling wind and lashing rain, and back again just as quickly. Brendan Behan's famous quip that 'the weather in Ireland is so changeable that you wouldn't know what [clothes] to pawn' is taken to its utmost extreme here. An instinctual sense to look seaward on a frequent basis develops, especially when the sky is unsettled, to have some forewarning of what's on the way. You learn to gauge the shifting moods by the configurations and relative proportions of silver, white, blue, green, grey, or near black towards the horizon's rim.

All the clichés about the striking and constantly changing nature of the light in the west of Ireland are entirely justified: visual stimulus simply abounds in the presence of the ocean. Glancing west, perhaps fast-scudding, angrily dark clouds are sweeping Inisfarnard or the more distant Skelligs with a near-solid phalanx of gunmetal rain showers, yet are thrown into stark contrast by brilliant sunshine on the flanking sea and islands. Twin concentric arcs of electric-toned rainbows may frame the scene, the inner ring marking a crisp transition from bright to dark. Minutes or even seconds later the picture is likely to be barely recognisable, over and over, throughout a day.

Plenty of times too though, the weather adopts a certain state and just sticks with that for days. That can mean either dry or wet periods, which in the latter case includes anything from monsoon rain to brief but torrential cloudbursts; from constant successions of passing squally showers to light drizzle or thick mist or fog. If there really are 40 or 50 Inuit words for snow (linguists still debate the truth of that), a similar number would be needed for all the different forms of moisture that descend from the sky in these parts, and it seems that may actually have been the case *as Gaeilge*.

Most people in Beara seem to find the mist and fog oppressive, with visibility through the murk restricted to only metres at times. I love it, though saying so can provoke looks of wide-eyed amazement when discussing the weather with other customers in a local shop, for example. Beyond the mysterious, otherworldly atmosphere it creates, in the back of my mind there is always the thought that much of the lush and very special local wild flora owes its presence to the high levels of humidity.

Walking in the woods in misty or foggy weather is like entering a dreamy alternate dimension, in which the outlines of trees and rocks have dematerialised into floating, shape-shifting, ethereal semi-solids. When patchier or swirling, the drifting vaporous banks and wisps expose and then shroud again ever-changing framed views of the surrounding woods, mountains and sea. All the forest-dwelling ferns, mosses and other plants exult in these conditions, becoming glistening, luxuriant and succulent, some of them even semi-translucent.

Elements that might normally be easily neglected are thrown into prominence. The gossamer silk threads of a spider's web, tautly bridging the airy void between two wet stalks, are sequined with glinting aqueous beads of varying sizes, each one a lens refracting an optically inverted version of the ghostly world behind. And the only sound breaking the thick, heavy silence is that of slow dripping from the leaves or twigs all around.

The Gulf Stream delivers a constant supply of warm waters direct from the Caribbean right to Beara's doorstep, ensuring that temperatures are nearly always mild compared to most of Ireland. So frosts are less frequent and less severe, and when 15 centimetres of snow falls in Bantry, for example, probably less than three arrive here, and last for just a short time before melting. Only once has there been really heavy snow since we moved to Beara: in February 2018, with perhaps 20 centimetres, gathering in drifts of a metre or more deep in places.

The woods were a place of extra wonder in those couple of days, transformed into a scene of eternal winter from the children's fantasy *Chronicles of Narnia*. Every non-vertical twig, bough, or trunk held aloft a tall bladed ridge of powdery snow, while the contours of the land and rocks underneath were made unrecognisable under the thick, sound-dampening whiteout.

Persistent rain and other forms of 'bad' weather used to often get me down in Dublin and other places where I lived in the past, but, surprisingly, never in Beara, even though there's more of it. That may be partly because I was keenly aware that it would be part of the deal when considering moving here, and accepted it in advance as a price well worth paying. But more important, I believe, is that aspect already alluded to: living in a wilder environment like this, all the forms the weather takes just seem part of the natural rhythms and essences of the place.

But nor in Beara is there any scarcity of sunlit, balmy days, with only a light breeze – or none at all – throughout the year. And then it's not unlike living on the Mediterranean, with endless azure skies meeting wide-open sapphire seas. *Nel blu, dipinto di blu,* as the song goes. Or else divided from one another by rocky promontories and islands, in mesmerisingly lovely scenes that could be mistaken for the Aegean. But a past incarnation, without the present-day clutter of resorts, hotels, bars and luxury villas to spoil things.

Those are among the many moments in which, living in Beara, it can feel as if you've won a much bigger jackpot than any of those they sell tickets for.

Several months after we moved to Eyeries, my mother came from Dublin to stay with us for a short holiday, but her health was poor and she was unsteady on her feet. For the previous decade and a half, she had lived in a terraced ex-council house in Inchicore with a large back garden, as well as a smaller one to the front. There she had planted lots of native flowers, shrubs and trees, creating amazing wildlife-friendly patches. It was a real sight to come down her street of very respectable suburban houses, each one with a perfectly clipped lawn or concreted car-parking spot in the front garden, and then see her wild jungle in the middle of it all, bursting at the seams with life.

The contrast between her south-facing back garden and those of the neighbours was even more extreme. The many birches, hazel, blackthorn, whitethorn and rowan she had planted around the margins had grown to form a thick shelter, creating an internal suntrap paradise. When the weather was fine, she used to spend much of the day there in the company of her adored tabby cat Boetie, in the midst of bumblebees, butterflies and numerous other pollinators in her unrestrained riot of a wildflower garden.

She managed to visit the land in Bofickil only once during that holiday, and with my help was able to slowly walk a little way down into the woods. We went as far as an extremely charismatic old oak near a stream, its torso hulking and bent, and, like the other trees, absolutely dripping with hanging ferns and mosses. We stopped there for a while to soak in our surroundings, and then turned back.

Several months later she became much more seriously ill, and I was making ever more frequent trips up to Dublin to see her. As her health deteriorated further, she had to be admitted to Harold's Cross Hospice, but after a few months they told me that they wouldn't be able to keep her any longer because of bed shortages, and so I had to start working out what to do. The house in Eyeries was too small, and the stairs too steep, for her to come and live with us there, so we found another rented house for all of us to live in at Faunkill and The Woods, close to the farm.

My mother was originally from a small coastal town in South Africa's Western Cape Province named Knysna. She had been constrained to leave South Africa in the late 1950s at the age of only nineteen, due to a deep involvement in the anti-apartheid movement there, arriving in London after a long voyage by steam packet up the west coast of Africa. A few years later she met my father, who was from Westmeath. I was born in London and we lived there until I was five, at which point we moved to Dublin where I grew up. I was an only child, so my mum and I were fairly close, but throughout my childhood I was always allowed a high degree of freedom to explore and experience life, including the wild outdoors. I'll remain forever grateful for that.

Although she always loved Ireland, she felt increasingly less at home here as the economic boom took off in the second half of the 1990s, and gained momentum into the new millennium. For her, society was placing ever more emphasis on aspects of life she was unable to relate to: money, property, status and self-interest. Conversely, those values closest to her heart, and which had been so much in abundance here previously – community, openness, sharing and inclusion – seemed ever scarcer. (I think she was right, although those shifts were far from confined to Ireland, as she would herself have agreed.)

Partly as a consequence, over the last decade or more of her life her thoughts turned more and more to South Africa, focusing in particular on Knysna. She would have loved for me to visit the country with her, but for decades I was too stuck into other things to go, and then her declining health reached a point where it became a barrier to her going back herself.

After little more than a week in Faunkill, she became too sick to remain at home with us, and had to go into Castletownbere Hospital where she was very well looked after by a lovely and kind staff. Throughout that time she'd frequently ask me to read out loud to her passages of a favourite book, *Memories of Knysna*, a collection of short pieces about the locality's past, and the various characters who helped make it so colourful. Those accounts commonly featured the Knysna indigenous forests, which my mum had often spoken about throughout my life as a unique and wondrous place, with immense trees bearing such exotic names as outeniqua yellowwood, ironwood and stinkwood.

My mum died only about seven weeks after coming down to Beara, but it meant so much to me to have been there with her when she passed. I buried her ashes beside a pointed rock that stands upright naturally like a headstone, in a prominent part of the farm with sweeping views out over the woods below, backdropped in turn by the Atlantic stretching to the horizon. I still always think of her whenever I'm near there, or when passing that wizened old oak near the stream, which is usually at least a few times each week. It is her tree.

5

A Dying Forest

My plan had always been to conserve the native woodland that had developed naturally over about two-thirds of the non-commonage part of the farm. But, despite its deep beauty, I quickly realised that something was very badly wrong, and it became apparent that, actually, I had an ecological car crash on my hands. Apart from the tree trunks and mosses, there was virtually no vegetation from about chest or head height down: everything else had been stripped bare. Where the ground was flattish, if you hunkered down it was possible to see for a considerable distance, because there was almost nothing living to block your view.

A healthy forest consists of several layers. There is the canopy – the crowns of the larger trees like oak and birch, an understorey of smaller trees, such as holly, and a ground layer of flowering plants and ferns. In wet western parts like Beara, there is a further layer on much of the woodland floor: the mosses. In the Bofickil woods, however, the understorey was largely either absent or much reduced, and a whole stratum, the ground flora and undergrowth, was simply missing, aside from a few ferns and other plants like woodrush. The cause of all this wasn't long in revealing itself, as a large herd of feral goats (domestic goats gone wild) had a constant presence in the area, along with smaller numbers of sika deer.

Our ancestors began domesticating goats in southwest Asia – the first birthplace of agriculture – at least 8,000 years ago. They proved extremely useful to us, with an unrivalled ability to eat practically every sort of vegetation, and to reproduce rapidly. As farming spread around the world, so did the goat, and they have been an invaluable means of taming wilderness, converting 'useless' natural habitat highly efficiently into useful milk, cheese, meat, and hide.

In Ireland, there is much folklore associated with the animal, and some believe there exists a distinct 'native' breed in the wild, usually called the 'old Irish goat', ignoring their distant origin and human introduction. They certainly are fantastic-looking animals, with their shaggy coats and the billies' long, impressively curved horns. To see them nimbly perched on rocks on a bare mountainside, deftly negotiating the most precipitous terrain, can be a memorable experience.

But the backdrop of a bare mountainside is far from coincidental: goats are nothing less than living, walking strimmers. As a result, they've been an unmitigated ecological disaster in many parts of the globe, stripping away all native foliage they can reach, augmented by an ability to scale trees, as I witnessed myself in Bofickil on several occasions. Often described by ecologists as 'desert makers', they are responsible for helping to push native species across the planet into extinction, with fragile island ecosystems especially vulnerable.

On the Galápagos, for example, the endemic giant tortoises (the largest in the world) were in danger of dying off, because introduced goats were eliminating all the native plant life on which the tortoises feed. Only with the implementation of conservation measures, which included removing the goats, did the natural habitat begin to return, assuring the future of a species that played a significant role in bringing Darwin to his theory of evolution. 'Immense herds' of goats were kept in eighteenth-century southwest Ireland, and it's highly likely that they contributed greatly to the disappearance of remaining vestiges of native forest.

Their effect on the Bofickil woods was no exception. Neighbours told me that at one point before our arrival, the herd in the immediate area numbered over a hundred. By the time we came, this had been reduced to around 25 through culling, but even a group that size was more than sufficient to keep all woodland and other natural habitat over a couple of square kilometres in a state of severe degradation.

The origin of the goats in our area wasn't entirely clear, but anecdotally it seemed that a small number – which then proliferated – were released by a group of people who had been living an alternative lifestyle nearby a decade or two previously. These people had also turned the acre of land where they were based into the local epicentre for a whole host of invasive non-native plant species, which were spreading rapidly. Given that they had no doubt been seeking a more 'back to nature' approach to life, there was more than a little irony in the fact that they had inadvertently caused huge damage to the local native ecosystem. Clearly having your heart in the right place isn't enough in itself, and can actually bring very destructive consequences if not informed by at least a minimum of ecological savvy.

Sika deer, on the other hand, were brought to County Wicklow from far-east Asia in 1860, and were introduced from there onto the estates of Lord Lansdowne, on the northeastern side of Beara, four years later. They're smaller than the red deer, of which the most important herd in Ireland is found in and around Killarney National Park. Despite being generally considered native, the red deer was probably also introduced, but from much closer: the north European mainland. While the red has no presence in Beara, sika are now widespread on the peninsula, and extremely numerous in some parts, especially around Lauragh, Kenmare and Glengarriff. They have a similarly negative, if less locally concentrated, effect on native woodland to that of the feral goats.

By eating almost every bit of native greenery below what is known as the 'browse line', including all tree seedlings, the goats and sika had effectively been preventing the trees from reproducing in the Bofickil woods. Because tree seedlings are highly nutritious, and therefore no doubt extra tasty, many herbivores tend to favour them over grass and other vegetation, and hence selectively eat them out over and above everything else. I have since witnessed this phenomenon myself on many occasions with goats, sheep and deer.

Consequently there was a total absence of any seedlings, saplings, or trees younger than a couple of decades; in ecological terms, the woods were very much out of kilter, lacking a varied age structure. If such a situation persists for long enough in any forest, as trees age it will shrink and eventually die away, which is exactly what was starting to happen in Bofickil. In addition, there was none of the rich variety of wild flowers and other plants associated with native woodland: nearly all the ground flora had been cleaned out.

Both the goats and deer also had a highly damaging

affinity for peeling and eating the bark from the trunks of established trees, especially holly, but also rowan, sally (willow), whitethorn, hazel, young oak and others. The bark is the living section of the trunk, part of the less than 3 per cent of the wood in a tree that is actually alive. If bark-stripping extends all the way around the trunk, the tree dies, since the bark plays an essential role in transporting water, nutrients and sugars up and down between the tree's leaves and roots, as well as forming a protective skin against pathogens.

The upshot was that the Bofickil woods were thickly littered with dead trees, their decorticated trunks identifying the cause. Furthermore, any trees that were blown over in storms had their previously inaccessible leaves constantly stripped away until they too died (most trees that are knocked down by the wind would otherwise survive).

The woods were, quite simply, being eaten to death.

To make things far worse, by removing all competition in the form of native vegetation, the overgrazing and browsing by goats and sika had cleared the way for invasion by a range of non-native plant species. These included Chilean myrtle, giant rhubarb, fuchsia, montbretia, Japanese knotweed, pheasant berry, bamboo and sycamore.

But easily the worst of the lot was *Rhododendron ponticum*. With only mosses or leaf litter remaining on the forest floor, the overgrazing had prepared exactly the sort of seedbed rhododendron finds ideal for germination. There were mature stands of this plant present in several parts of the land, and their offspring seedlings and bushes were vigorously sprouting and growing everywhere.

My ecological knowledge was limited enough back then, but I was aware that, left alone, rhododendron is a death sentence for any native woodland, its thickly tangled growth shading out all native tree seedlings and other plants. A single flowering bush is capable of putting out up to a million tiny wind-borne seeds per year, and each one that germinates can in turn be flowering and producing seed itself within ten to twelve years. The result is that, if not dealt with at an early stage, huge areas can very quickly become choked in true *Day of the Triffids* style.

Rhododendron also contains deadly toxins that discourage animals, whether mammals or insects, from feeding on its leaves. Herbivores such as the goats and sika in Bofickil sense this (presumably through taste) and therefore avoid it to selectively focus on any native foliage, further facilitating takeover by the rhododendron. Its leaf litter forms such a dense and toxic layer on the lifeless floor underneath that even fungi are unable to push up through, and its flowers' nectar is poisonous to native pollinators.

In Killarney National Park, Ireland's largest and most important surviving tract of native forest, colossal efforts over many decades have gone into trying to control the same problem. All to little avail, with the plant occupying great swathes of the park and constantly gaining ground, in large part due to the discontinuation of the highly successful summer work camps run by an organisation called Groundwork. For over 30 years, their thousands of volunteers came from all over the world, and together managed to eliminate rhodo from about half of the oldest, most biologically valuable and remote parts of the park – the western oakwoods – using a science-led, systematic approach.

A dispute with the park authorities (the National Parks and Wildlife Service, or NPWS) ended the programme in 2009. The main disagreement appears to have centred on whether volunteers should be able to continue to spend part of their time monitoring and keeping the areas they had cleared rhodo-free, or instead have to focus entirely on parts visible to visitors from the road through the park. Groundwork has since brought evidence, undisputed by the NPWS, that many of the cleared sectors have since become seriously reinfested with mature flowering plants.

Ultimately, the core of the problem seems to have been rooted in two very contrasting perceptions of the primary role of the park: as a sanctuary for wild nature, or just a cash cow and a means of drawing tourist money into the wider area. In any case, the entirely unnecessary squandering of decades of immensely hard toil, international goodwill and hard-earned, accumulated, ecological knowledge simply beggars belief.

Just like the Bofickil woods, Killarney National Park is also very severely denuded by high numbers of sika and red deer, feral goats and sheep from neighbouring farms. As a result, there are no native tree seedlings, the sole exceptions being high up in the crooks of older trees and other such spots the grazers can't reach. The first and most obvious step in restoring the ecology of the park would be to remove *all* sika, feral goats and sheep from the park, leaving only the red deer. Even then, the population of that species would also have to be kept at a low enough level to allow the natural regeneration of native flora, including trees. Why this approach wasn't adopted decades ago is quite unfathomable.

In addition to overgrazing and invasive plants, wildfires regularly occur in dry periods within Killarney NP, or spread in from neighbouring commonages, causing immense damage to the forests and wildlife. This is *only* made possible by the park's wrecked condition, since native Irish forest in a healthy state doesn't actually burn. Essentially, Ireland's flagship national park, and one of only two designated UNESCO biosphere reserves in the condition, is slowly dying as a result of these combined factors, all of which stem from the overgrazing. That such a situation has been allowed to persist for so long – both sika deer and rhododendron were already recognised as serious problems by the mid-1970s – is a monumental national disgrace.

Uragh, another NPWS-managed ancient native woodland in a spectacularly beautiful setting by the shores of Lough Inchiquin in Beara, is in exactly the same state, but without the rhododendron – for now. The entire forest floor has been picked clean of any native plants by sika, goats and sheep, many sections of the surrounding deer fence having collapsed. And it's unlikely to be long before rhododendron arrives in the Uragh woods, since it's present nearby; when it does, it will find conditions in the woodland perfect for invasion.

The picture is depressingly similar in the vast majority of surviving fragments of native woodland throughout Ireland. Only 19 per cent of Atlantic woodland, for example, is in a favourable state, according to a 2012 study. This is such a tragedy, given that these are some of the last remnants of once almost unimaginably rich habitats that covered most – probably around 80 per cent – of this island, but are now down to around a mere *1 per cent*.

Another invasive exotic (non-native) species, the pheasant, also became common in the Bofickil woods for several years. These birds, native to Asia, are bred and released into the wild in substantial numbers for shooting, but around two-thirds avoid that fate. Others are taken by foxes and other predators, are run over on roads, or die of other causes, but about a third of those freed survive. In the first years after I came to Beara, I saw pheasants only very rarely on the land, but over time their numbers increased. When I was walking through the woods or surrounding open spaces, they would often burst from cover with a loud clatter of wings and squawks, and their ground roosts were everywhere.

By inverse proportion, the numbers of common lizard (Ireland's only native reptile) basking in the sun on rocks, as well as frogs and slugs (including the protected Kerry slug), noticeably diminished. These changes are unlikely to have been unrelated, since pheasants are known to prey on exactly such creatures, as well as small mammals and invertebrates. A phenomenal 61 million are released every year in Britain (in Ireland the figure is unknown), where they are blamed for the sharp decline of some native wildlife. This includes the adder, Britain's only venomous (but not generally dangerous to humans) snake, which is facing imminent local extinction from most regions.

Thankfully, pheasants have since grown fewer again in and around the woods – perhaps local releases have lessened; hopefully the native species they prey on will be able to recover as a result.

It may surprise many people to learn that invasive exotic (non-native) species are recognised by ecologists as the second biggest driver of global species extinction, only barely pipped at the post by resource extraction like logging, hunting and fishing. The reason is that the species that make up a native ecosystem have evolved alongside one another over aeons, constantly adapting to each other's evolutionary changes in an ecological process known as coevolution. The ecosystem therefore develops natural checks and balances, preventing any one species from becoming dominant.

Sessile oak, for example, has evolved ecological relationships with more than 280 different species of native phytophagous (plant-feeding) insects, while the figure for willow is 450 and birch 334. Just like rhododendron, oak has natural chemical defences (tannin) in its leaves against attack by insects and other herbivores. But native animals have had all the time necessary to evolve a partial immunity and other strategies to overcome these defences to some degree, in the sort of 'arms race' that is so fundamental to evolutionary processes.

By contrast, any native insects that feed on rhododendron leaves will likely die of poisoning, because they haven't had a chance to adapt, presumably unlike those in the plant's home range around the Black Sea and the Iberian Peninsula. There is strong evidence that the increasing prevalence of non-native plant species is a major factor driving the current sharp decline of insect populations across the world, and consequently many insectivorous bird species also. In comparison, native plants like oak will never predominate to the point where everything else is pushed out, simply because they are eaten by so many different insect species, along with deer and other mammals. And all these connections also provide huge benefits to the wider ecosystem in so many other ways.

But when species are artificially transported between every corner of the globe in a random and forced manner, as people have very unwisely been doing at an ever-increasing rate for centuries, they are often released from the ecological constraints that previously applied. Even so, many struggle to survive outside their natural environments, while others just get by without causing major problems. But a small minority – generally held to be about 0.1 per cent of introduced non-native species – become invasive. This means that the native ecosystems in which they find themselves are unable to restrain them, and they take over, causing immense damage.

The separation between native and exotic species is far from black and white though (we'll look at this in more depth in a later chapter). For example, very often the farther away geographically that species originate, the more potentially damaging they are likely to be, since coevolution with native ecosystems is correspondingly more remote in time. Most of those from the nearby European continent, like the red deer for example, will have been coevolving with what are considered native Irish species until relatively recently in ecological terms.

Just as a variety of species brought from abroad are causing havoc here, so are some of our most familiar and loved plants and animals doing the same elsewhere. An Australian ecologist who visited the Bofickil woods in 2019 told me of working on programmes to eliminate our native holly there, where it is overwhelming indigenous rainforest ecosystems. The red fox and domestic cat, also introduced by Europeans, are responsible for the extinction of dozens of native animal species on the same continent, with cats alone estimated to kill *over 2 billion* animals there every year. Purple loosestrife – a gorgeous native wildflower that's common in the wetter open areas around the Bofickil woods – is a major problem in the wetlands of the northern United States. Each plant can produce 2.5 million seeds per year, forming dense stands that exclude native plants. Along with European ivy, it's one of the top six invasive plants in the US.

The most crucial thing to understand about invasive species is that they tend to make most headway in ecosystems which are already heavily compromised by human activities. The relationship between the elimination of native vegetation by artificially high densities of herbivores in our few remaining native Irish forests and the spread of rhododendron is a prime case in point. There are other examples in an Irish context, some of which I'll look at later on. And the list of invasive species in Ireland extends far beyond the few mentioned here, with 140 species presently listed by the National Biodiversity Data Centre, a number that is continually growing.

The invasive threesome of feral goats, sika deer and rhododendron was dragging the Bofickil woods into an intensifying spiral of ecological meltdown. If that process had been allowed to continue, rather than measures being taken to arrest it when they were, within a few more years things would have snowballed to a point where it would have become very difficult to stop. A first priority was to start working to get rid of the rhododendron and other invasive plants, an extremely labour-intensive operation that I carried out in my spare time over several years.

That task will never really fully end, because seeds continually blow in from outside. In fact, taking out rhododendron in just my own place would have been almost pointless, since it was growing in neighbouring properties all around. And so over time I went about asking permission from around a dozen or more different owners to remove the plant from their land also. That was perhaps made a little easier when one neighbour was told after calling the vet to his sick cattle that they were suffering from poisoning due to feeding on rhododendron leaves.

To tackle the overgrazing issue, I applied for a state scheme that would provide funds to erect a deer (and goat) exclusion fence around some 21.5 acres of land on the seaward side of the main road, where most of the woods are. As well as permitting the existing woods' return to health, the process of new trees colonising open ground – which still comprised about a third of this area – would be able to start up again, creating new woodland.

Officially, wherever feasible the Native Woodland Scheme seeks to grow new trees principally through natural regeneration (i.e. trees' natural ability to reproduce by seeding into surrounding land), rather than planting. In practice, though, planting is almost always a major component. I was adamant, however, that there should be no planting of the species already present, and that all new forest should be allowed to come through natural regeneration. This gives rise to a much more natural forest (oddly enough), consisting of *wild* trees.

Because so much of the landscapes of these islands are now laid bare, there is often an automatic assumption that new trees must be planted by human hands. But that's completely untrue: trees were reproducing without difficulty for hundreds of millions of years before people arrived on the scene. The principal means by which that is now prevented is through overgrazing, either by livestock or artificially high numbers of wild herbivores. Take away the overgrazing and wild trees will generally arrive by themselves in abundance, except where there are no mature trees left in the vicinity to send out seeds, in which case planting is required. But there should be no doubt that, as woodland ecologist Oliver Rackham put it, 'Tree-planting is not synonymous with conservation; it is an admission that conservation has failed.'

Self-seeded wild trees are adapted to the local environment, and germinate and do well only if and where soil conditions and other factors are to their liking. So willow and alder tend towards wetter places, sessile oak preferentially seeks out drier stony spots (hence *Quercus 'petraea'*, from the Latin for 'stone'), rowan (mountain ash) higher ground, and so on. There is, however, no shortage of exceptions to any such generalisations, and most of the tree species in the Bofickil woods seem to be pretty flexible regarding where they will grow. Naturally regenerated trees also avoid the trauma of having their roots ripped from the ground and replanted elsewhere (practically all planted trees are put in bare root). For all these and other reasons, they usually grow much more vigorously and healthily than planted trees.

The degree of contrast between a wild-grown forest like Bofickil and a plantation, even where a mix of native species is used, really does have to be experienced at first hand to be fully appreciated. They are just entirely different entities. Apart from the great diversity of shapes already mentioned, wild trees grow from spots and in ways that would never occur with planting, such as from a fissure in the face of a rock escarpment, spreading horizontally to reach out from under the cover of other trees above. Or from the carcass of a dead tree, the roots of the young sapling growing down through the rotting wood to the soil below, the old passing its energies on to the new. Or two saplings of different species developing side by side, intertwining with one another as they grow.

The possibilities really are practically endless, and in sharp contrast to the often banal monotony of planted trees, native or otherwise. And the enormous diversity of forms in naturally regenerated wild forests is another factor behind their greatly enhanced structural diversity, and hence exponentially increased value as wildlife habitat, compared to plantations. Crucially, natural regeneration works *with* nature, as opposed to people continually trying to impose our will on it, an approach we very much need to leave behind. The latter is not only questionable from an ethical viewpoint: it often fails or has other, sometimes unforeseen, negative effects.

James Lovelock, the British scientist who in the 1960s invented a means of detecting chlorofluorocarbons (CFCs) in the atmosphere, and formulated the hugely revolutionary Gaia theory, described the results of planting some land he had in Devon with native trees. He had done so with the intention of creating a natural forest, but after a couple of decades many of the trees had died, while the rest were barely hanging on: the whole exercise was a complete flop. However, he also noted that, by contrast, another piece of ground nearby, with which he had done nothing except exclude grazing animals, had spontaneously turned into rich, flourishing woodland over the same period through wild trees seeding in. Years later he wrote: 'Planting a tree does not make an ecosystem any more than putting a liver in a jar fed with blood and nutrients makes a man.'

Over the course of a week or more, contractors put up a two-metre-high fence all around the 21.5 acre parcel of land on the seaward side of the main road, a hugely challenging and demanding job given the extreme roughness of the terrain. As a result, the men doing the work were all nearly at the end of their tethers towards the finish. Just as they were about to complete the final stretch of fencing, a neighbour asked if that last piece could take a more circuitous route so his view would be less affected, a change that would have meant extra work.

The man in charge – Dan Joe Cronin from the Borlin Valley near Glengarriff – told me that if he were pressed to do so, he would instead be sorely tempted to 'take off walking to Castletownbere, buy a bottle of whiskey, and never come back'. We took the hint, and the fence went the direct route to the original starting point, closing in the land, and the goats and deer out.

Erecting the fence cost the taxpayer nearly €37,000, a very considerable sum in 2010 given the limited size of the area inside. It was also an eyesore, especially at first, and involved the use of heavy machinery – including a 12-ton digger for driving in the 2.4-metre-long stakes with the bucket. The result was damaged and compacted land in many places. And fences are far from being a long-term solution in the very wet conditions of the west of Ireland: stakes quickly rot, wire mesh loses its tension, and within a decade or less a fence can be starting to fail if not continually maintained.

Additionally, the savage storms that frequently come hammering in from the Atlantic can knock large branches or even entire trees onto a fence, crushing sections and compromising the overall integrity. Therefore, fences must be checked regularly along their entire perimeter, and sometimes repaired, which can be difficult when the location is remote, inaccessible or, as is often the case, both (in some places materials even have to be helicoptered in). Fencing is also far from ideal from an ecological standpoint, with a number of downsides including acting as a barrier to the movement of larger native species. For instance, the badgers living in a sett just outside the fence in Bofickil come and go from the woods through a large pipe that carries a stream under the road and deer fence.

However, the choice at the time was a straightforward one: either fence off the land, or watch the forest continue to be grazed and browsed to death by the goats and sika.

6

Reaching Through Time

As Liam began attending the village primary school, and Seánie the playschool, getting to know people in our new community became ever easier, and it slowly dawned on me just how fortunate we had been. We had come to Eyeries solely on the basis of the farm in Bofickil, with no prior knowledge of the local social dynamics. But I was aware that these can differ greatly from one area to another, and have a crucial effect on quality of life, in some senses much more so in a rural district than in an urban one.

The differences in way of life between a city and the countryside should not be underestimated. Not because country people are somehow innately different to 'city slickers' – in my experience they aren't – but chiefly because the urban combination of constant 'action' and relative anonymity is absent. Possibly largely as a consequence, many people who try to make that change realise after varying lengths of time that it's not for them, and return to the city. That can often be for personal reasons, but the social environment can play a major role too.

I remember visiting a friend from Dublin who was living for some time in Connemara in the early 1990s, and her descriptions of the various distinct categories of 'blow-ins' (people like myself, not originally from an area) who were living there. They had all formed themselves into very separate cliques, and seemed to have as little as possible to do with anyone from outside their own particular group, or with any of the local people. Not surprisingly, my friend didn't stay there long. Such a scenario sounded awful to me, but often it really is down to the luck of the draw when moving to a new place.

What we found in Eyeries was quite the opposite. There was a good sprinkling of other blow-ins, but most people were from the area, which made the community feel rooted. Just as importantly, people generally seemed not to care too much where anyone else was from, and were just getting on with living alongside one another in a relaxed way. To my mind, that's the way it should be: we're all just people, after all, wherever we happen to be born or brought up.

My neighbour Michael might often try to 'rise me' (wind me up) about being 'only an effing Dublin jackeen', and I'll throw 'culchie' back at him. But it's always purely to have the craic, with never any badness (or 'blackguarding', to use the local term) whatsoever intended on either side. Just like any other place in the world, the people around Eyeries are a mixed bunch, but it all seems to work and, by and large, there's a pleasant, communal atmosphere. We were extremely lucky to land into that.

My mother's passing meant that, in addition to grieving, there was a lot to be sorted out, especially with regard to her house in Inchicore, which we decided to sell. She had always had a tendency to accumulate stuff, but this had been greatly accentuated in the last few years of her life. And everything was mixed together: things that were really important to keep, others that might be useful – either to ourselves or to someone else – and a lot that had to go straight to the waste recycling centre, all jumbled together in vast quantities. So going through it all was a gargantuan task, made much worse by the fact that I'm allergic to house dust, and would start sneezing and my eyes watering within minutes every time I would go at it.

I decided the only way to survive the process, both physically and psychologically, was by making periodic trips up to Dublin, thereby breaking it all down into less overwhelming segments. Each time, I'd trawl through a great pile of odds and ends, bring many (estate) carloads to the local second-hand shops, many more to the recycling centre, and finally drive home to Beara with the car loaded to bursting with furniture and other material I wanted to keep.

Going through all my mum's things was a very emotional experience at times, with all sorts of mementoes, old letters, and so on coming to light. So it was a constant challenge not to end up sitting there for hours on end poring over bits and pieces, making no real headway at all with the monumental job at hand. Some of the material I needed to sort out had belonged to my father, who had died many years before. One day while sifting through some of his stuff, I came across a couple of sheets of foolscap paper with what was a letter in his very distinctive hand-writing, written in April 1971, and addressed to the editor of *The Irish Times*.

It had obviously been a very rough first draft, in which he was working out what he wanted to say, and how. There were lines through many of the sentences, cancelling out (without making illegible) earlier ideas, with replacement phrases and additional notes scribbled in here and there, wherever space would allow. He had even thrown in a couple of animalesque doodles, just to add to the overall confusion. So I struggled at first to get a handle on the subject and content of the letter.

It had been written in response to an article that had appeared in the newspaper some days earlier on pollution in the lakes of the Irish midlands, near to where he grew up and used to go fishing 'with pole and line, summer after summer as a kid'. Learning of the situation had clearly made his blood boil:

> I wonder how many readers read this report. Were they shocked? Or do they just accept it as inevitable, the price to be paid for so-called progress, and then pass on to other pages to read column upon chockablock column of political doings and rantings – all absolutely irrelevant in the light of the irreparable damage that is being done to the narrow strip of earth/air/ water on our planet which constitutes the biosphere? [...] It's amazing how many people regardless of social class or political outlook are shy of this vital question. Why?

Also included were references to the worsening ecological state of the Mediterranean and Baltic seas, and several lines of poetry in Irish – in which he was fluent – by Máirtín Ó Direáin, lamenting the disappearance of wild fish as a result of human activities:

> *Tá réim an éisc thart le fada,*
> *Sibhse anois iarmhar na mara,*
> *Gach fear mar dhealbh mharmair,*
> *Ar shaol bhur sean go seasta.*

He finished his letter by paraphrasing Seán O'Casey's 1924 play about the Irish Civil War, *Juno and the Paycock*: 'The blinds is comin' steadily down, but does Joxer want to know?'

It's difficult to find the words to convey just how deeply moved I felt to find such a letter written by my dad. What amazed me was the fact that, half a century ago now, he was conceptualising a local issue in terms of our relationship with 'the narrow strip of earth/air/water on our planet which constitutes the biosphere'. And, even more so, that he went so far as to dismiss most of what passes for politics (which were *extremely* important to him) as 'absolutely irrelevant' compared to the 'irreparable damage' being done to it. The sentiments he expressed are rightly and necessarily voiced ever more frequently nowadays, and that trend will almost certainly continue into the future. But I think it was a pretty farsighted piece of writing for the time.

Sitting there amidst the chaos and dust, holding that letter in my hands, it felt as if my father had found a way of reaching to me through time, of telling me that what I was trying to allow happen with the land in Bofickil was good and worthwhile. For me, it was a valorisation from probably the one person from whom it could ever have meant most.

It was a few years before a couple of vitally important characteristics of the Bofickil farm began to properly hit home. For starters, the fact that the land had been left unused for so long meant that, crucially, it had been thoroughly spared the attentions of heavy machinery.

It's true that, over the centuries, Herculean human labours had clearly gone into many of the same actions as are now carried out by diggers and tractors. Rocks – some of them massive – had been stacked into field walls, which served as much as repositories for unwanted stone picked from the land, as to create field boundaries. Land was drained through the construction of souterrain-like underground culverts – which still exist in places, flanked and capped with large flat stones, and then back-covered with soil in such a way that only the openings are visible.

Michael also told me that streams would once have been regularly cleared with a spade to improve drainage, removing any *scrá* (accumulated sediment and vegetation) that formed. Tree branches were cut and drawn out of the woods for firewood, and peat harvested with the *sleán* from the six acres near Ardgroom where the farm has turbary (turf-cutting) rights. But all this had been done almost entirely through human brawn alone, occasionally augmented by horsepower, greatly limiting the extent of the impact on the landscape. It must have been an extremely tough life, one that we would now hugely struggle with, at least in the western world.

With the arrival of diesel-driven machinery from around the 1950s, what was once impossible, or would have taken weeks of backbreaking work, could be achieved in a matter of hours and with little effort. Clearing, draining, eliminating, flattening, rendering uniform; creating endless tracts with all the variety of a golfing green. As tractors, diggers, chainsaws and other similar means became increasingly accessible, land that has avoided such a fate has become correspondingly ever scarcer, in a process of total transformation that continues unabated across Ireland. Over time, I developed a growing appreciation of the fact that the Crowley place had escaped such a fate, for a number of important reasons beyond just the most immediately obvious one (to me, at least) of aesthetics.

Firstly, as a result the landscape remains a highly cultural one, with the signs of past human occupancy preserved. And this area is simply awash with the remains of the prehistoric, and more recent, past. There is a possible, but unconfirmed, wedge tomb marked within the boundaries of the farm on archaeological maps, although my own feeling is that it's probably a natural formation. However, within a further few hundred yards of the same boundaries are a definite wedge tomb, a stone circle, a Bronze Age copper mine, a *lios* (stone ringfort) complete with souterrain, and the tallest ogham stone in existence, at 5.3 metres. It's virtually certain that there are many more remnants that are still unknown, and all around are other intriguingly ambiguous features that make you wonder as to their origin – that is, whether they are natural or man-made.

Similarly, the land retains intact the craggy marks of deep geological time, especially those resulting from glacial action, reminders of just how very recently the human era began. But it's in ecological terms that the dividends are greatest, for a diverse landscape is simply far better for wildlife, due to the increased potential variety of niches available. However, despite all the arguments in favour of treating the land gently, there is a rapid and relentless homogenisation taking place throughout the length and breadth of the Irish countryside, with flat monocultural banality the ideal always strived for. And there is practically unlimited mechanised power available with which to impose it. Everywhere, the ancient forms and features that tell the story of the land, and make it special and rich, have been – and are being – erased forever at a savage rate.

Far less obviously, but of no less importance, the Crowley place was never subjected to the deluge of agricultural chemicals – artificial fertilisers, pesticides, herbicides, animal antibiotics and others – that is now the norm in modern farming. Michael told me of his father regularly drawing seaweed up from the shore on his back in a big wicker basket to fertilise their land in Reentrisk, near Allihies on the west of the peninsula, in the 1940s. Synthetic fertilisers became widely available in Beara and elsewhere after the Second World War, following the discovery of a means to convert atmospheric nitrogen into a usable form earlier in the century. Industrial quantities of nitrate- and phosphate-based fertilisers, as well as slurry, are now regularly spread on most farmland throughout Ireland and beyond in order to boost productivity, whether of grass for grazing animals, or planted crops.

These chemicals are disastrous for the environment on numerous levels. They eliminate or repress much of the underground life that is so essential to the healthy functioning of soils (and therefore ecosystems), such as earthworms and other invertebrates, microbes and mycorrhizal fungi. Many wild plant species also disappear, as artificial nutrient levels – especially nitrogen – accumulate far beyond those that occur naturally in soils.

Perhaps even worse, most of the vast amounts of fertilisers and slurry spread on farmland are not absorbed by the target plants or soil at all. The excess instead washes into streams and rivers, where it causes eutrophication in the same way as raw sewage, with algal blooms and oxygen depletion severely damaging aquatic ecosystems. Drinking water is also polluted, as residues seep into wells; and when they inevitably flush into the sea, coastal dead zones result where sufficiently concentrated.

The desperately sad truth is that, beneath a thin veneer, there was nothing much green at all about the 1950s and '60s 'Green

Revolution', as it was called. In reality, it was a catastrophe for natural ecosystems across the planet, which paid an extremely high price for increased food production, based on the promotion of ubiquitous chemical- and diesel-fed monocultures. In Ireland, farmland rich in wildflower meadows, patches of wetland, extensive diverse hedgerows, pockets of unfarmed scrub and other species-rich habitats all began disappearing. As elsewhere in Europe, these changes were greatly accelerated by the introduction of the Common Agricultural Policy (CAP) in 1962, which has pushed for maximum, but sterile, productivity at all costs ever since.

The farm in Bofickil was extremely fortunate to have bypassed this many-fronted blitz. The streams contain a great abundance of creatures including aquatic insects, with myriad pond skaters on the surface and a great variety of larvae on the streambeds, attracting such birdlife as grey wagtails and dippers. The absence of chemical pollution was likely also a major factor in the fantastic blossoming of the land that had been taking place prior to the arrival of the goats, and which has fully resumed over the last decade with the erection of the deer fence.

After a couple of years of efforts, Cork County Council finally granted us planning permission to build a new house beside the old cottage in Bofickil. This came as a huge relief since, for a time, it looked as if we might never actually get it. As feared, the main impediment turned out to be the access road, but in the end getting the deer fence put up gave me a clue as to where it might be routed. The contractors levelled a particular area of incline to gain access for their digger, and the path they made ultimately became part of a new driveway leading down to the house.

The trials and tribulations of the planning stage over, the next step was building the house, which was becoming increasingly urgent, as renting was putting a serious strain on our remaining funds. Having read up on the subject, I decided to attempt to build the house as close to passive standard as we could afford. *Passivhaus* is a concept that originated in the Nordic countries, whereby most of the windows of a building are faced towards the south, high levels of insulation are incorporated throughout, and a variety of other design measures taken to minimise heat loss. It creates a living environment in which the passive heat of the sun alone is sufficient to warm the internal spaces (hence the name), and no heating system is required. In Ireland's milder but more overcast winters it doesn't work in quite the same way, and some very minimal form of heating is usually necessary, but building along these lines still makes enormous sense with regard to energy efficiency and comfort.

However, constructing the house in this way made the whole process substantially more complicated and nerve-wracking. And since I was managing every aspect of the build as well as doing a lot of the work myself, the project proved to be hugely demanding, both physically and, much more so, mentally. This all had to be balanced with running my sculpture business, very real financial worries, and all the many other more usual pressures of life. Sadly, my marriage to Giuliana was also failing, leading to our separation several years later, and all these things combined to make this an extremely difficult period.

The one thing that got me through it all, more than anything else, was being able to regularly spend time in a wild and natural place: the woods.

Whenever I felt as if I was carrying the weight of the whole world on my shoulders, within only a few steps into the woods I would feel that start to lift, often in the most indescribably powerful way. It was as if the galvanised steel farm gate in the deer fence were a portal, swinging open to reveal another tier of reality in which all the pressures of everyday life were hereby suspended until further notice. My mind would then go to a very special, deeply peaceful, place.

But the transformation I underwent often extended far beyond just mood. It could be intensely physiological, as if there was an immediate surge of positive energy throughout my body, leaving the whole feeling much lighter, more relaxed and connected. That might sound exaggerated, but if anything it doesn't even come close to doing justice to the benefits I have gained from entering the woodland environment down through the years. Not necessarily always to quite the same degree, but absolutely without fail.

In those moments everything else just dissolves away, leaving me feeling only the here and now of maybe the dappled sun on my face, fat insects buzzing drowsily past my ear, and the gentle gurgling of a nearby stream. Or the dripping exuberance and heady mixture of fragrances that permeate the forest air after rain, hitting you with a constant succession of differing aromatic head punches. And there is always the possibility – likelihood, actually – of unexpected encounters during the course of a wander in and around the woods.

A family of wrens, for example, the fresh-out-of-the-nest

juveniles a bunch of tiny hopping, threeping, round balls of scruffy feathers, attended to with frequent beakfuls of insects by frenetically working parents. There might even be a sighting of a badger, fox, hare, lizard, or some other member of the local fauna. Or, in summer, perhaps a close-up of one of the fantastically colourful dragonflies and damselflies that are so common in the more expansive woodland glades, zigzagging back and forth as they hunt for flying insects. An awareness that they have been doing so virtually unchanged since at least the Upper Carboniferous (325 million years ago) and Lower Permian (250 million years ago) eras, respectively, only adds to the intoxication.

In autumn the chance might be granted to watch, through binoculars, a pair of jays busily gathering acorns for the winter. For the rest of the year, hearing their raucous screeches echoing through the woods, or a glimpsed bright flash of blue and white, is about as much as you're likely to get of this ultra-shy bird, whose Irish population constitutes a unique subspecies (as with the coal tit). In winter there is the common joy of finding yourself immersed for several minutes in a passing 'flocking' of dozens of small passerines, working their way through the forest as an apparently non-discriminatory multi-species troupe. A brightly coloured horde of squeaking and pippering blue, great, coal and long-tailed tits, goldcrests (Ireland's smallest bird, weighing in at a mere 5 grams), and maybe even a treecreeper or two, all scouring the branches together for invertebrate snacks.

Even without meeting any particular fauna, which is rare, the mere fact of being in such a multi-layered natural environment is sufficient for a deep rejuvenation to be effected in me, every time. To give just one example of what that might mean, there are spots at the tops of high precipices where, standing near the edge, you're at canopy level with the trees growing lower down, or are even looking down on their undulating bunched tops. In such places, the gaze can directly zoom out from the filigreed minutiae of nearby mosses and lichens growing on the rocks and trees all around to the open expanse of the Atlantic and its horizon, framed by the surrounding leaves and branches. Thus a single glance almost at once encompasses worlds that verge on the microscopic, and the proportionately infinite.

Time as measured by the clock loses its significance in the woods, becoming just another human construct whose relevance belongs only to other jurisdictions. Just an hour or two provides a plenty sufficient pit-stop of visual, physical, cognitive and sensory stimuli that would last for weeks, if a fast of any contact with the woods were to be suddenly imposed for some reason. Were I to be thrust into a nightmarish ordeal along the lines of Brian Keenan's *An Evil Cradling*, which describes his abduction and forced isolation in Lebanon, I would call upon my stored memories of being in the woods to help keep me sane.

In the forest, ecological time, which is only truly measured in scales stretching far beyond our own lives, potentially comes into view, if not quite within full grasp of the mind. And it takes on the cyclical form of continual renewal our ancestors were familiar with, rather than the relatively recent, linear one of 'progress' we are now forced to live by. Constantly 'doing' is replaced, for the duration, by just *being*, and the opportunity to imbibe some of the wonder of it all. Of how the water, mineral and air molecules that make up the elements of life's systems have been endlessly exchanged and recycled over the course of billions of years. Of how that which is now an oak, a thrush, a woodland stream, a moth, you and me, was once a mammoth, a pterodactyl, a carboniferous rainforest, a trilobite.

There is true liberation and healing in forsaking the worry and discord of the human sphere for a while, before re-engaging with renewed energy, and clarity around what really matters, and what doesn't. Wendell Berry's sublime poem 'The Peace of Wild Things' manages to catch in written word these aspects of being in nature perhaps better than anything else I know of, and if you haven't yet had the pleasure of reading it, I'd strongly recommend doing so.

After spending time in the woods, I leave as a different person, recharged to my very core. All is once again right with the world. Those feelings, a combination of deep joy, serenity and hope, have never lessened over time, and continue to be a huge positive in my life, one which since coming to Beara I would struggle to go without. In moments, it goes beyond a meditation, to the closest I have come to what might be described as transcendental experience.

There is an accumulating weight of evidence to show that contact with nature is one of the most beneficial things we can do for our physical and mental health. And the wilder and less managed the particular nature is, the better it works. It shouldn't be at all difficult to understand why. Like all other species, we evolved over millions of years in natural environments, rather than the modern constructed one of straight lines, rigid angles, unyielding surfaces, computer screens, manufactured uniformity and deadlines.

These impositions, to some degree self-inflicted, increasingly govern and regulate our existence today, but they are alien to us. Our minds and bodies are hardwired to respond well to being in nature – it really is as simple as that. For example, studies conducted in hospitals have demonstrated conclusively that patients in rooms looking out over trees and other greenery heal or recover from illness significantly more quickly than those in rooms that do not, all else being equal.

The Japanese concept of *shinrin-yoku* ('forest bathing'), which means spending fully relaxed time in a natural forest, has been steadily gaining traction around the world. Scientific research has shown that it provides enormous health benefits, reducing blood pressure, lowering cortisol levels, boosting the immune system, and improving concentration and memory. This is increasingly accepted as fact by medical practitioners, and it has been – or is in the process of being – adopted into the official health programme of several countries. Certainly my own experiences have convinced me beyond all doubt of its validity.

As regards the idea of 'bathing' in forest, I have always felt there to be remarkably strong analogies between diving into a natural body of water and entering the Bofickil woods, especially on a hot, sunny and breezy summer's day. Inside the woods, the air remains much more cool, moist and still, with shimmering shafts of sunlight penetrating down through the canopy of leaves above, recalling the effect of swimming underwater. The exploration of this very theme – the many similarities between swimming in a natural place and being in wild native forest – is a recurrent thread running through Roger Deakin's lovely book, *Wildwood*:

> In the woods, there is a strong sense of immersion in the dancing shadow play of the leafy depths, and the rise and fall of the sap that proclaims the seasons is nothing less than a tide, and no less influenced by the moon.

When the Bofickil woods figure in my dreams at night, as they occasionally do, I always find myself able to float weightlessly through the air, going where I like as if released from all gravitational restraints. I then use my fantastical powers to explore and experience fully the three-dimensionality of the woods, hovering along between the trees, among branches, or soaring above the canopy. That is one sort of dream from which I am always especially sorry to waken.

Walking the mountain commonage and looking down on the woods below can resemble simulated flight, though without the silent jetpack buoyancy of my dreams. When the trees are in leaf, they form a rich mosaic of broccoli tops in myriad shades of green, ranging from the delicately bright and cheerful lime of the birches, through the stronger verdancy of oak, to the dark opacity of holly and ivy. But the canopy is far from flatly even: the great discrepancies in ground height below, variations in tree sizes, open glades, wind-knocked trees, and other factors all combine to give a highly contoured surface. In some places, certain trees, usually oak, stand above their surrounding neighbours in a diminutive version of the giant Brazil nut and *ceiba* 'emergents' of tropical rainforests. Diminutive purely in stature, mind, not presence.

Seen from the mountain above, in autumn the canopy mutates into a lacerated mottle of russet, beige, yellow and orange, becoming ever more threadbare as the leaves are shed to reveal the underlying architecture of the trees. Winter nudity brings out each species' own signature traits in shape and texture, with pockets of birch a distinctive purple-brown wispish haze (recalling a certain song by a certain Jimi Hendrix).

Oak is silvery-grey and much more clearly defined, like the tracery of a thirteenth-century Gothic window, while ivy and holly become more evident in their seasonally unvarying sombre duskiness. Every other species similarly distinguishes itself in some way: massed hazel branches have a reddish hue from afar, and the grey of whitethorn can often appear tinged with pale green through heavy lichen encrustation. And when the wind blows forcefully, the trees, whether wearing their full summer garb or in a state of winter undress, all swirl together in woody communion with the ocean's wild churning, just beyond.

As for night flights into the woods, only once have I ever physically ventured in there after sundown without a torch for backup. The landscape that night was floodlit by an exceptionally luminous winter moon, tracking only barely above, sometimes touching, the black rocky silhouette of the adjacent mountain. Entering the woods was an eerie and yet deeply enchanting experience, an exploration of a surreally bright spellbound realm of contrasting silver and shadows that was at once wholly familiar, and yet unknown to me. Passing through a silent monochromatic negative of the daytime forest I had come to know so well, it felt like taking part in an arthouse movie in which the use of colour film had been eschewed for its excessive gaudiness. It was a glimpse into yet another of the woods' seemingly limitless incarnations.

Finally moving into our own house was a wonderful moment, celebrated in the by now customary manner of a bottle of *vino 'nero' italiano*, as the sun went down over the Atlantic. Since we were a mile or so to the east of the first rented house in the village, the view was different but no less spectacular. If anything, it was much more elementally diverse, encompassing the woods, mountains, a heavily inletted coast, and several more islands, while still retaining a good segment of open ocean. That evening the setting sun cast a long flash of sparkling gold towards us, streaking across and between the Skelligs, Deenish, Scariff, Inisfarnard, and the tip of Kilcatherine Point, underneath a drama-filled coppered western sky.

The house turned out to be a very pleasant and comfortable one to live in, with the flow of internal spaces working out well in practice, rather than just as we had imagined and hoped when planning it all out on paper. Although much more focused on energy efficiency, and larger, the new house had much in common with the cottage in Kilmainham. The design similarly drew heavily on traditional vernacular architecture, with the eastern Mediterranean – but also very Irish – colour combination of white and primary blue again predominating. We used natural materials wherever possible, such as thick, rough slates as a floor covering, the exact same as those on the roof. The outside plaster, and all the edges around doors and windows inside, were roughly rounded and undulating, giving a nicely 'organic' feel to the building. Everyone who came to visit or stay was very complimentary, and there was of course a satisfaction in that.

But for me there was never a sliver of doubt regarding the house. I saw it, and will always see it, as nothing more than a necessary means to being able to live close to what *really* counts: the land, the woods, and the increasingly rich webs of life for whom they are home.

7

Temperate Rainforest

In the years after the deer fence went up, I was privileged to be witness to the most stunning, magical transformation of the land inside. Native tree seedlings began to pop up everywhere and, rather than being immediately eaten to death, were able to carry on growing into adolescence and beyond, giving rise to what has since become new young forest in areas that had previously been just grass. Where trees were already present, a rich dormant ground flora began to reawaken, with a great profusion of woodland flowers appearing, many of them species that I had presumed were completely absent.

Tapestries of bluebell, lesser celandine, wood anemone (my favourite), bugle, primrose, dog violet, pignut, sanicle, wild angelica, herb Robert, wood sorrel, opposite-leaved golden saxifrage, marsh violet, yellow pimpernel, barren strawberry, wood avens, enchanter's nightshade, germander speedwell. All these, and a plethora of others, would burst into florescence in a rolling display lasting from early spring into late summer.

The visual effect was one of wildly splashing impressionist colour about the blank canvas of a previously barren woodland floor. Slowly at first, but at an ever-increasing velocity thereafter, life in all its vibrancy was coming back to the woods. The many wetter open areas similarly exploded with their own palette of yellow flag, ragged robin, cuckoo flower, heath spotted-orchid, devil's-bit scabious, sheep's bit, and purple loosestrife, to name just some of the many wildflowers that emerged. All this helped create the conditions for a great boon in insects, which in turn attracted additional numbers of birds. More and more, the whole place buzzed with flying creatures and rang with birdsong. The change was radical on practically every level.

Seeing that coming to life unfold (it has never slowed) has often reminded me of the early scenes in a much-loved picture book I had as a child, and which was passed on to my own boys when they were small. *Where the Wild Things Are* by Maurice Sendak tells of a young boy named Max, who's sent to his bedroom without supper for making mischief. As he stands there in his wolf costume, the room around him begins to morph, scene by scene, into a wild forest.

The walls and bedposts become trees, and the ceiling turns into a night sky full of stars and a bright moon. Max finds himself in a marvellous wonderland, in which he goes on to have the most fantastic adventures, before finally getting back to his bedroom to find his supper waiting for him. For me, those first images of Max's bedroom conjure perfectly the metamorphosis I have observed in the Bofickil woods, as they have gone from a partially empty sterility and dying state to the chaotic and tangled fullness of a healthy forest.

Moving to Beara precipitated a full immersion on my part in the literature of forest ecology, and ecological science in general, that will never end. I fervently devoured everything I could lay my hands on, beginning with British woodland specialists Oliver Rackham and George Peterken. Soon I was moving on to internationally renowned biologists and conservationists like Edward O. Wilson, Michael Soulé, Aldo Leopold and Daniel Janzen. A very synergistic process was at play, whereby, parallel with learning from spending time in, and working to restore, the Bofickil woods, I was able to sponge up a framework for it all from some of the best ever minds on the planet.

No doubt there were plenty of gaps in what I absorbed, as I focused on those aspects that were of most relevance or interest to me, in contrast to a more academically structured study of the same subjects, for example. Nevertheless, it was one of the most intensely exciting times of my life, as I learned about a whole new world of wonder to which I had hitherto been largely blind. This included mind-expanding insights into some of the very ecological mechanisms that make our home planet tick.

Developing out of that self-education, the most startling, thrilling realisation soon began to take hold, though at first I struggled to believe such a thing could really be true. What I was restoring wasn't just native woodland: according to all the scientific definitions, it was in fact very clearly rainforest. As opposed to the tropical rainforest mainly found in Latin America, Central Africa and South-East Asia, the woods in Bofickil are a prime example of an entirely separate biome: the far more rare *temperate* rainforest.

The main giveaway indicator of any sort of rainforest, anywhere in the world, is the presence of epiphytes. These are plants that grow on other plants – generally trees – without being rooted in the ground, hence excluding climbers like ivy or woodbine (honeysuckle). Epiphytes don't take any sustenance from the trees they grow on, depending entirely for moisture and all their nutrient requirements on what comes their way from the surrounding air, and in any accumulated organic matter on the surfaces they cling to. They can therefore only survive in places where high levels of moisture arrive on a frequent basis in the form of rain, drizzle, mist, fog, and so on. Airborne water, and lots of it, is the catalysing element.

The Beara Peninsula certainly isn't short of such conditions, with between 1.5 and 2.75 metres of precipitation per year, depending on altitude (by way of comparison, Dublin gets around 0.75 metres). Even more important than the actual amount of water that falls is the number of 'wet days' each year, i.e. days with over 1 millimetre of rain, which in Beara averages out around 200 or more, with relative humidity at 75–85 per cent. Southwest Ireland's position means that its climate is largely conditioned by the Atlantic, and in particular by the Gulf Stream, which brings a continual supply of warm waters from the Caribbean. The resulting very mild and wet conditions, called 'hyper-oceanic', are perfect for rainforest, which once clothed practically the entire landscape.

Just as in tropical rainforests and cloud forests, with their great abundance of bromeliads, orchids and other epiphytic plants, so too are the trees in Boficikil similarly thickly clad. Mosses, lichens, a variety of ferns, including polypody and Tunbridge filmy, as well as navelwort, herb Robert, wood sorrel, kidney saxifrage, St Patrick's cabbage, woodrush and many others form a rich carpet on trunks and boughs alike. It's not unusual to find actual tree species that have taken root in pockets of debris in larger, more mature trees. (In the temperate rainforests of New Zealand, 28 different species of epiphytic vascular plants alone, i.e. excluding mosses or lichens, have been found growing on a single tree.)

Even before human impacts, temperate rainforest was always much more limited in global extent than the tropical equivalent, only ever constituting a very small fraction – perhaps a tenth – of the latter's land area. But its location in temperate zones also made the land much more attractive for agriculture, and therefore subject to far more drastic reduction due to both clearance and grazing pressure. As a result, it now has an extremely restricted distribution globally. However, examples of temperate rainforest do still survive in several parts of the world where suitable conditions occur. These include the coastal forests of British Columbia in Canada, the Valdivian forests of Chile, and those along the west coast of New Zealand's South Island.

And, in what seemed a most incredible coincidence, I learned that also among them are the Knysna-Tsitsikamma forests of South Africa, next to where my mother had grown up, and of which she had always spoken with such wonder.

In the years following my mum's death, I was regularly in touch by telephone with her sister Jill, who still lived in Knysna. We would have long, enjoyable chats about all manner of things, with the forests both here in Bofickil and in Knysna a common feature. Back in the 1960s and 1970s, Jill and her husband Ian had a farm on the other side of some of the forested hills from the town, and would often see baboons, more rarely leopards, and even, on a few occasions, elephants, while passing through. One day while having one of our telephone conversations, she casually let me know that her health wasn't great, and that if by any chance I was considering visiting South Africa some time, and would like her to still be around, I should consider doing so sooner rather than later.

My last visit to the country had been at the age of 14, over 33 years previously, and I had only ever been once before that. My mum would very much have liked for us to go together before she died, but for a variety of reasons that had never happened; so, in a sense, I felt the need to make a trip to South Africa as part of coming to terms with her passing. And I also had a strong desire to see examples of temperate rainforest in another part of the world, feeling that an acquaintance with the African forests had the potential to bring a deeper understanding of the ecology and other aspects of my own place in Beara. The sheer level of fluke in the presence of the same biome in both the Bofickil farm and my mother's home place so far away was simply too great to ignore. It seemed that fate had decided it was time to go, and so I booked a return flight to Cape Town in a travel agent's office near the National Monument on Cork's Grand Parade, which I was restoring at the time.

As well as family stuff, I wanted time to explore and try to get to know indigenous forests all along the east coast almost as far as the border with Mozambique, a journey of over 1,600 kilometres each way. On that basis I decided a full month was the minimum necessary. But while hugely excited about the trip, at the back of my mind there was a very distinct fear: that what I would experience in the forests there would be so magnificent – in extent, age, richness of wildlife – that I would never again be able to enjoy the woods in Bofickil to quite the same degree as before. Nevertheless I was intent on going, and the day soon came to depart. After arriving into Cape Town and spending a couple of days with cousins there, I hired a car and drove up the coast to Knysna, stopping off for a night along the way in the town of Hermanus to do some whale-watching.

Seeing Jill in Knysna for the first time in many years was, as always, a great pleasure, the last occasion having been a visit she made to me while I was living in Italy. I stayed with her over two stints totalling about twelve days, and we established a routine in which we would meet for long, leisurely chats over breakfast on her garden terrace every morning, discussing life and the world. Jill was among those people I feel luckiest to have known, for her great kindness, no-nonsense approach, genuine wisdom and vibrant sense of humour. She died at a good old age only a few years later, making the trip even more timely and meaningful.

Those mornings on the terrace were also memorable for the great variety of spectacularly coloured wild birds that were constantly active all around us in the trees and bushes. After breakfast I would drive out to the forests in the nearby hills, and spend the fullness of each day hiking, exploring, taking photographs and drinking in the essences of the places I visited. There was never any shortage of lovely spots to stop for a picnic lunch, such as by a waterfall plunging into a crystal-clear pool, bathed in sunlight, with huge, brightly coloured dragonflies zipping about hunting over the water and surrounding tree ferns.

Throughout that month in South Africa, I felt as though my mum was there with me at all times, but in moments like these that sensation was especially acute. I was struck by the strange circularity of her life's journey, which had taken her from the environs of a temperate rainforest in one hemisphere, through the traffic and turmoil of London and Dublin, to a final resting place in another. She would have loved the poetry in that.

One of the highlights of Knysna was getting to meet and spend time with a family friend, Hattie Thesen, who had known my mum. Together with her life partner Debbie, she was running ecological awareness-raising adventure activities for groups of schoolchildren on the edge of the forest. Many of the kids were from desperately poor townships, ranging from the local area to the outskirts of Cape Town. I was able to witness first hand the sheer delight on their faces at having the chance – in many cases very possibly for the first time in their lives – to engage with a wild place. By doing what they do, Hattie and Debbie are making an inestimable contribution to the education of a generation that is more cut off from nature than ever before, but on whom its future will ultimately depend.

Hattie also managed to find time to bring me into particular parts of the forest I might otherwise have missed, and to talk me through some of its basic ecology, about which she is extremely knowledgeable. Her father Hjalmar had been a passionate and lifelong nature conservationist, who in the 1960s turned the game reserve he owned into a permanent nature sanctuary. That was the world in which Hattie had grown up, and she was well connected with other conservationists working locally, such as Gareth Patterson, who carried out much of the most recent research on the enigmatic elephants of Knysna forest.

The few elephants that remain are the last of a population that probably once numbered around a thousand, but which was almost wiped out by hunting and habitat loss as the surrounding more open *fynbos* was converted to agriculture. As a result they are extremely secretive, and for a time it was thought possible that they had actually died out, with no sightings for many years. However, DNA evidence Patterson gathered between 2001 and 2008 suggested that there was still a herd with at least five young cows, the most vital element for a potentially viable future. I was very grateful to Hattie for the many insights she was able to give me into the zone's specific ecological dynamics.

The Knysna forests have been heavily affected by human activity, especially since European colonisation and settlement over the last few centuries, being exploited for timber and cleared over large areas for farming. Despite that, they still extend over some 568 square kilometres, making them the largest natural forest complex in southern Africa. The forests are big enough to get lost in and never be seen again (as occasionally happens), and contain colossal trees, such as outeniqua yellowwood, with trunks measuring several metres across at the base, and heights of up to 45 metres.

The variety of tree species far exceeds that of any Irish native forest, with about 90 different trees and 55 woody shrubs. Some of them have bizarre features, such as forest knobwood (*Zanthoxylum davyi*), with a trunk entirely studded in fearsomely sharp fat spikes up to 10 centimetres long, like a giant medieval battle mace. Presumably these evolved as a protection against elephants, or other mega-beasts (megafauna, to use the proper term) no longer in existence.

But of all the tree species I encountered in the South African forests, the one that made by far the greatest impression was the strangler fig, which has the most amazing life cycle. There are around a dozen species of strangler fig throughout the world, but they all share certain essential characteristics. The fruit of the fig is an important food source for a whole host of forest inhabitants, including many species of birds, monkeys and bats.

After digestion, the seeds are dispersed in their poop in the sort of exchange of ecological services so vital to the functioning of the living world. Often deposited high up in the canopy, if they happen to land anywhere there is any bit of collected humus – in the fork of a branch, for example – they germinate and grow, initially as epiphytes. This is a pretty clever evolutionary trick, because, by starting life high up where most of the light is, they effectively leapfrog the intense struggle to reach the sunlight from the relative darkness far below.

The fig grows very slowly at first since, as with any other epiphyte, the available resources are limited. But as soon as it's able, it sends a long thin root tendril down towards the ground, which may be 30 metres or more below. The moment the tip makes contact with the earth, everything changes. The fig is now no longer an epiphyte, having access to all the water and nutrients it wants, while also benefiting from the strong sunlight hitting its leaves high in the canopy above. It therefore begins to grow very quickly, with more root tendrils stretching down to the ground all around the tree trunk. These then thicken, turning into fat stems, and where they touch or interweave with one another, they fuse together, creating a dense lattice-like structure wrapped around the host tree, constricting its trunk.

Meanwhile, up above in the canopy, the leaves of the fig are shading out those of the supporting tree, which is now finding it increasingly difficult to survive, as its roots also have to compete with those of the fig. Often it eventually dies, and its trunk then rots away, leaving a hollow cylindrical tube of the intermeshed and merged stems of the fig, which by now are self-supporting. The fig tree is described as a 'hemiepiphyte', since it starts life as an epiphyte but doesn't remain one. (Figs aren't selective about the structures they use for support: perhaps the most famous examples in the world are those that envelop sections of the ruined twelfth-century temple complex at Angkor Wat, Cambodia.)

It would be easy to see something repulsive in how the strangler fig operates, taking advantage of the host tree in such a way that the tree's death often ensues. Indeed, a couple of people I spoke to about figs in South Africa saw them as a parasitic pest to be removed from trees wherever possible. But that view misinterprets what is, in fact, just another among countless examples of how incredibly wondrous the workings of nature are. The fretworked stems of the fig covering the trunk and branches of the tree beneath provide innumerable niches for a huge variety of fully epiphytic plants, which in turn support a host of wildlife, and the whole thing becomes practically a mini-ecosystem high up in the air. The fig also plays a vital role in the forest by providing food to so many of the animals that live there.

A pride of lions taking down a zebra or kudu, for example, while obviously not especially beneficial to that particular animal, is an essential and enriching part of the natural ecosystem on the African plains. It would be absurd to argue that lions don't belong somewhere like the Serengeti, just because they prey on other species. (Although in truth, all over the world predators have long been eradicated wherever and whenever possible; we'll touch on this again.)

The exact same should apply to the strangler fig's survival strategy, or any other natural ecological interaction anywhere. That includes processes that might seem nasty or cruel to our eyes, such as actual parasitism, for example (the fig is not parasitic). All of them are a part of what makes this planet so fascinating, beautiful and, not least, functional, helping to create a habitable environment for all living things, ourselves included.

In attempting any real understanding of the natural world, the very subjective human lens of what constitutes good or bad must largely be set aside.

I'm often asked about my attitude to ivy, which is the closest we get to a strangler fig in this part of the world. Just as with the fig, many people consider it detrimental to the trees it grows on, and therefore something to be eliminated. When I was in my early teens, a friend's family had the use of an old isolated gate lodge near the shores of Upper Lough Erne in County Fermanagh, and we sometimes spent time there over the summer. It was a wonderful place, where we would pass the days canoeing, swimming and exploring the surrounding pieces of native woodland. One of the activities we experimented in was cutting out sections from the stems of ivy (thereby killing it) on one or two of the big old oaks nearby, in order to 'help the trees'. It's still common to see the results of the same action on trees everywhere.

I know now that such an approach gets it very wrong

from an ecological perspective. Ivy is a native plant and a hugely important part of a natural forest ecosystem, its waxy water-shedding leaves providing loads of wildlife with all-year-round places to hide, shelter and nest. The flowers and berries on mature ivy are also a fantastic source of pollen and nectar for flying insects, and food for birds. (Mature ivy is distinguishable by its oval leaves; young ivy, with the three- or five-pointed leaves, doesn't flower or fruit.) This is especially so because it flowers in the autumn, and its fruits ripen over the winter, when there is much less sustenance available generally.

Furthermore, the forest is greatly 'thickened' by the presence of ivy, reducing wind speeds and helping to create the damp, stable, non-extreme climate many woodland inhabitants such as moisture-loving ferns and mosses prefer, particularly in winter, when most of the trees have dropped their leaves. In short, ivy, no less than the strangler fig, is an ecological powerhouse in the forest ecosystems of which it is naturally a part.

Does ivy damage the individual trees it grows on? Ironically, in the Bofickil woods quite a few trees were actually spared death by having thick ivy stems winding up their trunks, because these prevented the goats and sika from stripping the bark all the way around. But in a more general sense: no, ivy isn't harmful to trees, at least not in the way most often imagined. It is not parasitic, taking nothing from the tree except support. It can rob some of the tree's light, and lead to the loss of branches – or even the whole tree being knocked over – in winter storms, since it doesn't lose its leaves as most of the trees it grows on do. Its stem can also sometimes exert enough pressure to alter the growth form of the trunk or branch it's twisted around, creating amazing sculptural forms.

But none of that does the actual forest, nor usually the tree itself, any harm, as I'll discuss further on. On the contrary: just as with the strangler fig, it's all a part of the natural scheme of things, and is highly beneficial to the overall ecosystem. And *that* really is the level we need to be considering first and foremost, rather than what might be good for this or that particular organism or species, which mostly misses the point of what nature is, and how it works.

After Knysna, I continued heading northeast up the coast as far as St Lucia, close to Mozambique, spending time walking in a string of pieces of temperate and subtropical native rainforest along the route. The itinerary was mainly based on a volume I had picked up in a Knysna bookshop, *Ferns of Southern Africa,* which proved an excellent means of zeroing in on the wildest and wettest forests.

In one of them, Dlinza, near Eshowe in KwaZulu-Natal, there was a high boardwalk that brought you right up to into the canopy level, and above, at a height of 20 metres. Alongside one section was an awe-inspiring strangler-fig-covered tree, which I spent many hours gazing at, even returning the next day for a second helping, there was so much to take in. The writhing limbs of the fig gave opportunities for an incredibly rich hanging garden of epiphytes, all of which was habitat for an abundance of insects and birds.

While walking in the depths of the same forest, I encountered a blue duiker – a very tiny antelope (less than 0.7 metres long) with spiky horns. Despite being to all appearances wild and healthy, he allowed me to approach to within a few metres, so close that I had the bizarre experience of being able to see clearly in his eye a reflection of myself and the forest behind. Of all the possible media through which to catch a fleeting glimpse of your own image, in the eye of a living wild creature must surely rank among the most haunting.

I also visited several national parks, where all the really iconic megafauna like elephant, lion, buffalo, rhino, hippo and crocodile can be seen. Contrary to what might be expected, though, that was nowhere near as memorable as the times I spent in the forests. In the parks, you're constrained to your car, and the animals are generally so used to traffic that they act as if it wasn't there. On the positive side, that allows the visitor to observe the wildlife up close, behaving relatively naturally.

And there were some spine-tingling moments, such as one occasion in Imfolozi watching a solitary adult lioness calling and playfully rolling on her back nearby, just like a big kitten. She continued in that mode for maybe five minutes after I stopped until, in response, her mate came striding up the incline on my other side directly towards me (well, towards her), his mane flowing in the breeze, before passing right next to the car. Raw, unadulterated, rippling power and self-assurance on four legs; a presence that oozed from every pore the message 'You do *not* want to mess with me.' When the pair met, there was some deep groaning and playful nuzzling of heads in friendly greeting, before they moved away together, relaxedly sloping off up the hill side by side as if they owned the place.

Something in the subconscious cannot but be deeply stirred by such scenes, triggering as they must the most primal instincts stemming from millions of years of potentially being on the menus of large, fierce and sharp-toothed things ourselves. The hairs were standing on the back of my neck – a reaction that apparently also occurs when we are being watched by a predator we can't see, an evolved sixth sense that few of us now have any need for.

Yet on the whole I found the parks experiences removed and abstract, as though it were all happening elsewhere, watched on a television or computer screen rather than the other side of a windscreen. The high surrounding fences, even though usually far out of sight, combined with that sense of detachment, gave me the constant and inescapable feeling of being in a large open-air zoo, instead of the actual wild. At times it bordered on working my way through a box-ticking exercise.

Walking in the forests was altogether in contrast to that, being far more immediate, personal and vivid. It was made so by feeling the ground under my feet, and leaves brushing against bare legs or chest (I would generally wear only short trousers and hiking boots). Added to that was hearing the wind or bird song in the canopy above, and being able to stop to look more closely at a particular tree, fungus or insect. Or just stand or sit for a while in quiet contemplation of a special spot, such as by a river at the bottom of a deep gorge in full spate after rain, with the trees, ferns, flowers and everything else growing from mossy rock still oozing water droplets in the fresh sunshine. It was in all senses an interaction, rather than a detached observation, and felt deeply real and meaningful at all times.

While I saw plenty of often highly exotic-looking birds through my binoculars, apart from the duiker the only mammals I encountered in the forests were chacma baboons and vervet monkeys. But, even so, there is a very different, quietly exhilarating, quality of feeling in being on foot in a place with the knowledge that leopards, elephants and other large animals may be around, even if hidden. The sounds were at times transfixing, with a cacophony of otherworldly birdcalls echoing through the forest. In one part of the Knysna forests, I was genuinely very close to having to put my fingers in my ears, the aggregated rasping of frogs was so deafening. Elsewhere there was instead a deep, roaring silence.

Although only small fragments of forest remain relative to what once existed, spending time there was an unforgettable and humbling experience. Nothing even remotely comparable in size, age, wildness, or fauna still survives in Ireland. That is a deep pity, and a gaping lacuna in our national heritage, especially considering that most of the island would once have been mantled in rich, thick, old-growth forest. Happily though, my fears about being underwhelmed on returning to the woods in Bofickil proved totally unfounded. On the contrary, the time spent in African forests very much worked to further heighten my appreciation, by bringing an acute awareness of the many things that make Irish temperate rainforests so special and dynamic. I'll take a look at some of these in the next chapter.

8

The Dynamism of
an Irish Rainforest

At first sight, the tiny, delicate and translucent fronds of Tunbridge filmy fern are easily mistaken for another of the mosses with which it grows in thick, luxuriantly glistening mats on banks of rock and tree trunks. All three of Ireland's filmy ferns are present in Bofickil (the others are Killarney fern and Wilson's filmy fern), but *Hymenophyllum tunbrigense* is by far the most common. There are patches scattered throughout the woods, especially on north-facing surfaces where conditions are more humid and there is less competition from light-demanding plants.

Despite its name, the fern is now extremely rare in most of England, so much so that colonies are sometimes actually stolen there. It was a great surprise to come across the very same species in Knysna and many of the other African forests I explored, where, just as in Ireland, it's native. In fact, small populations are widely dispersed around the globe, being also present in parts of the Americas, New Zealand and, coincidentally, the Apuan Alps in Italy. It really was bizarre to see such a familiar sight so far away, like a tiny piece of home inserted into a very different context.

Another plant, this time a flowering one, looked practically identical to the wood sanicle I know so well from the Bofickil woods, although actually a different but closely related species. Such coincidences caused me to contemplate that some species must have survived in both what became Ireland and southern Africa in an effectively unaltered state since the separation of the planet's once single land mass, Pangaea, some 175 million years ago. The existence in the Knysna forest of an endemic species that has remained pretty much unchanged for around 500 million years – the predatory Knysna velvet worm, with cousins in Australasia, Malaysia and South America – suggests there may have been something to that. There were plenty of other commonalities between the Bofickil woods and the forests I saw in South Africa, the most obvious being in the lush, humid conditions, and corresponding abundance of epiphytes, ferns, mosses and lichens.

But I found enormous differences between Irish and African temperate rainforests too, in part because they are respectively located in cool and warm temperate zones. Seasonal variations in temperature are much less pronounced in South Africa, and, as a result, the forests don't change throughout the course of the year the way they do in Ireland. That constant transformation, it's worth remembering, also sets rainforests in temperate Europe apart from their much more extensive subtropical and tropical brethren. Coming home to Bofickil, I was much better able to enjoy and value the perpetual transmutations manifested in almost every aspect of the woods through the course of each year.

In autumn there is the vast array of different fungi types of all shapes and colours, pushing their way up through the thick, freshly falling leaf litter above. In winter the bareness of the trees, when days of heavy rain are more likely to swell normally riffled streams flowing down off the mountain into roaring torrents of boiling and splashing peaty cream froth. The explosions of colour in spring, when a kaleidoscope of woodland flowers blossoms; and the total shift in mood in summer, as swollen buds open out into new leaves in the canopy above, creating striking shafts of sunlight through the partial gloom.

(As an aside, hoverflies and other flying insects like to populate these tunnels of luminescence. Apart from a blur of wings, they hang almost immobile in space, picked out as if in a spotlight against the varying degrees of shadow behind. They then momentarily zip-zigzag about, playfully buzzing off one another as if in a teasing dance, before resuming their airy posts. A most sublime sight is to look at one of these hovering insects through a good pair of binoculars from as close up as the focusing ring will allow, on mine around 1.5 metres away. First, the binoculars black out everything around, concentrating attention on the subject. But they also greatly accentuate the contrast, with the insect itself magnified to fill much of the field of view, every detail in crisp focus and lit up by sunlight. Meanwhile everything in the background is unfocused and darker, aside from perhaps hazy starbursts here and there. I find the visual effect just mesmerising.)

Other than extent, antiquity and diversity of tree species, there is one measure in which native Irish forests really do come up short in comparison with those in other places, such as South Africa and even continental Europe: the range of larger animals they harbour is very limited. Ireland has a low diversity of native fauna in general, for which there are several reasons beyond the island's relatively restricted variety of natural habitats and size.

Firstly, the early closure of the land bridge to the continent as the ice receded around 16,000 years ago prevented many species from getting to Ireland. Only those that made it beforehand, arrived without human help afterwards, or were brought in deep prehistory and have since become naturalised are generally classified as native, although in my view that warrants reconsideration (see Chapter 13). Secondly, many of those species that did somehow manage to be in Ireland were later driven into extinction by human activity. Mammals that were lost included the wild boar, lynx, wolf, European wildcat and bear. Woodland-associated species were especially badly affected, as Ireland went from mostly forest cover to virtually the lowest in Europe.

In the first years after we arrived in Bofickil, the biggest non-avian native fauna were badgers, foxes, hares, stoats, wood mice, lizards and frogs. While every species has its own charms and place within an ecosystem, that group doesn't quite compare to elephants, leopards and baboons. Still, badgers, for example, are fascinating and amazing-looking creatures, with their white and black striped heads and formidably long claws for digging. Their paths, scats and ground-scratchings (for such delicacies as earthworms and the tubers of pignut) are everywhere in the woods.

A few years back, I received a visit from an ecologist, Kieran Flood, who had studied badgers extensively, and was able to outline to me some of their complex (possibly matriarchal) social structure, territorial behaviour, setts, latrines, and so on. Although generally nocturnal, I sometimes catch glimpses of them mooching through the woods, and their gorgeous – but somehow slightly comical – faces and body shapes also feature regularly on camera trap videos.

What the South African trip brought home to me most of all is just how very dynamic the Bofickil woods are. In addition to the seasonality, the frequently extremely violent storms have a lot to do with that, tearing off branches and knocking down trees of all sizes, some very large. In winter, often they are those with a heavy covering of ivy, which catches the wind like a sail.

Many of the trees are naturally reinforced at the crossover point where trunks submerge underground, with reduced versions of the flanged buttress roots found on such tropical giants as mahogany. But sometimes even adaptations like this aren't enough, and they are brought crashing down regardless, especially when the direction of wind gusts is constantly switching, a characteristic of some storms. Over the following years, the openings thus rent in the canopy stimulate all the plants on the woodland floor, including young trees, which take advantage of the sudden jump in sunlight pouring in to rush up and fill the gap. Most of the fallen trees themselves survive to carry on growing, sending new stems up vertically from the branches, trunk and upturned rootplate, greatly enhancing structural diversity and increasing the variety of niches for forest wildlife.

Storms can have other unpredictable effects. Storm Hannah, which arrived in late April 2019, brought a deluge not only of rain, but also of salt-laden sea spray, burning off almost all the leaves that had so far opened, and reducing woodland growth for that year. Winter floods often change the course of streams in places, as the rush of water pushes up over banks to carve out new channels. Or a fallen tree or branch in a stream might gather debris, creating a blockage until the flow is diverted in a new direction. Similar mechanisms have caused many sections of stream to become much more braided, and have given rise to plenty of pools, ponds and shoals, as build-ups of material dam the flow. All this has been an enormous boon for wildlife, even attracting occasional visits in more open areas from water-loving species like mallard ducks and herons.

Just as significant a factor in the continual flux of the Bofickil woods has been the natural regeneration unleashed both within the woods and in the mosaic of open, unwooded parts of the land since the deer fence went up. Light-demanding, fast-growing 'pioneer' species with tiny wind-borne seeds weighing as little as 0.0001 grams, like birch and sally (willow), often open the way in the unwooded areas, helping to create the shelter and soil conditions other species prefer. Before long, oak, hazel, rowan, holly and all the others begin to follow, although these species themselves often act as pioneers too.

A striking aspect of this process of change has been the wide range of speeds at which it has been happening. While in some areas scattered young seedlings were only slowly and timidly beginning to appear after several years, in others a rapid and radical transformation started immediately grazing ceased. In these, where previously there had been only grass, they were soon thronged with numerous mushrooming trees, and within only six or seven years the canopy was closing in overhead, at a height of perhaps 4–5 metres.

It hasn't always been easy to explain the very fast succession (to use the ecological term) to woodland in some areas, and the slower pace in others. Availability of water is clearly important, and in general the wetter areas have been much quicker to revert to forest than those with thin rocky soils in raised spots, which are more likely to become parched in a drought. Similarly, areas sheltered from the wind coming in off the sea behind already established trees or rocky hummocks tend to regenerate faster than more exposed places. For both reasons, low-lying hollows have usually re-wooded more quickly.

Whether there are mature trees in the direction of the prevailing southwesterly wind is also a factor for species whose seeds are wind-borne, like birch and sally. But there have been so many exceptions to these and other criteria as to make me think there must be at least one other, less obvious, element at play. I strongly suspect that to be the presence or otherwise of a mycorrhizal (fungal) network underground, waiting to tap into germinating seedlings. But I'll come back to that.

The main pioneer tree species in wetter ground here in Bofickil, sally, is seen as a weed by many people in Beara because of its capacity to colonise ground quickly and grow extremely fast. Along a raised 'ditch' on one boundary with a neighbour, there is a row of remarkably evenly spaced old sallies. Interestingly, while putting up the deer fence, Dan Joe Cronin told me that these had almost certainly developed from fence posts made from freshly cut branches in the past, since these will readily take root. Sallies are exceptionally valuable to insects, supporting an outstanding 450 different species, more than any other native tree here. That won't come as a surprise to anyone who has ever witnessed the immense numbers buzzing around the outpouring of bright yellow catkins (hanging flower spikes) in early spring, for example.

The limbs of sallies have a tendency to crack away from the torso without completely detaching, or else to slowly fall over, either way continuing to grow horizontally, serpent-like and close to the ground. Along with seeding, this is a principal means by which the species colonises open ground adjacent to existing trees. In older individuals, the deeply fissured, often reddish bark harbours a wealth of mosses, polypody, and other epiphytes. Anything but a weed, sally is an ecological goldmine, a central pillar of woodland biodiversity, and a very beautiful-looking tree to boot.

In truth though, that description is no less valid for any of the other wild native tree species present in the Bofickil woods, each one in its own special ways.

In addition to the arrival of new young trees everywhere, in the absence of browsing, the previously existing trees also began to transform. As well as continuing to grow in stature and girth of course, most of the adult trees started rapidly sending out abundant new stems from lower down on their trunks, especially basal shoots near the ground.

Quite a lot of the hollies and other trees that appeared to have been killed by bark-stripping goats turned out to be still alive below ground, with fresh shoots sprouting from around the base and lancing skywards alongside the old dead trunks. Over the years, as the dead sections rot away, they have gradually been collapsing back down to be absorbed into the soil, feeding the surrounding ecosystem and leaving just the new stems standing in their place. As time goes by, all this combined new bushy growth has become very copious, together with new young trees and other vegetation giving an entirely altered character to the ground layer of the forest.

Another notable change has been the great number of ivy and woodbine stems, some of them the thickness of heavy rope, traipsed across, and hanging loosely from, tree branches almost to the ground, like jungle lianas. (I was fascinated to learn that woodbine flowers exude their beautifully aromatic scent more powerfully in the evening and night-time, when the pollinating moths the plant wants to attract are out and about.) Previously these vine-like growths would have been dragged down and devoured by the goats and sika deer.

All this increased vegetation has had the effect of making the woodland considerably denser, in many areas a veritable mass of extremely biodiverse multilayered growth. As mentioned already, that is hugely beneficial in many ways, reducing the speed of circulating air, helping to create the damp and stable conditions most woodland species thrive in. In sum, the woods are now far more productive with regard to the amount of 'stuff' (or biomass, to use the proper jargon) that grows, all of which is great news for the thousands of different types of organisms that call them home.

An interesting aspect of the natural succession to woodland in Bofickil has been that, as grassland turns first to scrub, and then matures further, it goes from being easily walkable, to an impenetrable thicket, and then back again. In the intermediate stage, it becomes a dense tangle of young trees, high gorse, bracken and briars. But with time, as the canopy closes in overhead, light levels are reduced and much of the undergrowth and less competitive trees die away, making it possible to pass once more underneath.

So for several years thickly successional areas are lost to human interaction, but (largely for that precise reason) become fantastic havens for nesting birds and a great abundance of other creatures. Afterwards there is a wonderful feeling in once again exploring newly reaccessible areas, the complete transformation à la Sendak's *Where the Wild Things Are* making the experience fit somewhere between a reacquaintance and a first-time meeting.

Mirroring that which occurs with the courses of streams, the principal routes I take when walking through the land are continually forced to shift. A section of frequented 'path' (insofar as it exists) is suddenly blocked by a storm-thrown tree, or more gradually by the spontaneous growth of new woodland in the form of scrub, or the increased bushiness of older trees. When that happens, entirely new ways have to be carved out, hacking through dense briars, furze and maybe bracken between naturally regenerated trees, over ground untravelled for years.

Thus the mental maps of the woods carried in my head require constant revision and updating, to take account of freshly established detours, and the mini-territories they reopen. In almost every conceivable way, the unconsidered assumption I held before coming to Bofickil that forests were relatively immutable environments over long periods of time has been forcefully – but delightfully – cast aside. Here at least, the level of dynamism is phenomenal.

With practically every visit to the woods and their surroundings, there are exciting new discoveries or encounters to be had. It might be in finding that a corner left unvisited for a spell has undergone an especially rapid phase of successional metamorphosis. Or meeting a species of bird unseen for a year or two, such as blackcap, bullfinch, goldfinch, cuckoo, or reed bunting. It could be a new patch of primrose, or a self-seeded crab apple sapling, both of which are among the less common species in the Bofickil woods. There are, for example, only about half a dozen mature apple trees in the whole place, each of which stands out as a pink-tinged white blotch in the spring when looking down on the woods from the mountain commonage.

These trees are not the progeny of discarded apple cores from domesticated trees, but are instead examples of one of their fully wild ancestors, *Malus sylvestris*, with yellow-red fruit of only two or three centimetres in diameter. Crab was described by woodland historian Oliver Rackham as a 'non-gregarious' species, a lovely way of saying that in a forest it almost always occurs away from others of its own kind, conjuring images of anti-social, crabby cranks. (Which may be where the word 'crab' apple comes from: either that or the acid taste of the tiny fruits.) That observation certainly holds true here, with no two growing anywhere near one another.

Other tree species that are less explicably rare in the woods are ash (there is an abundance of mountain ash, or rowan) and alder, despite both being common nearby. (Archaeological evidence has shown that alder was the largest component species of forests in the immediate area from at least as far back as 2500 BC, until around 1400 BC, when it lost its dominance.)

As the woods began to return to a more ecologically healthy state, it became easier to piece together, detective-style, which patches were older, and which had developed more recently, that is, over the last half-century or so. That had already been fairly apparent in the existing trees themselves. As you'd expect, in the more 'ancient' areas, the trees generally have thicker trunks and are much more characterful in terms of shape, their fantastically contorted limbs writhing every which way.

Other features, such as a more deeply fissured bark, or an abundance of 'witch's broom' in the birches, equally set them apart. Many also have fat, intertwining ivy stems twisting up around the trunks, melded together where they cross, and at times resembling the strangler figs I saw in Africa. By contrast, trees in the patches established within the last 50 years – the teenagers, in tree terms – tend to be much less gnarled, and of more uniform age and shape. The trunks are mostly more thin and straight, as a result of racing up for the light in hot competition with their neighbours.

But what also became clear, as a great multitude of flowering plants appeared on the woodland floor in the absence of grazing, was that the older sections of woodland have a *far* richer ground flora. The variety and profusion of flowers and other plants present is generally enormous, in contrast to newer areas of forest, which often have just a few species. Some, such as wood anemone, seem to be particularly characteristic of the older woodland; indeed, it figures on most lists of what are called 'ancient woodland indicator' species for Ireland and Britain. That's explained by the fact that wood anemone is a clonal plant, and colonises new ground principally by sending out rhizomes underground to form new patches, but at a rate of only around 0.4 metres per year.

So while the formation of new woodland through natural

From little acorns ... strange as it may seem, almost single-handedly
rebuilding a ruined eighteenth-century stone cottage in Kilmainham,
Dublin, was in many ways the first step on a journey that led me
to restore a wild rainforest on the Beara Peninsula, West Cork.

Above: The only parts of the original cottage that weren't
buried under a mountain of earth.

Below: The reconstructed version several years later,
just before I left for Italy.

The belltower of the eleventh-century Romanesque *duomo* from my balcony in Via Caffaggio, Carrara. So many happy hours were spent in that seat, reading in the sun or listening to the sounds of life all around, during my seven years studying sculpture there.

During my time living in Italy.

A painting of the old Crowley house, probably done some time in the 1960s when Eileen still lived there, from the top of a steeply sloping field called Glann.
(Artist unknown; with grateful thanks to Joe Harrington for permission to use.)

A view of the old house in Bofickil as it was when
we bought the farm in 2009, also taken from the top of Glann.

My good friend and neighbour, Michael Harrington (Caupey),
enjoying a laugh (very possibly at my expense) at our kitchen table.

One of the older oaks on the land. From the very first moment I laid
eyes on such sights, I have been deeply in love with this place.

The view out west from the 'first top' of our mountain commonage.
The nearest island is Inisfarnard, beyond which are Deenish and Scarrif,
with the Skelligs barely visible in the haze to the right.

The devastation caused by overgrazing in Killarney National Park, Ireland's largest surviving remnant of native rainforest. Our place in Bofickil was in a very similar state when we arrived, including serious infestations of rhododendron and a host of other invasive species.

Feral goats were mainly responsible for a complete lack of regeneration of native trees and other flora in Bofickil. The forest was, quite simply, being eaten to death.

The lower reaches of this old oak forest in Lauragh (Kerry) are completely submerged under a sea of invasive rhododendron. No light gets through the dense canopy, preventing any native plants bigger than mosses from growing. Once the existing old trees die, there'll be only rhododendron left.

This is what a natural forest in formation looks like: a chaotic tangle of scrub, here composed of birch, oak, hazel, willow, holly and wild apple. Despite being extremely species-rich in its own right, with the potential to mature into rich native forest, scrub is still often vilified, bizarrely even by many nature conservationists.

In the years after the deer fence went up, I was privileged to be witness to the most stunning, magical transformation of the land inside, with a rich dormant ground flora reawakening, like these bluebells.

A carpet of flowering bugle in one of the wetter sections of our woods.

Wood anemone, very possibly the best indicator of the more 'ancient' areas of forest in our place and my absolute favourite woodland flower.

regeneration is often quite rapid, the associated biodiversity can be slower in following along behind, depending on the proximity to source populations. Similarly, some species have difficulty crossing open spaces to more recently formed fragments of woodland, or their ecologies require the presence of old trees. These are all yet more reasons why the longer a forest is allowed to age naturally, the more species-rich, and thus ecologically valuable, it becomes. It is also further grounds – and this cannot be stressed enough – for prioritising native woodland expansion around existing patches of older natural forest.

During the centuries in which the Crowley land had been farmed, each pocket of remaining woodland, however small, had effectively served as a refuge. Not only for the trees themselves, but also for all the other associated species that make up a forest ecosystem: plants, animals and, not least, fungi. Logically, these *refugia* were located in the many areas that were of little use agriculturally, such as steep rocky slopes with escarpments and scree, which were more likely to be left to their own devices. These patches, and their surroundings, are the parts that now show all the hallmarks of relatively older forest, with more recently regenerated woodland on the flatter, more fertile areas in between.

In other cases, single, very large, old spreading trees appear in the midst of younger 'infill' woodland, much of which is likely their own offspring. The lowest branches of such venerable 'wolf trees' (that's the proper term, not me trying to add descriptive flavour) often snake horizontally just above the ground, and are laden with a thick cloak of moss, adorned with copious polypody fern and other epiphytes. These trees are usually situated on, or next to, the stone ditches that mark old field boundaries, and some of the oaks in our place have been estimated as seventeenth century.

In neighbouring farms where the land is still used for pasture, there is the exact same scenario, minus a century or so of reversion to the wild. Clumps of trees are surrounded by open fields, with occasional lone individuals or hedgerows along the stone walls in between. So looking around, it's easy enough to picture how the land under the woods in Bofickil would have been in the past, before the trees spread out into open areas, turning into a forest.

Ultimately though, regardless of the similarities and divergences between the forest in Bofickil and those in Knysna and beyond, I felt there to be a shared fraternity (or sorority, to use the sisterly equivalent) between them, as places retaining a relative wildness. At times when in the Bofickil woods, I imagine they are connected by an intercontinental underground network, and that by resting a hand on a tree, an arboreal salutation will be passed on to all those I met on that amazing trip, and others around the world.

So occasionally, on the off chance that it's somehow more than just my fantasising, that's exactly what I do. My fingers then vanish to the hilts into a deep, soft, cool and moist green cushion of tamarisk, haircap, little-shaggy, rough-stalked feather and other epiphytic mosses. And there you have it, in writing: not quite an open admission to tree-hugging, but pretty damn close.

Soon after moving to Beara, I introduced a few examples of a native tree that was absent from the land, although there is at least one living wild in the immediate vicinity. *Arbutus unedo*, or strawberry tree, now only grows naturally in a few parts of the southwest, apart from a small outlier population by Lough Gill in County Sligo, but it may very well once have been more widespread. The Anglican bishop of Cork and Ross wrote of coming across it during a visit to Beara in 1700:

> On the south side of Daad O'Huologhan [Hungry Hill] towards the bottom of the hill near the sea, grow at least a hundred of the arbutus or Cane Apple trees, called in Irish apples Cahannah, some of them 24 or 26 foot high. [...] In the same woods grow oaks, birch, hazel, crab trees, heath, fern, furzes and holly, which seems to thrive better than the rest. [He also mentioned seeing several eagles in Beara, and that 'There are many wolves there.']

There are still a few scattered arbutus growing in that same locality around Adrigole today.

The tree is one of an anomalous bunch of about seventeen species known as the 'Lusitanian group', after the ancient Roman name for the southwestern part of the Iberian Peninsula. The natural distribution of these species includes parts of Ireland – mainly, but not only, the southwest – and southern latitudes of Europe, primarily Spain, Portugal and Italy, but they are mainly absent from Britain. In fact, I had first known arbutus as *corbezzolo* while living in Italy, since in the Apuan Alps it's a common member of the native flora up to altitudes of around 600 metres. Curiously, it rarely seems to attain real tree size there, as it does in Ireland.

The English name 'strawberry tree' comes from the round red fruit, which someone must have found to be not particularly pleasant to the taste, hence the Latin *unedo*: 'I eat only one.' I propagated cuttings I took from wild arbutus and, once they developed root systems, planted them in various spots around the land, protected until the deer fence went up by timber stakes surrounded by wire mesh. Half a dozen survived, some of which have since done very well and grown to a good size.

There were at least six other Lusitanian species already present on the land in Bofickil: Kerry slug (a faunal member of the group), Irish spurge, St. Patrick's cabbage, kidney saxifrage, Irish eyebright and large-flowered butterwort. (The last, incidentally, is one of three insect-eating plants present, the others being pale butterwort and round-leaved sundew.)

Various theories exist regarding just how the Lusitanian group came to be in Ireland, so far from their other areas of natural distribution. These range from introduction via human movements in prehistoric or even more recent times, to being relicts of populations that were once widespread in intermediate zones but have since died out elsewhere. For me, the apparent lack of associations with phytophagous (plant-eating) insects points towards arbutus being what is called an archaeophyte, i.e. a plant that was introduced by people in antiquity, whether knowingly or not. Whatever the true explanation, they clearly find the mild and humid conditions in the southwest of this island, which have been described as 'Mediterranean-Atlantic', greatly to their liking.

All over Beara, including the nearby bog where our farm has turbary rights, the stumps and roots of ancient trees have been revealed by peat exploitation for fuel in the past. Many of these woody skeletons are pine, and pollen analysis of peat cores taken in the immediate area confirms that the species comprised around 10 per cent of the forests in this region until circa 1900 BC, when it began to disappear. As in practically all the rest of the country, pine was unable to survive the successive onslaughts of forest clearance, most probably due to its inability to coppice (i.e. grow back from the roots when cut down), as most deciduous trees do in the absence of overgrazing.

Pine was reintroduced into the Irish landscape from Scotland in the eighteenth and nineteenth centuries, hence Scots pine, as we usually call it. Interestingly, however, research by Jenni Roche and Alwynne McGeever showed that a population of pine in an area called Rockforest in the Burren, County Clare, is indigenous, with pollen records indicating an unbroken continuity of presence stretching back at least sixteen centuries. In more open areas of the land, I planted a good number of pines, some of which had been painstakingly grown from seed collected at Rockforest by an ecologist I know, Daniel Buckley.

Aside from the fact that it was here in the past, the tree is great for wildlife, contributing to a web of life that includes red squirrels and pine martens, for example. There were healthy populations of both species not far away, and Finbarr Caupey told me he had seen a squirrel on their farm next door a few years ago. My hope is that, with a bit of luck, a few might even make their way back to the Bofickil woods over time.

9

Recess of the Wild Wood

As I learned more of the history and prehistory of our immediate locality, it was deeply fascinating to discover that both the townlands in which the farm is situated owe their names to forest. Bofickil derives from *Badh Fiadh-Choille*, or 'Recess of the Wild Wood' in Irish, while Faunkill comes from *Fan-Choill* – 'Sloping Wood': good indications of the past character of the land.

Most Irish townland names are thought to have been 'fixed [by] the eighth century', and we can assume both names came into use before then, confirming that the area was still heavily wooded at the time. Throughout Beara, a high proportion of place-names originated in woodland words, especially *doire* (oak wood), which gave Dereenacush, Derrymihan, Cleanderry, Derreenaloig, Derryconnery and Derrynabrack (oak wood of the badger), to name just a few. In fact, local historian Cornelius Murphy estimated that 'over 10 per cent of townland names in Beara contain the element *Doire*'.

As with the rest of Ireland, most of the peninsula was once mantled in rich, thick, old-growth forest, inhabited by wolves, bears and many other wild species. The first people to enter that environment were almost certainly small groups of hunter-gatherers, who would have been present, or visited, in pre-agricultural times, prior to 4000 BC. Archaeologists now believe these nomadic peoples altered Irish wooded landscapes far more substantially than previously thought, often managing wild resources in ways that blur the distinction with actual farming. At Mount Gabriel on the Mizen Peninsula to the south of Beara, for example, there are signs of strong periodic woodland disturbance from around 6400 BC.

The first known evidence of actual human settlement in Beara dates to the Neolithic Period, with a significant site at Cashelkeelty, less than 10 kilometres to the east of Bofickil, lasting from roughly 3900 to 2900 BC. These were the first real farmers, with a culture heavily based on cattle, and they initially cleared patches of land of its cover of forest using slash-and-burn – still a common practice in the tropics – and ring-barking. The effect of livestock in preventing the regeneration of trees is also likely to have played a decisive role in transforming initially isolated fragments of land into a more open state.

A later period of natural woodland regeneration shows that these settlements were then abandoned for over a thousand years until the Bronze Age, when people returned. As populations and their herds expanded, so did the forest recede. Pollen analysis of a peat core taken only several hundred metres from the boundary of our Faunkill commonage, in the adjacent townland of Barrees, shows a collapse in tree cover around 1350 BC. (Spores of all three filmy ferns are also frequent in the record, substantiating rainforest.) In Bofickil, the woods may well have begun to disappear even earlier than this, as indicated by the presence of a wedge tomb at the western side of the townland dating to between 2000 and 1500 BC, along with other remains.

Just beyond the commonage 'high top' is a Bronze Age copper mine (bronze is an alloy of copper and tin), which radiocarbon analysis of charcoal determined to have been active around 1650–1450 BC. The technique used to glean the copper was to superheat a rockface that showed traces of the green ore with an intense fire of birch hardwood, which burns very fast and hot. Cold water was then thrown over the surface, the sudden drop in temperature shattering the rock and making it easier to break out. Large, heavy beach stones with an oval, flattish shape were used as hand-held hammers for pounding the rock, and when one fractured, it was discarded and another pressed into service. Broken stones of this type still litter the area surrounding the cave-like mine workings, along with heaps of tailings from which the copper had been extracted with more wood fires.

When I first saw the site, I marvelled at the sheer effort required to haul the great quantities of firewood up from the forest below. But it later struck me that, at that time, the hills would still have been largely wooded themselves, and the timber there, all around (see Chapter 10). Now there is little other than rock, sheep and *fionnán* (purple moor-grass, a very coarse, long, and usually sandy-coloured grass that grows in large tussocks).

Condensed down, the evidence for prehistoric Beara clearly shows an ebb-and-flow dynamic between people and wild forests that continued over thousands of years, a pattern that echoes other parts of Ireland. The Barrees pollen record indicates enormous pulses of woodland clearance around 1350 BC, 800 BC, 500 BC, 250 BC, AD 700 and AD 1700, each of which was later followed by its extensive return, bar the last. However, the overall trend has been a downward one throughout. Each time they contracted, the forests were replaced by pasture (highlighted in the pollen record by a corresponding spike in grasses), along with some minor level of cereal-growing.

Without the protection afforded by trees, nutrients were leached away by rainwater, as well as being lost from the soil in the food produced for people. They wouldn't have been sufficiently replaced by the small amounts of manure generated by livestock, or the spreading of seaweed as a fertiliser. The final phase of each cycle was then an almost complete collapse of the conditions necessary to survive, as the environment became increasingly degraded, followed by human abandonment.

Periodic natural deteriorations in climate, bringing wetter and cooler conditions, have commonly been blamed for the disappearance of Irish forests in prehistory, but that ignores the obvious fact that rainforest thrives on rain – the more the better. However, a worsening climate after 1000 BC *does* seem to have caused people to further intensify their forest clearing and agriculture to compensate for reduced food production. Deforestation, land degradation and consequent depopulation were solely due to human activities, primarily related to farming.

An absence of people and their animals allowed the return of woodland, with new trees seeding into what had been farmland. Over centuries, layers of woody debris in the form of fallen leaves, twigs, branches, whole trees when they died, and other vegetation would again accumulate steadily, all turned into rich humus by the forests' natural processes.

I see these at work in the Bofickil woods, where there is a constant and extremely copious rain of organic matter onto the woodland floor, even outside the autumnal fall, all of which then rots down, adding to the soil. Less visibly, the tree roots speed up the breakdown of rock, releasing minerals that, along with water, are brought up from sometimes deep below to the surface, making them available for use by other organisms.

In short, human activities would deplete soils, while forests built them back up again. Each time soil levels and fertility improved over centuries of woodland, the land became attractive for agriculture once more, and farmers would return and start clearing, recommencing the cycle. This pattern carried on into the historical era, as it did across most of the rest of Ireland and elsewhere in Europe, with disturbances like protracted warfare or epidemics, such as the mid-fourteenth-century Black Death, also allowing woodland to return. That there was an awareness of the phenomenon is well demonstrated in the age-old Irish saying '*Teóra h-uaire do cuir Éire, Teóra monga, agus teóra dhí*' (Three times Ireland was cultivated, thrice wooded and thrice bare).

Gerald of Wales (Giraldus Cambrensis), who wrote a book about Ireland – *Topographia Hibernica* – based on his visits in the late twelfth century, described the Irish countryside as still more wooded than open. The Norman invasion of 1169, which paved the way for Gerald to come, is unlikely to have made much of a dent in forest cover, since those areas where it was highest were neither attractive to the settlers, nor easily subjugated.

We should, however, be wary of the temptation to consider these remaining forests as 'primeval', even at that time. Almost everywhere there is likely to have been a very long history of hunting, logging, grazing, burning, coppicing and other human impacts, going right back to the Mesolithic and probably beyond. Where woodland persisted, or was able to return, its species composition and other ecological characteristics would have been very strongly altered, and this is borne out in the palaeoecological evidence from Barrees and other places.

As revealed in the pollen record and preponderance of related place-names mentioned earlier, prior to the collapse that began around AD 700 surviving forests were widespread in Beara. Almost a thousand years later at the tail end of the medieval period, one of the first maps of the peninsula dating to around 1558 shows they had partially recovered, with extensive woodland (and wolves) in some parts. In Glengarriff, for example, it still covered almost 21 square kilometres in 1580. However, these forests all either greatly contracted, or were entirely erased, by the huge clearances that took place across the entire country in the seventeenth and early eighteenth centuries with the tightening of English control. The extent of surviving woodland in Ireland at the pivotal moment of 1600, before this final tidal wave of deforestation, isn't clear, with maps missing or incomplete for many areas.

The date of 1600 is important on a couple of counts. First off, it's the accepted threshold for determining what can be considered 'ancient' woodland in the United Kingdom, including Northern Ireland, although in the Republic the year 1660 is used instead. Very little forest older than that date still exists in Ireland, although a list of 123 ancient – or possible ancient – woodlands (AW/PAWs) in the republic has been compiled. As above though, these would generally have been even far more severely altered by human activity in the centuries between Gerald of Wales' visit and 1600. Indeed, historical accounts of many Irish forests bear out a sustained heavy exploitation.

For example, in the Desmond Survey of 1584, the trees of Glanageenty (now a PAW near Tralee, County Kerry) were described as mostly consisting of 'underwood of the age of fifty or sixty years'. Its spindly oaks were deemed 'fit for house timber but not large enough for the making of ships or castles'. Post-1600 exploitation and planting with non-native, sometimes invasive, species in those few woodlands that did survive down to the present day can only have further weakened ecological integrity. Combined with the fact that they are now also highly fragmented, and much of the native fauna is missing, the result is that these mostly tiny patches are only very pale shadows of what they would have been even at the start of the seventeenth century.

Secondly, the Battle of Kinsale, which brought about the definitive end of independent rule by Gaelic Irish chiefs, took place in 1601. The new English colonial class that was increasingly taking ownership of the land had a much more rapacious attitude to the remaining forests. Richard Boyle, later 1st earl of Cork, stands out in particular for having destroyed huge areas of remaining forest all over counties Cork (including parts of Beara), Kerry and Waterford in the early seventeenth century. Most of the lands in question had been seized from the FitzGeralds after the Desmond Rebellions of 1569–83 were put down, and parcelled out to Sir Walter Raleigh and other soldiers in reward for their services. Boyle began buying them out, mostly at extremely low cost, from around 1602 onwards.

By making 'great havoc of [i.e. felling] the woods' on the estates he amassed, especially for ironworking, Boyle was able to become, reputedly, the richest subject in all the three kingdoms of England, Scotland and Ireland. He is now sometimes described as the 'first colonial millionaire', setting a precedent for centuries of immense fortunes made all over the world from colonial-related *ecocide*: the wholesale liquidation of natural ecosystems. (I had ample occasion in 2012 to ponder Boyle's role in deforesting Munster while restoring the very grandiose funerary monument he had erected for himself in Youghal, east Cork.)

In many parts of the country, however, including Beara, the serious destruction of forest in this period really began in earnest only after the much more extensive land expropriations under Cromwell, half a century later. Nonetheless, the year 1600 remains particularly important when discussing ecological history in an Irish context. Woodland historian Eileen McCracken estimated that 'In 1600 about one-eighth of Ireland was forested'; although sometimes challenged, that figure of 12.5 per cent has remained a primary reference point ever since.

For her English counterpart, Oliver Rackham, it was much lower, with only around 2.1 per cent of Ireland under forest in the first half of the seventeenth century; in his view, most of the deforestation of this period happened after that. And he considered that, by the time the first Ordnance Survey maps were made between 1830 and 1844, only about a tenth of that remained, i.e. a minuscule 0.2 per cent of the country.

Until the Cromwellian conquest of Ireland from 1649 to 1653, the townlands of Bofickil, Faunkill, and most of the rest of the Eyeries and Kilcatherine districts were in the possession of a Randolph O'Lynchigh. Like most other Irish landowners in Beara and elsewhere who hadn't already been dispossessed, his lands were then confiscated. He and his family may have been transported, either west of the Shannon to Clare or Connaught, or even overseas to the Caribbean. Most likely though, they managed to stay on in the area, joining their own former tenants in status (there are still a few Lynches in Beara).

Almost all the County Cork parts of Beara (i.e. the south and west), including O'Lynchigh's former lands, were granted to a man named Arthur Annesley for his support of the Parliamentarian side in the English Civil War. The entire Kerry side of the peninsula, as well as many other parts of Ireland, fell into the hands of William Petty, physician-general in Cromwell's army during the conquest.

Petty had later overseen the Down Survey, a series of maps made of most of the country in 1656–8 for the purpose of divvying up forfeited lands among members of the English governing class, and he himself was one of the greatest beneficiaries. The parish-scale maps indicated existing forest and other land features in considerable detail, but, unfortunately, only the barony-scale maps have survived for Beara. Several decades later, around 1690, Annesley's very substantial estates in Beara and the Bantry area were bought up by a family named White.

In effect, for the next couple of centuries almost the whole Beara Peninsula, along with huge tracts of land elsewhere in Ireland, was in the possession of just two families: the Whites and the Pettys (who later became the lords of Lansdowne). Like Boyle, both made themselves extremely wealthy on the back of deforesting the lands they had acquired. The bulk of the timber was made into charcoal for iron smelting, an activity the two dynasties were engaged in until the middle of the eighteenth century, by which point almost all the forests had been exhausted. The rapid erasure of the hitherto surviving forest in Beara would therefore have taken place over the course of those hundred or so years, i.e. roughly 1650–1750.

The bishop of Cork and Ross's 1700 account of the mixed forests with arbutus near Adrigole, quoted in Chapter 8, shows that, at least in some localities, forests still remained at that point. But with the exception of a few small fragments in places like Uragh, Lehid, Derrylough, parts of Glengarriff and perhaps Dunboy, very little is likely to have lasted on the peninsula beyond the next 50 years. In all probability it was around this time that most of any forest left in what would become the Crowley place was cleared, a couple of centuries before it was able to begin making its way back following Phillip's departure for Montana in 1909. That chronology also accords perfectly with the pollen record from the adjoining townland of Barrees.

What happened in Beara at this time is fairly representative of the destruction of forest across the rest of Ireland, which was extremely fast and near total. It was in this period that much of the island's missing native woodland fauna was also lost: the wolf, red squirrel (although a few may have survived), goshawk, capercaillie, black grouse, great spotted woodpecker, possibly wild boar, and undoubtedly a plethora of less obvious species. Others, such as pine marten, declined dramatically, almost disappearing completely.

New colonial landowners were seeking to turn forests into quick cash, while at the same time making the land available for agriculture, and depriving Irish resistance of cover: there was no agent orange in the seventeenth century. In 1632, Richard Boyle, who by this time had been made earl of Cork, wrote:

> The place where Bandon Bridge [west Cork] is situated is upon a great district of the country and was within the last twenty-four years a mere waste bog and wood serving as a retreat and harbour to woodkernes [native guerrilla fighters], rebels, thieves and wolves and yet now (God be praised) as civil a plantation as most in England.

Such comments, and other written documents from the time, reveal unambiguously that the motives went beyond greed and the drive to secure conquests, to the idea that the colonists were engaged on a righteous, divinely sanctified, civilising mission. They saw their task as extending not only to the subjugation of the island's remaining wild fauna (e.g. wolves), flora, and the very land itself, but equally its native populace. Subjugation readily and frequently became outright annihilation, with the then more common word 'extirpation' regularly used in state papers of the time relating to Ireland.

Up to a third of the population of Munster is thought to have been 'extirpated' in the crushing of the Desmond Rebellions (1569–83). Untold numbers died during the Nine Years War (1593–1603), and an estimated 20–33 per cent of people in the entire country during the Cromwellian invasion (1649–53). Numerous other, more minor, colonial conflicts took a heavy toll too ('between 1546 and 1603 there was not a year when government forces were not engaged in operations in some part of the country'). Official policy regularly dictated that all 'Irishry' – 'manne, woman and childe' – be put to the sword wherever they were found, leading to vast uninhabited tracts, written accounts of which were unashamedly left by many of those in command.

The extraordinarily high mortalities were also largely a consequence of the scorched earth tactics employed by the English military, which caused severe and widespread famine. In 1596 the English poet Edmund Spenser, who had served as an officer in the Munster campaign, described the state to which the province had been reduced:

> Out of everye corner of the woode and glenns they came creepinge forth upon theire handes, for theire legges could not beare them; they looked Anatomies [of] death, they spake like ghostes crying out of theire graves ... in a shorte space there were none almost left, and a most populous and plentyfull countrye suddenly lefte voyde of man or beast ...

It was total war, to borrow a twentieth-century term. And though historians tend to stop short of the word 'genocide' in relation to this period of Irish history (the contexts in which the term may properly be applied are quite specific), it can be hard to see what separates them. By the time the Down Survey was carried out in 1656–8, for example, the population of the whole Beara Peninsula had dropped to a mere 621. Just as for wolves, bounties (often of strikingly similar amounts) were offered on the heads of any woodkernes. Chasing them down was seen as 'a pleasant hunt', as Robert Blennerhassett, whose family had received lands in County Kerry, wrote in 1610. The hunting of wolves and men – either for sport, payment, or both – was deemed essential to pacifying the land, and practised for centuries.

It was of course highly convenient that carrying out 'God's work' also brought such opportunities for enormous gains in land, riches, power and status. For centuries, an identical approach, but on a vastly greater scale, was taken to indigenous peoples, forests, other natural ecosystems and their wildlife with the European conquest and colonisation of other continents. Very often the same rich individuals were behind it; for example, a group known as the 'West Country Men', which included Sir Walter Raleigh, was involved in establishing colonies in both Ireland and, later, the Americas.

That the supremacist ideological and methodological templates developed in subduing Ireland were directly transferred to the New World is well accepted. And colonial expansion in both was influenced by translations of Spanish texts concerning the earlier exploits and moral justifications of the *conquistadores*, such as Pedro Mártire d'Anglería's *De Orbe Novo* (1530). It seems even the 'papist' identity of the authors, and those they were exalting, could be overlooked when it came to picking up tips on how to get the better of 'savages', whichever side of the Atlantic they might be on.

As historian Kenneth Nicholls noted, there are strong parallels between deforestation in seventeenth- and eighteenth-century Ireland and what has been carrying on apace in the tropics and elsewhere over more recent times, with no signs of slowing. We invariably tend to think of forest destruction in terms of trees being cut down, and that was certainly a big part of the picture throughout that time.

Much of Ireland's remaining forests were rapidly consumed in an orgy of unsustainable extraction that mainly went into making charcoal for iron production, but also a variety of exportable goods such as barrel staves and plank. As McCracken wrote: 'In his diaries [Richard] Boyle recorded transactions involving about 4,000,000 staves (approximately 500,000 cubic ft) between 1616 and 1628.' Pure wastage was also a part of the equation, with trees either killed by ring-barking or (with oaks) bark-stripped for use in tanning leather and burned or left to rot.

However, though less obvious because of its contrastingly continuous, slow and non-dramatic nature, grazing by livestock effectively prevented both the stumps of cut trees from resprouting, and the natural regeneration of new seedlings. It would thus have been just as responsible as the axe, saw, or flame for the loss of forests. To quote Nicholls:

[Cromwellian] Land surveyors were interested in woodland as an economic resource and tended either to ignore degraded or scrubby woodland, to lump it in with pasture, or even to class it with bog as 'unprofitable'. Such woodland was obviously regarded as fit at most for the grazing of livestock, a use which if sufficiently intense would lead to its ultimate disappearance through preventing regeneration. It is likely that it was this, rather than deliberate clearance, which led to the disappearance of many Irish woods.

The higher trees are above sea level, the slower they grow, and so any upland forests would have disappeared even more quickly due to grazing pressure. In the southwest, the 'immense herds' of goats kept subsequently are likely to have had a significant hand in this, as noted in Chapter 5.

A century before the Great Famine of 1845–52, the forests of Ireland were effectively all gone, as famously described in the eighteenth- or early nineteenth-century *Caoineadh Chill Chais* (Lament for Kilcash):

Cad a dhéanfaimid feasta gan adhmad?
Tá deireadh na gcoillte ar lár; [...]
Níl coll, níl cuileann, níl caor ann,
ach clocha is maolchlocháin;

What shall we do for timber?
The last of the woods is down; [...]
There's no holly nor hazel nor ash here,
but pastures of rock and stone;

Few historic accounts of Beara touch on the disappearance of the forests, but a valuable exception was left by James Anthony Froude, an English historian who spent time on the peninsula in the 1840s, and leased Derreen House (Lauragh) in 1868–71:

> The long peninsula shut in between the fiords of Bantry and Kenmare was then [in the 1580s] covered from end to end with forest, inaccessible except by water, or penetrated by a few scarce discoverable horsetracks; inhabited by wolves, and by men who were almost as wild, and were human only in the ineffable fidelity with which they concealed and shielded their hunted chief [Gerald of Desmond]. The enormous trees which lie in the bogs, or the trunks which break on all sides out of the ground, prove that once these hills were as thickly wooded as those which have escaped the spoiler [...]. Now, the single fault of the landscape is its desolation. Sir William Petty [...] considered the supply of fuel to be practically as inexhaustible as we now consider our coal measures. He set up refining works on the shore of the harbour, and [...] ore was brought over there, till the last available stick had been cut down to smelt it. Nature still struggles to repair the ruin, and young oaks and birches sprout of themselves, year after year, out of the soil, but the cattle browse them off as they appear; and the wolves being destroyed which once scared the sheep out of the covers, and gave them time to renew their natural waste, civilization itself continues the work of the destroyer, and dooms the district to perpetual barrenness. Of the forests of oak and arbutus and yew which once clothed the whole of Kerry, the woods at Killarney have alone escaped; those and some few other scattered spots, which for some special reason were spared in the general havoc.

Aside from the explicit racism, what stands out here is Froude's eyewitness testimony that, with the wolves gone, grazing cattle and sheep were blocking the attempted return of forest by eating the many native tree seedlings.

That the defeated Irish culture had a strong affinity with woodlands seems apparent in the quite severe penalties laid down under the old Gaelic Brehon laws for wrongfully damaging trees. This reflected the very special place given to trees in mythology, spirituality and other aspects of life from far back into pre-Christian times up to the very recent past, as exemplified in the many still-existing ancient 'fairy trees' dotted around the country. Ogham, the earliest form of script used in Ireland (mostly in the fifth and sixth centuries AD), based each letter on a different tree species, and for that reason is sometimes called the 'Celtic tree alphabet'.

But the often prevalent narrative that it was the English who cut down all Ireland's forests is clearly also highly oversimplified. According to all serious estimates, the vast bulk – somewhere between 87.5 and 98 per cent – of the island was already open by 1600. In fact, it's notable that of all the major forest clearance events shown by pollen analysis of the Barrees peat core, by far the most severe were those that occurred over the millennia *before* AD 1000.

These earlier phases of deforestation were equally likely to have been largely the result of a lack of regeneration due to grazing by domestic animals. That conclusion is very much reinforced by the extremely prominent place held by pastoral farming, especially of cattle, in Gaelic and pre-Gaelic society, culture and economic life. As is still the case in many parts of the world, wealth and social status were to a great extent based on the number of cattle owned. Indeed, much of the known medieval history of Beara seems to have centred around *creachta* – warlike cattle raids, in which the men of other clans were often killed, and the women taken captive.

Following the 1601 Irish defeat at Kinsale, cattle were routinely slaughtered en masse (along with the people) by crown forces in Beara as a means of stifling resistance: bovines were very clearly still central to rural economies in Ireland at the time. The Gaelic practice of 'booleying', in which people seasonally moved and followed their cattle within a landscape, was one of the main grounds on which the natives were condemned as barbaric by English colonists, who equated it with nomadism and a lack of civilisation. Here's Nicholls again:

> Although the amount of cultivation has certainly been underestimated, the importance of pastoralism in the medieval Irish economy cannot be overstressed. The Irish chiefs and notables possessed enormous numbers of cattle; in 1601 the son, grandson and cousin of Turlough Luineach O'Neill each possessed two thousand head. Like some other pastoralists, the Irish no doubt tended on occasion to overstock their pastures, and certainly the pressure of stock must have been one of the most important causes of the destruction of the natural woodlands.

But the gradual retreat of forests caused by livestock in pre-1600 Ireland – going right back to Neolithic times – was likely to have gone on mostly unperceived by the people living at the time. This would have been largely down to a phenomenon called 'shifting baseline syndrome', which I'll look at in Chapter 11.

Even so, there is also much truth to the 'nationalist' version of events, with the new colonial order ruthlessly and very rapidly wiping out almost all the forest that had managed to cling on up to the seventeenth century. Some historians, including Rackham, have sought to frame the loss of the last Irish forests as a consequence of the enormous demographic growth that took off towards the end of the eighteenth century. But as Nicholls pointed out, the forests were already long gone by then, ruling that out as a serious contributing cause.

In any case, the debate around who was primarily behind transforming the island of Ireland from an overwhelmingly wooded landscape into virtually the most deforested region in the whole of Europe looks set to roll on into the future.

Yet there is another, entirely different, perspective, which not only renders such arguments about culpability largely redundant, but is ultimately the only real truth of the matter. It requires taking a step back, and looking at things from an ecocentric (ecosystem-centred), as opposed to anthropocentric (human-centred), viewpoint. That is, from that of the forests themselves, and of the thousands of species that inhabited them. Seen from that angle, *people* – of whatever ethnicity or creed – were responsible, pure and simple.

From Mesolithic times, our ancestors – again, of whatever ethnicity or creed – on this island unrelentingly reduced the extent and viability of wild forest until it was practically all gone, a process that even now still goes on. The only respites were due to wars, plague, famine, environmental depletion, or other such limiting factors, but these were nothing more than temporary blips on an otherwise continuously downward trend.

The picture is little different among other societies all across the world, whether pre-agricultural, agricultural, or industrial; past or present (see Chapter 13). Tragically, destroying natural forests everywhere our species has gone on the planet seems to have been, and continues to be, a pretty universal human trait. Even the 'rolling Tuscan landscape', with which I became so enamoured during my seven-year stay in Italy, is the artificial product of human actions over millennia, having once been dense natural forest. But, just as in Beara, the pendulum swings in both directions. For example, much of the Amazon, Congo and other apparently pristine rainforest around the world is now known to have been open farmland in the past, as demonstrated by ancient overgrown monuments found deep within, and other evidence.

The oscillation between forest and human-created landscapes over thousands of years has been a fairly universal phenomenon, but generally with a plunging overall trajectory. Once sufficient numbers of people and the technological capabilities were there, whether in the form of fire, domesticated livestock, efficient hand tools, chainsaws or heavy machinery, the pattern has always been much the same: drastic forest clearance. (It's essential to be aware, however, that today indigenous communities all around the globe are very often the staunchest defenders of their forest homes and other natural ecosystems against the onslaughts of more 'advanced' society.)

Some scholars, including Edward O. Wilson – generally acknowledged as the most ground-breaking biologist of the last hundred years or more, consistently expanding our horizons of thought in diverse directions – have a particular take on why we have such a destructive effect on forests. Fascinatingly (and quite convincingly in my view), Wilson believed the reasons to be very deep-seated biological ones:

> Finding themselves surrounded by forests that once covered most of Earth's habitable land, Neolithic peoples set out ten thousand years ago to convert them into cropland, pasture, corrals, and scattered woodlots. What they could not chop down, they burned. Successive generations, their populations growing, continued the process until today only half the original cover is left. [This was written 20 years ago; it is significantly less now.] They needed the food, of course, but there is another way of looking at the relentless deforestation. People then as now instinctively wanted the ancestral habitat. So they proceeded to create savannas crafted to human needs. *Homo sapiens* did not evolve to be a forest dweller, like chimpanzees, gorillas, and other great apes. Rather, it became a specialist of open spaces. The aesthetically ideal environment of today's transformed world is the much-treasured landscape, for better or worse our ersatz savanna.

If that seems far-fetched, consider the fact that, as a species, we lived and evolved for millions of years on the plains of central East Africa. And it was probably only relatively recently in evolutionary terms – around 60,000 years ago – that our *Homo sapiens* ancestors successfully migrated out of Africa and began to spread across the rest of the planet's land masses.

(Exactly how this played out is still far from settled, however, and the thinking around it is continually developing.)

Just as with all other species, our behaviour now – at both individual and group levels – is undoubtedly partly the result of the evolutionary path that has taken us here. It seems that even some of our earlier cousins like Neanderthals cleared forests by fire and other means to mould environments in directions that suited them better. As Wilson also pointed out: '... history makes no sense without prehistory, and prehistory makes no sense without biology'. However, when it comes to people, there are of course always other key determining factors interwoven with biology, above all cultural.

Can we overcome a seemingly innate tendency to destroy wild forests, and then prevent them from returning, identified by Wilson as partly the result of an instinctual drive to recreate our species' natural savannah habitat? I think the answer is yes, but we need to be aware not only of that tendency itself, but of the mechanisms by which we carry it out (especially the largely unseen one of grazing animals), and move beyond. Since culture is such a key driver of human behaviour, a profound transformation in our cultural relationship with forests and other natural ecosystems, to one of respect, and indeed reverence, is vital.

It is not an exaggeration to say that our own very survival as a species will ultimately largely hinge on whether we can do so – or not.

An Gorta Mór, the Great Hunger of 1845–52, happened above all for reasons relating to history, politics and ideology, rather than the natural calamity that came in the form of a potato blight. Throughout the period, undisputedly huge quantities of food were being exported from Ireland, often under armed guard. A generally estimated more than 1 million people perished – around one-eighth of the entire population, either from direct starvation or hunger-induced disease.

Over twice that number were forced to emigrate, mostly to North America, to escape the horror and death. A high proportion of those who did so succumbed to fever themselves during the crossing in overcrowded and rancid 'coffin ships', or were drowned in shipwrecks. Millions more left over the following decades, ultimately cutting the population of the country by half. The poorest parts, especially those along the western and southwestern seaboards, were by far the worst affected. The Beara Peninsula was utterly hammered.

In themselves, the population statistics for our two townlands tell a story of unfathomable suffering and loss. In 1841 the population of Bofickil was 179, while that of Faunkill was 123. By 1851 there were only 85 people left in Bofickil – a drop of over 50 per cent, while by 1861 numbers in Faunkill had plummeted to only 32, an even more catastrophic crash of almost 75 per cent. The 1841 population of Beara as a whole was around 39,000; today it is just 6,000, although the decline continued long after the Famine, numbers only stabilising in the 1970s.

It is impossible now to even begin to imagine the heart-rending scenes that must have taken place here during that time. People would have been forced to watch helplessly as loved ones died the most horrible slow deaths, starting with children and elders. They were often then followed into mass graves – if there was anyone left to do the burying – by every last member of their families, one by one. Whole communities disappeared. The relatively luckier ones who managed to leave, and survived doing so, had to forever abandon everything they had ever known, frequently including their own families.

Contemporary accounts from the district go some way towards helping make more tangible the human cost of the disaster, in a way that raw statistics alone cannot:

> The streets of Castletown[bere] are swarming with beggars whose haggard and famine-worn countenances frighten and appal the stranger, round whom they flock with utmost pertinacity, praying and beseeching for something to appease their appetites while the shrill screams of the children for food thrill through the brain.
>
> Our town [Bantry] at six o'clock this morning was a scene of unparalleled misery and destitution. At that early hour two hookers [fishing boats] arrived at our quay laden with 240 human spectres from Berehaven [Beara] who had quitted their homes of wretchedness to find shelter in the workhouse. I saw them crawl from where they landed ....

The physical testimonies left behind by those who died or emigrated are still there all around in the landscape, including beneath the trees in the Bofickil woods, the oldest of which must have borne witness to the unbearable agonies that occurred. A detailed Ordnance Survey map from 1842 shows a number of buildings, including a village-like cluster of dwellings known as a *clochán*, in various parts of what are now our woods. But on the subsequent edition, made in 1901, they are all either gone, or only their outlines still appear, indicating rooflessness.

It's not unlikely that the inhabitants were evicted during the

Famine by the bailiffs of the landlord, Richard White, who by then had been granted the title earl of Bantry. All over Ireland at the time, people were being put out of their homes for an inability to pay rent, and their mostly tiny, miserable one-room cabins 'tumbled' (pulled down) to prevent reoccupation. Michael Caupey told me that the ruins of the *clochán* were still in evidence when he was young, but little is visible of them now.

The slowly crumbling remains of other stone buildings do however survive elsewhere in the woods. And in several flattish, gently sloping areas, the parallel ridges of potato beds are still clearly discernible in the ground, now grown over with trees. It is almost certain that the last time they were cultivated was during the Famine, and that they would have been despaired over before being finally abandoned after repeated crop failures in those dark, cruel years.

Throughout the woods are old stone field walls, in places with longer protruding stones set as steps in a diagonal row up the side. They are now covered over, like almost everything else, in thick spongy carpets of mosses, punctuated by navelwort, polypody and other lithophytic plants (i.e. growing on bare rock). Other, less easily deciphered, remains are everywhere, enduring reminders that the area where the woods are now was once part of a much more peopled landscape, filled with human voices, laughter and song.

The desperately sad fact is that it was their passing that ultimately opened the way for the woods to start returning to *Badh Fiadh-Choille*, the Recess of the Wild Wood, just as I had seen in Prague and Tuscany. Despite their extreme beauty and biological wealth, the woods are, in that sense, a post-apocalyptic landscape. As with the Chernobyl district in

Ukraine, the demilitarised zone between the two Koreas, and other places vacated by people, they are yet another poignant, if small-scale, example of how nature can return – and does best – when left alone.

And the Bofickil woods likewise pose an ever more urgent and vital question, encapsulating what is probably the greatest challenge of our time: how can we achieve a paradigm shift away from the past and present situation, in which only either nature or people do well, towards a future in which both are able to survive, and indeed thrive, together?

10

An Unlikely Sheep Farmer

The Crowley place came with almost 40 acres of mountain commonage, which is like saying there was a quarter share in 160 acres, for example, although it was actually a bit more complicated than that.

Commonage is usually on lands that are less productive agriculturally – particularly uplands, which in the past were used communally by tenant families living nearby for grazing their animals. Joint ownership was then formalised with the break-up of the big landed estates, when in the late nineteenth and early twentieth centuries the British state loaned most tenants the funds to buy out their farms from landlords. These concessions around land ownership were very hard-won, coming only after what was, in places like Beara, a long and extremely bitter battle for rights, referred to as the Land War.

The division between the two townlands of Bofickil and Faunkill carries on up the mountain commonage from the main stream running through the woods, with a deep cleft of bare rock marking the first stretch almost up to the 'first top', as the neighbours call it. Beyond that there is a hollow, known locally as the Valley of Goulagh, behind which the land recommences its rise up to the 'high top' of the commonage, at 262 metres above sea level.

This marks the beginning of a ridge of the Slieve Miskish Mountains, which rises steadily through the commonages of other townlands for about five kilometres. It passes Lackawee (572 metres) and a couple of other high points before arriving at the pinnacle of the corrugation, Maulin, at 621 metres. Though modest in elevation compared to the Apuan peaks I was familiar with in Italy, for example, being situated so close to the sea makes them feel much higher than their altitude in metres alone might suggest.

I once walked from the front door of the house we were renting in Faunkill to the high top of our commonage, and from there carried on along the crease of the ridge as far as Maulin, before retracing my steps. By the time I got home around eight hours later, my legs were trembling with fatigue, more so due to the roughness of the terrain than the nominal distances covered. The average incline of perhaps around 35 degrees up to the high top of the commonage might not sound particularly steep, but walking up it gives an altogether different impression, and even the fittest are likely to struggle for breath most of the way up. The Faunkill side is extremely rough, but the Bofickil flank is even more so, with a greater abundance of high, sheer rock faces, or cliffs, as they're called in Beara. (People have died in other parts of the peninsula from falling down these, or 'getting clifted'.)

Our farm has one of four shares in the Bofickil commonage (the Caupeys also own a share), while on the Faunkill side we have one of nine shares. With a share of say, ten acres, in a commonage, you can't lay exclusive claim to any particular ten acres of it. Instead, you have the right to co-use the whole area, along with everyone else with one or more shares. (Although in many instances shareholders have agreed among themselves to divide up, or 'stripe', commonages into private areas.) What that means in practice is that there really is nothing that can be done with commonage except what everyone else does, i.e. graze it with sheep or, less commonly nowadays, cattle. As things stand, anything else would be to interfere with other shareholders' rights.

For the first six years after moving to Beara, I made no use of the commonage, other than to often walk to the top for the stupendous views. But with time I began to give some thought to the idea of putting livestock on the mountain as a source of additional income. Although my sculpture business was doing well, earnings were uneven and unpredictable, being reliant on whatever contracts might be given the green light at any particular time. The nature of the work entails both peaks and troughs, and slack periods when there was nothing definite on the horizon could be a cause for anxiety, even if something always seemed to crop up in the end just as things were getting tight.

I was initially interested in Galloways, a tough Scottish breed of mountain cattle, and Finbarr and myself installed a welded steel cattle crush in preparation. But Michael persuaded me that sheep would be a more practical option on the mountain, due to the extreme roughness of the ground.

In all the wildest imaginings of my youth, living in Dublin, London, Paris and Prague and trying hard to be cool (with questionable success), ending up farming sheep would have been among the very least likely scenarios I foresaw.

In terms of probability, I would have ranked it alongside farming kangaroos in the Australian outback, or llamas in the Peruvian Andes. And, to be honest, it wasn't a prospect I relished even all these years later in Beara. Chasing woolly beasts around a mountain in the lashing rain (as I afterwards had to do on countless occasions), or mending fences in Atlantic gales (as I also had to do), were most definitely *not* high up on my list of fun activities. But the land was there, and needs must, so in 2015 I bought a dozen Scotch blackfaced ewe (female) lambs from Michael, five Scotch/Cheviot crosses from another neighbour, Batty O'Neill, and stuck them all up the mountain.

Over the following five years I learned a fair bit, usually the hard way. As, for example, when I first marked the sheep green (everyone has to give their sheep a distinguishing mark), making them more difficult to spot on the hill by providing quite effective partial camouflage. (I know, pretty obvious in retrospect; purple was soon adopted instead.) Or once, while trying to take them down off the mountain in the rain, I found myself crawling in my oilskins out along a ledge of slippery rock overhanging a sheer ten-metre drop in an attempt to pull two particularly uncooperative members of the flock out of the precipitous spot from which they were refusing to budge. After a half an hour or so of very dangerous and futile effort, no doubt spiced with quite a few profanities, I realised I was seriously risking my life out of nothing but pure pigheadedness, and left them for another day.

In moments such as these, I often rued the day I ever decided to get sheep, and the neighbours no doubt greatly enjoyed watching some of my more ridiculous antics while trying to coordinate dog and sheep. But, saying that, there were surely as many times when I found myself up the mountain on a glorious day, with the knowledge that I probably wouldn't be there at all otherwise. Every way you look, the views are breathtaking.

From the high top, they extend out over Bantry Bay, Bere Island and the Sheep's Head Peninsula to the south. The long fissure of Kenmare River (actually a bay, not a river) lies to the north, with the Iveragh Peninsula, Deenish and Scariff islands, and the Skelligs where it meets the ocean – jewels set in scintillating lapis lazuli. To the west, the open Atlantic stretches out past the tips of the peninsulas and islands to the horizon, while looking eastwards Carrauntoohil and the MacGillycuddy's Reeks mountains, in the winter often mantled in white, rise up into the clouds. On the right day, just being up there at all can be serious food for the soul.

About 8.5 acres of our own ground slope up towards, and adjoin, the commonage on the non-seaward side of the main road. Most of this area was very similar to the mountain in character, apart from scattered clumps of wild native woodland lower down near the road, covering perhaps a quarter of the land. For the first few years after we bought the farm, a neighbour used this ground for sheep. Like the 21.5 acres across the road had been before the deer fence went up, it was grazed bare, with little at ground level but *fionnán* and *raithneach* (bracken fern). There was the same total lack of natural regeneration of any trees, as well as almost no floral diversity among the ground layer: it was like a bumpy billiard table with protruding rocks and the odd older tree. But I then asked for the land back, and left it ungrazed.

Within less than a year, the trees were naturally regenerating freely, with copious self-sown wild seedlings of birch, sally, rowan, oak, hazel, whitethorn and other native species springing up in the open everywhere. All around an ancient copse of blackthorn that had been slowly contracting, new suckering stems began pushing up through the bracken over a wide area, powered underground by their elders. Where the bracken stands were very thick, they inhibited the growth of saplings of other tree species, casting very dense shade on the ground and dying off en masse in the autumn, smothering any young trees trying to struggle up from below. But where it was patchier, bracken actually seemed to benefit young trees coming up between the fronds, by providing them with shelter from the often fierce winds gusting in off the Atlantic.

It was in this area that I buried my mum's ashes, and in exactly that spot a rowan later appeared, subsuming some of her substance. Like the old oak in the woods below, it too is her tree.

After a couple of years I started letting my own sheep into those 8.5 acres, but only for a short period in mid-winter, when the deciduous trees have dropped their leaves, and are therefore much less susceptible to damage from browsing. Even then, however, the sheep sometimes stripped the bark from saplings, killing them. But the absence of grazing for most of the year also released the richest and most diverse constellation of native wildflowers and other plants throughout, along with the ever-increasing numbers of trees.

Among those that have appeared in great, quivering multitudes are devil's-bit scabious, heath spotted-orchid, sheep's-bit, bog asphodel, bird's-foot-trefoil, water mint, selfheal, creeping forget-me-not, Irish lousewort, marsh pennywort, and a host of others. Eyebright, an interesting little plant that parasitises the roots of other species, has also become common. All this fecundity is a rich font of nectar, which in turn helps attract a great profusion of insects. Included among them are many butterfly species, such as small tortoiseshell, peacock, red admiral, painted lady, orange-tip, large white, small white, speckled wood, gatekeeper, ringlet, green-veined white, grayling, small copper, meadow brown, silver-washed fritillary, holly blue, common blue and small heath.

Another, marsh fritillary – a gorgeous creature with chequered orange, yellow and brown wings – lays its eggs on the leaves of devil's-bit scabious, the main food plant for its caterpillars. Although a declining and threatened species across Europe, including Ireland, due to habitat loss and other factors, marsh fritillary is now a fairly common summer sight on this piece of land, as well as across the main road in many of the areas protected by the deer fence.

Curiously, even in the open areas, many of the oceans of flowers that have burst forth in the absence of overgrazing are woodland species like bluebell, wood sorrel, lesser celandine, dog-violet, wood anemone, pignut, bugle and primrose. These all seem to have been lying dormant, especially in areas of dense bracken. This fern re-emerges from the ground in late spring, just a little later than the leaves of deciduous trees open, similarly allowing woodland plants to get their growth and flowering phases done before it closes in above. In the summer, bracken also creates humid, low light and wind conditions akin – if more extreme – to those underneath forest. So these flowering species have likely been hanging on under the *raithneach* since the last time the area was wooded, centuries before.

Bracken dominance is considered by many ecologists to be a sign of land that 'wants to be wooded', but is prevented from being so by overgrazing, and there's a lot of truth to that. On the other hand, while bracken prefers dry, fertile ground, soils that are wet and infertile or rocky and thin are equally happy with woodland, just perhaps of a slightly different species mix. The truth of it is that most of Ireland 'wants to be wooded', whether bracken is present or not.

As with a small colony of the relatively rare and protected Killarney fern I discovered concealed under a rocky overhang, the woodland flowers are ecological relics of a far richer, more diverse, past. And their long wait is being rewarded at last: in a delayed emulation of the larger area behind the deer fence across the road, much of the rapid woodland colonisation throughout the 8.5 acres is now twice my height or more. The ground flora is largely already there, biding its time for the return of the natural habitat it was designed to be a part of, now happening all around. Although starting from a poorer baseline, wild nature is flooding back in the most spectacular way into these 8.5 acres too.

In addition to the exclusion of the sheep, this explosion of life was also made possible by the gradual disappearance of the feral goats, probably due to a continuation of the culling that had already been in course before our arrival. I did however also hear that they had moved on to another area farther east, so perhaps they are still around, somewhere else. Although sika deer continue to sometimes pass through, for the moment numbers seem to be kept somewhat in check through being taken by local hunters for venison. That's in sharp contrast to many other parts of the peninsula, where densities are extremely high and, according to what I've heard, increasing all the time.

When not away with work, I often walk up the mountain commonage to the first (or, less frequently, high) top with the dog and a pair of binoculars, finding it great for both body and head. Being relatively high up, there is always a good chance of meeting ravens – 'the vultures of the north', or choughs; both members of the crow family are common here. There might also be a hunting kestrel, peregrine falcon, or even, on a couple of very exciting occasions, one of the spectacular white-tailed eagles reintroduced to the southwest of Ireland over a decade ago. Generally speaking, though, there is very little birdlife on the hill, apart from hooded crows and meadow pipits. In fact, there is very little life of *any* sort.

While traversing the commonage, I often come across native tree seedlings, such as rowan, sally, oak, or holly here and there. Those that are accessible to sheep – i.e. nearly all of them – always disappear soon after, chomped in what would be only a mere mouthful or two. A pretty unspectacular and premature end to something that would otherwise have the potential to grow into one of our most impressive native land plants.

A very odd few manage to cling on alone on cliff ledges and other spots that the sheep can't reach. There they remain bonsai-like, pummelled by the wind into a stunted *leath-ceann*, or 'half head', i.e. bent right over, away from the prevailing wind. Scattered elsewhere are a handful of lone and battered old oaks, whitethorns and hollies that somehow managed to 'get away', i.e. grow beyond the height at which all their foliage can be relentlessly nibbled away until the tree dies.

Essentially, though, the only things that survive on the mountain are the ubiquitous *fionnán* and other coarse grasses like *Nardus stricta*, bracken, and some bitten-down heather and gorse. Otherwise, apart from a few flower species that are able to withstand the constant grazing, such as tormentil and heath milkwort, the hillside is a rocky moonscape, devoid of vegetation. But it's very clear that, just as is now happening in our own place on both sides of the road, the entire mountain would revert naturally to native woodland were that not being continually prevented by the grazing. I say 'revert', because it would once have been covered in rich, thick, old-growth temperate rainforest.

The evidence for that isn't just in the remains of ancient roots on the mountain, exposed in areas of eroding peat, or the peat cores from adjacent Barrees in which tree pollen dominates. The altitudinal limit for rowan, for example, has been put at 730 metres above sea level in this region, several times greater than the high top of the commonage at 262 metres, while Hungry Hill, the highest point in Beara, is still only 685 metres. But given the near total absence of native forests in our uplands, that 730-metre limit is likely based on the known occurrence of *individual* trees. When trees instead grow together as a natural forest ecosystem, as they would have in the past, they make their own microclimate within. As a result, they are much more impervious to the effects of wind, cold, or drought, significantly raising their resilience and the upper limit at which they can survive.

A good example of how forests create the environment that suits them can be seen when no rain falls for many weeks in Beara, and most of the local streams dry up. In contrast, those within the Bofickil woods keep flowing, albeit at a much reduced rate. While natural springs may play a role in this, the main factor is likely another. The mosses in a Costa Rican cloud forest, for example, were found to absorb 50,000 litres of water *per hectare* in just one fall of rain; those in a healthy Irish rainforest are unlikely to be any less effective, given their terrific abundance.

In the Bofickil woods, all the mosses and other vegetation, as well as the porous and absorbent forest soils, act as a giant sponge, soaking up vast quantities of water in times of plenty, and then releasing their stored reserves gradually. Thus moisture levels are actually largely self-regulated by the forest ecosystem. It really is quite stupefying to witness the very same stream that has run dry on the mountain, but is still trickling away lower down in the woods, in a sort of surreal Maurits Cornelis Escher-style inversion of the laws of physics.

There's no doubt that, just as with other parts of Ireland, most of the peninsula was once thickly covered in rainforest, and would spontaneously return to such a state over time if allowed to do so. Only in some of the most exposed, westerly parts might the salt load from sea spray present a barrier. And standing up on the commonage looking down, it's impossible not to be struck by the magnitude of the contrast between the desolate barrenness immediately to hand, and the enormous plenitude of life in the woods below.

Straddling the border of Poland and Belarus is a great forest named Białowieża, which at 1,250 square kilometres is generally considered the largest and most natural stand left anywhere in Europe. Bison, lynx and wolves all live there, and bears are starting to show up again too. In his book *Natural*

Woodland, George Peterken estimated the numbers of distinct species it contained. He determined there to be around 990 vascular plants, 254 bryophytes (mosses and liverworts), 200 lichens, 1,000 fungi, 8,500 insects, 206 spiders, and 226 birds, the last three categories among a total of 11,000 animal species.

While Irish and British Atlantic rainforests like the Bofickil woods are recognised as extremely rich in their bryophyte diversity, no Irish woodland would come even remotely close to rivalling Białowieża in other categories. For one thing, as held by Edward O. Wilson and Robert MacArthur's 1967 theory of island biogeography, the smaller and more remote an island (or fragment) of habitat, the less species diversity it will harbour. Their very small size therefore puts Ireland's remaining scraps of native forest at a big disadvantage.

In fact, Peterken also noted that, by way of comparison, the ancient 390-acre Monks Wood in Cambridgeshire has 372 vascular plant species, 97 bryophytes, 34 lichens, and 337 fungi. Nonetheless, even this example is a powerful demonstration of how natural forests are by far the most species-rich land-based ecosystems, harbouring an incredible *more than three-quarters of all terrestrial biodiversity in the world*.

The amazing variety that is a living forest in places like the Bofickil woods – trees, insects, birds, flowering plants, ferns, mosses, fungi, lichens, mammals – makes a compelling case for allowing much of our uplands to go back to that, their natural state. And the difference with the bare hillside isn't just with regard to biodiversity but, equally importantly, *bioabundance*. The sheer volume of life of all sorts in the Bofickil woods really does have to be experienced at first hand to be believed.

There is no doubt in my mind that any one acre contains far more than all the hundreds of acres of nearby commonage put together.

Weighing upon the other side of the scales, as seen in the previous chapter pastoral farming has been practised for a very long time in places like Beara, since the first farmers settled in the Neolithic Period. For thousands of years, it was primarily based on cattle, even in the uplands, where they were grazed in summer and then brought lower down over the winter months, a system known as 'booleying' in Ireland, or transhumance elsewhere. It was only during the last 150 years or so that sheep took over on rougher and higher ground.

That last fact is significant ecologically, for cattle graze far less selectively than sheep, goats or deer, eating most vegetation without prejudice, rather than making a beeline for any tree seedlings as the others do. They therefore present less of a barrier to the resurgence of woodland scrub, wildflower meadows and other native habitats when stocked in low densities. (Although even cattle will damage or suppress natural vegetation communities unless numbers are kept at an absolute minimum, and land is grazed only seasonally.) Livestock farming remains an integral part of many people's identity and culture, and that must be respected, and supported, into the future.

There are, however, further important sides to the question that should also be factored in. The number of sheep such poor mountain land can support is very low, requiring supplementary feeding with sheep nuts or hay, especially in winter. Other costs are high, such as fencing, which needs constant maintenance and often complete replacement. Earnings from the sale of lambs and wool may cover only a fraction of the costs incurred, and even with farm subsidies, as an activity it often only barely breaks even on such marginal land. By way of example, in late 2020 the annual sale of our sheep's wool, weighing in at 43 kilograms and enough to fill a medium-sized car, earned me the grand total of €4.30 (*before* expenses) – not even the price of a single pint in the pub.

From my own experience, and from what I have seen around me, sheep farming in the uplands is an extremely tough life, with negligible and shrinking rewards. Ever fewer people are prepared to do it, and the number of sheep farmers in Ireland declined by almost a third between 1993 and 2015. Furthermore, climate change is predicted to render the activity ever more impractical in the hills over the coming decades.

But most crucially of all, at around 1 per cent of land area, Ireland has the lowest forest cover in the whole of Europe apart from Iceland. Statistics often put the figure at 11 per cent, but these are only accurate if lifeless plantations of non-native conifers, such as North American sitka spruce, are included in the definition of the word 'forest', which they absolutely should not be. A real forest is a hugely diverse and complex native ecosystem, composed of thousands of interconnected species, of which the trees themselves are but one element, if a fairly central one.

A real forest is most definitely *not* a rigid-edged block made up of a single tree species, planted in countless identical rows with almost no associated biodiversity. The latter should be called what it is: a plantation, or 'fibre farm', not a forest. In Ireland, plantations presently account for almost 90 per cent of total 'forest' cover, compared to a European average of just 3 per cent, a contrast well worth dwelling on for a moment.

Non-native conifer plantations, which are heavily subsidised by the state, not only look ugly and harbour almost no native wildlife, they are extremely damaging to the local biophysical environment beyond their own margins. They acidify the land and any nearby watercourses, and the chemicals used to fertilise ground and prevent insect attack create dead zones all around. The trees are generally industrially clear-felled as a crop in short rotation, leaving the ground a wasteland and causing huge runoff of silt and harmful chemicals into streams, rivers and lakes. And every time a plantation is harvested, the owner is contractually obliged to replant, locking the land and its surroundings into a perpetual cycle of ecological destruction.

The effect on local communities is equally negative. Owners of surviving family farms in many areas find themselves surrounded and hemmed in by unbroken walls of lightless and unvarying monoculture. Plantations are thus another contributory factor pushing out the people who live in many rural localities. Based on the unfounded pretext that plantations can help combat climate change (which I'll return to), the Irish government has plans to increase 'forest' cover to 18 per cent by 2046, through new plantations.

The great danger is that, with the ongoing decline in farm incomes, most of this will be foisted on what is presently farmland, driving even more people off the land. By contrast, allowing the return of *real* forest – i.e. naturally regenerated, wild and native – on a large scale would have hugely beneficial consequences in a variety of ways.

We tend to think automatically of the mountain landscapes across Ireland in places like Connemara, Wicklow, Donegal, or west Cork and Kerry as wild and pristine, as though they've always been that way. But of course the truth is they haven't. Before human impacts, most of the island of Ireland was covered in extremely species-rich native forest, which should be a huge and treasured part of the country's national heritage. But, instead, it is now practically non-existent, and a great majority of the few tiny fragments that do survive are in a dire and worsening state, largely because of exactly the same problems I encountered in Bofickil: overgrazing and invasion by non-native plant species.

Across most species categories, Irish wildlife populations are collapsing owing to a range of factors, but the ever-decreasing availability of the habitats they depend on, such as native forest, is primary among them. And just as human society requires food and other resources, so does it have just as great a need for the things that healthy forests and other natural ecosystems provide. These include climate stabilisation (in far more ways than just carbon sequestration), clean air and water, revenues from tourism, recreation opportunities, and the increasingly widely recognised health benefits that come from access to wild nature. Then there's another vital consideration.

The winter of 2019–20 saw huge problems with flooding across Ireland, causing immense personal and economic hardship for those affected. Exceptional floods, that should occur only once in 50 or 100 years, are now happening ever more frequently, in many places every few years. There are two principal reasons why this is becoming such an acute issue, the first of which is climate change – or climate breakdown, as it's increasingly, and more appropriately, called. The main effect of the build-up of latent heat in the atmosphere is on the hydrological cycle. That means we can expect an ever greater frequency of extreme rain events and storms in some parts of the world, including Ireland.

The second cause is the artificial land uses that are now so dominant on this island. In its natural state, with habitats like native forest, bogs, wetlands, flood plains around rivers and so on, the land would have been able to absorb colossal amounts of water, which were then released back out only gradually, at a rate that rivers and streams could cope with. As described earlier, I've witnessed this myself for years on a small scale in the Bofickil woods.

But the hills and lowlands alike have been shorn of their natural forests, and are forcibly kept in that state (plantations are useless in this role). Bogs, marshes, fens and other wetlands have been, and continue to be, drained. Rivers have been relentlessly straightened, and every attempt made to prevent them from 'encroaching' back onto their natural floodplains. Everywhere, originally diverse and complex landscapes have been rendered as close to featureless as possible. As a result, in periods of heavy rain the water flashes off the land, rushing downstream and causing floods that are immensely damaging for all those unlucky enough to be on the receiving end.

The degree to which we have so completely transformed the land is all just begging for very serious trouble. And these are problems that the hard engineering solutions currently applied in Ireland, such as dredging and raised concrete side walls, cannot hope to resolve. The volumes of water are just too immense, and they accumulate too fast. Such artificial measures simply increase the speed of water in rivers, making it even more difficult to deal with downstream.

By contrast, allowing natural forest to return to upland catchment areas, and rivers revert to their original, more natural winding and braided courses, full of native vegetation and debris, has proved to be a far more effective means of reducing peak flows and preventing flooding. It also costs only a fraction of the amount, as demonstrated so clearly at the town of Pickering in Yorkshire, for example. As climate breakdown worsens, so will the problems with flooding, until national and local authorities take on board that the only real long-term solutions will be nature-based ones.

In May 2019 Ireland became the second country in the world to rightly declare a climate and biodiversity emergency (the UK was the first), with the European Parliament following suit six months later. If these declarations are to be worth more than just the paper they were written on, native forests and other wild habitats must be allowed to return in the most natural way possible, i.e. through natural regeneration, and on landscape scales. So while it would be very wrong to force anything on farmers, for a whole host of reasons there is a crying need for deep change in how land is used and managed in Ireland.

Nature must be permitted to come back. Society needs it; our rapidly disappearing wildlife desperately needs it. How can that be achieved in ways that work for everyone, especially farmers and rural communities?

11

The Red Pill

Sculpture conservation takes me all over Ireland, often for extended periods with larger projects. One of the best things about that is coming home to Beara, since even a week or two away is enough to make me see it all again with fresh eyes, as if for the first time. When I get up on a Saturday morning, having returned from a job somewhere upcountry the evening before, and look out over the island of Inisfarnard and the Atlantic blue beyond, I still feel the need to pinch myself, to be sure it's all real.

And often – especially in spring – I'll make a point of waking before dawn to open the rooflight window of my bedroom, so I can go back to bed and listen to the dawn chorus of the wild birds in all its symphonic diversity of tones in the woods just outside. Lying there snug under the covers, drifting in and out of sleep, waves of rhythmic sound wash over me, the trilled notes of another universe penetrating to my innermost self.

There are so many things I love about where I now live. But the feeling of having a far more immediate and intimate relationship with place, the natural world with all its cycles, and by extension the very planet we live on, is the one that means most. Restoring a wild natural ecosystem – or, more accurately, removing some of the man-made impediments that were preventing it from restoring itself – has brought deep joy, fulfilment and meaning, to a degree that I could never have imagined possible. With its unending transitions and novelties, the forest is a cup that never runs dry, an elixir for thirsts that cannot otherwise be quenched, except through the 'time out' that only a wild place can provide.

On an intellectual level, it has opened doors to a multitude of much more enhanced and stimulating understandings of the workings of the world around us, many of which are more fantastic than actual fantasies. It really does feel as if a curtain that I barely even knew was there has been partially lifted, revealing a universe of wonders and deep significance beyond. And every single thing learned always raises many more questions in turn, making for an inexhaustible fount of marvel and fascination – one of the best sides to an in-depth engagement with nature and ecology.

From the very beginning, I have felt a powerful and profound sense of fusion with this piece of land and all the life within, and what I have given of myself to it has been returned in spades, and more.

But just as every dark cloud has its silver lining, so too are there very real downsides to discovering such a rich, lode-bearing vein in what life can offer. Principal among them is a heightened consciousness of how we are still destroying what remains of wild nature at a ferocious rate. That can bring a heavy and at times lonely anguish, which is further intensified by the knowledge that there are enormous barriers to a change in direction, not least because so many people remain largely oblivious.

An observation by the great American writer, ecologist and conservationist Aldo Leopold in the 1940s still holds perfectly true:

> One of the penalties of an ecological education [awareness] is that one lives alone in a world of wounds. Much of the damage inflicted on land is quite invisible to laymen. An ecologist must either harden his shell and make believe that the consequences of science are none of his business, or he must be the doctor who sees the marks of death in a community that believes itself well and does not want to be told otherwise.

Searching for a more contemporary analogy, it's worth invoking a scene from the 1999 science fiction film *The Matrix*, in which Morpheus offers the main character, Neo, a choice between the blue pill or the red pill. Taking the blue one will return him to a state of blissful unawareness, while the red will force him to see – and live within – an almost unbearable dystopian reality. Gaining an ecological education, as Leopold described it, is akin to opting for the red pill: afterwards there is no going back, either from the joy or the torment.

To truly appreciate just how astonishingly beautiful, complex, and precious something approaching real wild nature is makes it impossible not to see the present and increasing lifelessness of the land practically everywhere you look. And, in my experience, a personally lived, searing existential pain at the ecocidal destruction we are unremittingly visiting upon surviving living systems across the planet becomes an almost daily part of life. If, as I am, you're lucky enough to be able to just walk out the door to see the wonder of a *relatively* intact ecosystem, and so be constantly reminded of what is being lost on such a scale, that heartbreak can be even more acute.

Most people will hopefully have at least some knowledge of the great dying that is coming over the coral reefs, the 'tropical rainforests of the sea', due to overfishing and climate breakdown. And of the continuing annihilation of the world's great tropical rainforests in the Amazon, Congo, Southeast Asia, and elsewhere – the multitudes of smoke plumes rising from them now often visible from space. But it's less easy to perceive the fact that the landscape all around us in Ireland has undergone exactly the same process. It has been transformed from an unbroken mixture of forest and other natural habitats to an almost continuous stretch of artificial land uses that increasingly exclude wild nature.

The only difference is that on this island it has taken place over a much longer timeframe. So much so that, with the shortness of the human lifespan, it becomes almost impossible to realise that it has even been happening – at an ever-quickening tempo – at all. Indeed, most people take it for granted that the way things are now is somehow actually the natural state of the land. And every generation takes a new, ecologically poorer baseline against which to compare any declines over the space of their own lifetime. As a rule, the human mind struggles with time-scales that go much beyond that.

Generally missed therefore is that what is witnessed over the course of one life is only a very small segment of a blinking out that has been ongoing for hundreds and thousands of years. The result is that landscapes change beyond all recognition, with life's fabric torn apart, and yet the people living there have no idea that their surroundings were once a world away from that to which they are accustomed. Thus an incredibly rich and complex old-growth forest ecosystem, complete with every trophic layer (layers of the food pyramid), can be reduced down to just grass and sheep, for example, and the result still be almost unanimously considered 'natural'. This fairly recently conceived phenomenon of ecological amnesia has been termed 'shifting baseline syndrome'.

To give just one example of its effects, people living near the former home range of the Yangtse River dolphin, the baiji, which became globally extinct in 2007, soon forgot it ever existed. In the space of little more than a decade, the animal's erasure was effected not only physically, but mentally. Imagine that process playing out on a continual basis over hundreds and thousands of years, and it becomes clear how extreme ecological impoverishment is so universally normalised in the human mind and cultures.

We have been endlessly taking from the living world, without ever really giving thought to setting any serious limits. The further back in time, the more difficult it was to be aware that we were doing so, or of the disastrous consequences that must inevitably follow if we didn't stop, and start giving something back. Neither is now the case, and there are no more excuses for not acting as a society before our own unwillingness to wake up to what we are doing comes crashing back down on us, as it most surely will.

All the indications are that nature is collapsing in health, diversity and abundance at an intense speed all around us, with species populations and distributions being continually reduced and dying out everywhere across the globe. Ireland is no exception to this 'demographic winter', or *de*wilding, with conservation abjectly failing to do more than, at best, slow the rate of loss. A recent report found that over 90 per cent of our protected habitats are in bad – and worsening – condition, and one in five assessed species are sliding towards extinction.

President Michael D. Higgins summed it up with fierce anger and passion in his address to the first ever Irish National Biodiversity Conference, held in Dublin in early 2019: 'If we were coal miners, we would be up to our knees in dead canaries.' The hidden truth is that, despite the green image that is so carefully projected, Ireland is actually one of the most ecologically trashed and dysfunctional places on Earth. On land, an increasingly industrialised monoculture-based agriculture that gives no quarter to the wild is the prime culprit, but things are no better at sea.

On one occasion holidaying on the Dingle Peninsula when I was young, the sea was so full of sprat there seemed more fish than water; we were scooping them up in a bucket for our dinner. And I remember sitting over cups of coffee in Michael Caupey's kitchen listening to him and his cousin Johnny talking about the years they spent working together on Johnny's small boat, fishing the local waters. They spoke of how, up until the late 1970s, the surface of the sea in nearby Ballycrovane Harbour (Bay) and other local spots used to sometimes be literally 'boiling with fish' like mackerel, they were so plentiful. These days you can spend all day fishing off the rocks in season, and only if you're lucky will you catch just a few small ones.

But even the populations of the 1970s and 1980s, that seem

so abundant by today's standards, were only a pale reflection of what they had once been. The decline has been continuing for centuries, but has been speeding up as our technological capacity to scour the ocean of every single fish is ever further perfected. The seas have been, and continue to be, emptied of their wildlife and wrecked by overfishing on an industrial level. The resulting lack of prey is having knock-on effects throughout marine ecosystems, with serious declines among dependent sea birds and other species categories.

There are countless further examples of how human activities are killing off the living world at an accelerating speed; in fact an identical picture of loss presents itself almost everywhere you look. Take insects. The data from scientific studies conducted across Germany show a more than 75 per cent crash in numbers over the course of 25 years in 63 *nature reserves*. Equally shocking results came in 2021 from England, where a terrifying 65 per cent of flying insects have disappeared in just 17 years.

There are very few scientifically verifiable studies on insects, since, before they started to disappear, almost nobody thought them worth monitoring, they were so numerous. As a result, past baselines for comparison with the present are rare. But a leading expert, Professor Dave Goulson of the University of Sussex, estimates that 40 per cent of the million or so known insect species are at risk of extinction:

In the last 50 years, we have reduced the abundance of wildlife on Earth dramatically. Many species that were once common are now scarce. We can't be sure, but in terms of numbers, we may have lost 50% or more of our insects since 1970. It could be much more. We just don't know, which is scary, because insects are vitally important, as food, pollinators and recyclers amongst other things. Perhaps more frightening, most of us have not noticed that anything has changed. Even those of us who can remember the 1970s, and who are interested in nature, can't really remember how many butterflies or bumblebees there were when we were children. Human memory is imprecise, biased and fickle. You may have a vague nagging feeling that there used to be more than just one or two butterflies on your buddleia bush, but you can't be sure.

Goulson's words hint at a contributory dimension to the all-pervasive shifting baseline syndrome: our brains didn't evolve to be much good at perceiving gradual change, even that which occurs over the course of our own lifetimes. (Although in ecological terms, the decline of insects and other wildlife is happening in no more than an eye blink.) Many older people do, however, remember how when driving at night it was once often necessary to repeatedly stop to brush multitudes of moths and other insects from car windscreens and headlights. That's never required now.

The chief reason for the collapse in insect abundance and diversity – sometimes referred to as the 'insectageddon' – is a worsening lack of habitat, pushed out by ever more predominant intensive farming. Other factors to blame are the heavy use of agricultural pesticides, fertilisers and other chemicals, globalised diseases and, increasingly, climate breakdown. Light pollution, i.e. the ever greater prevalence of artificial light at night from houses, street lights, and so on, has also been identified as a major contributing cause, a demonstration of how seemingly innocuous extinction drivers can be.

Some people will likely wonder what difference it makes to them if there are less bugs to clog up their windscreens, or cause annoyance in various other ways. But what they need to realise is that all life is intimately connected, and a problem in one area of the natural world will inevitably have myriad other negative effects, many of which we cannot foresee. For example, insects pollinate about three-quarters of the flowering plants on the planet, including 35 per cent of the plants that produce the foods we eat.

They're also essential to nutrient recycling, perform a multitude of other vital ecological roles, and make up the bulk of the diet of many species of birds and other animals – which are in turn eaten by others higher up the food chain. So if insects disappear, all those connections, and the ecosystems largely built around them, also unravel and die, which is exactly what we are seeing happen across the planet. We are very unwisely putting to the test Albert Einstein's words of warning: 'If the bee disappeared off the face of the Earth, man would only have four years left to live.'

Thankfully, at least some people are keenly aware of what's happening, and the urgent need to do something about it. The 'All-Ireland Pollinator Plan', established in 2015 by the National Biodiversity Data Centre to encourage individuals and communities to put in place measures that favour flying insects, is a very positive development in that direction. Every farm, private or community garden, public park, schoolyard, cemetery, churchyard, roadside verge, roundabout, even window box, should be made as insect- and wildlife-friendly as possible.

Planting and sowing native species – or, far better again, just letting them come naturally, foregoing all herbicides or other chemicals, letting spaces go as wild as circumstances allow, or even just mowing lawns less often: all these steps and others are a help. As I saw in my mum's Dublin garden, every action, no matter how big or small, counts. But even so, I can't help feeling that, even with such brilliant initiatives as the Pollinator Plan, we are taking teaspoons to problems that are unfolding on the scale of mutually compounding tsunamis.

On a warm sunny day, the Bofickil woods can be so alive with flying insects as to be positively throbbing with the frenetic beating of tens of thousands of tiny blurred pairs of wings. The sonic amalgam includes every pitch and timbre, from fuzzy bass buzz to frantic high whine, with individuals becoming momentarily distinct as they skirt the ear, before quickly merging back into the background wall of aggregated sound. As Seánie said of the constant loud thrum when we were in there together some years back: 'It sounds like there's a plane flying over the whole time.'

I've counted up to 30 different species of insects of all shapes and sizes in a rainbow of iridescent metallic colours on a single purple-flushed umbel (flower cluster) of wild angelica. They come for the nectar, or else just to soak up the sun for a while before moving on. On days like this, walking in the woods can feel like traversing a magical living soup, the air is so thick with life and vibrating energy, extending from ground level right up into – and over – the canopy of leaves above. Switching to more scientific terminology, the levels of bioabundance are extremely high.

Sure, there are plenty of insect species that occur elsewhere that you won't find in the Bofickil woods. But a mosaic of actual wild natural habitats – native forests, wildflower meadows, naturally flowing rivers, bogs, other wetlands – will always provide insects and other wildlife with what they need way better than any man-made environments ever can.

I would never for a moment dispute the need to be far more accommodating of nature in our farms, towns, gardens, and so on, rather than continually pushing it to the margins in every way possible, as we have been. Nor would I want to appear to belittle the great potential in approaches like the Pollinator Plan for engaging and mobilising whole communities, while at the same time helping with the essential task of raising awareness of the bigger picture. A sea change in attitudes to the natural world among the general public is essential if we are to have any chance of resolving the current crisis, and every means at our disposal for bringing people on board must be employed with urgency. Such schemes are one of the best ways of achieving that, and are therefore crucial. As the saying has it, 'mighty oaks from little acorns grow'.

But I am also convinced that, ultimately, approaches large enough in scale to be in some way actually commensurate with the enormity of the collapse unfolding in our lifetime are vital.

Since the 1960s, farmers in Ireland and across Europe have been paid subsidies under the EU Common Agricultural Policy, including a series of agri-environmental schemes. Their requirements and objectives constantly shift as these schemes come and go, to the great frustration of farmers. But they all appear to have one thing in common: they are designed to be easily incorporated into box-ticking bureaucratic exercises, rather than to bring any real benefits whatsoever to nature. They are, in effect, a fig leaf.

For example, as a farmer I receive payments for attaching bird and bat boxes to trees, and leaving piles of builder's sand for bees, all of which are generally ignored by the birds, bats and bees. In my experience, farmers invariably agree on the absurdity of such measures, but like myself go along with them as a source of much-needed income.

The situation is, however, actually far worse than that: most of society is completely unaware that farmers are being continually pushed by official policy to destroy wildlife habitat, when exactly the opposite is what needs to be happening. Land with anything remotely resembling wildlife habitat, such as scrub, has until now been excluded from all farm payments. This is because one of the principal conditions for eligibility is that land must be in what is described as 'good agricultural and environmental condition' (GAEC).

While this sounds perfectly benign, in reality it's anything but: it financially penalises farmers who don't remove existing wild patches on their land, while other schemes pay them to take token actions that are useless to wildlife. Strange as it might seem, what birds, bats, bees and everything else really need isn't boxes stuck on trees or fence posts, or piles of builder's sand, but *actual wild habitat*.

I see the disastrous results of this policy across Ireland when away on sculpture projects, with precious surviving pieces of semi-wild land either cleared and levelled with diggers or repeatedly burned in order to make or keep land eligible for payments. I witnessed one example first hand during a more protracted sculpture restoration project I was engaged on upcountry, which I carried out in four separate stints over a couple of years. Right next to the site, where I was working outdoors, there was a tract of several acres of highly rich and diverse land, with oak, ash, elder, and many other native trees and shrubs.

Underneath were bluebells, celandine, wild garlic, and a great variety of ferns and other woodland flora. Interspersed among the clumps of trees were moss-covered stone outcrops and open wet patches, full of yellow flag, ragged robin and a great multitude of other wildflowers, all buzzing with flying insects like dragonflies and butterflies, and teeming with birds. It was a little piece of paradise, and having it there alongside made the first two periods of work a pure delight. It had clearly developed into that state through neglect, in turn probably because the land had been considered too rough and wet to seriously bother with.

But after I had been on site less than a week for the third phase of works, a 12-ton digger arrived and started clearing. All the abundance of wildlife I had enjoyed before was obliterated over the next few weeks, mostly in full view of where I was working. The trees were pulled out and piled up to one side, and any rock outcrops broken out with a hydraulic chisel attachment. The ground was dug up, perforated plastic drainage pipes laid and then surrounded by the broken rock and unearthed boulders, and the soil levelled back over the top. After I left, it was all seeded with a monoculture of one single species: high-productivity perennial ryegrass (PRG).

By the time I came back for the final spell of work after a longer interval, cattle had been put in and the land was being regularly drenched in slurry and chemical fertilisers. In essence, a treasure trove of wild biodiversity had been ripped out to make way for just two domesticated non-native species – PRG and cattle, fed by a constant deluge of artificial chemicals and fermented liquid excrement.

To anyone unaware of what had been there previously, by the end of the process it all looked like a blissfully green pastoral scene, a picture of how we've been conditioned to think the countryside should appear. But in reality it represented a devastating loss of yet another of our few remaining wildlife havens, full of rich, vibrant nature, and its replacement with ecologically empty barrenness. Exactly the same thing is happening everywhere, on an industrial scale and at a frenetic rate, transforming Ireland into flat, superficially green, sterile emptiness.

During the last couple of periods of work at that site, myself and the farmer who owned the land in question had a few casual friendly chats over the old stone wall that divided the property where I was working from his place. He told me that he had done the same to several other pieces of land, planned to do it elsewhere, and chiefly for one reason only: previously he wasn't receiving any payments for those patches, but afterwards he would. Relating this particular experience is in no way intended as a criticism of the man himself: trying to make a living from farming can be a very tough business – especially on more marginal ground, and this man's land was his livelihood. Like others destroying natural habitat, he was doing nothing more than what official policy is telling him to do via the most direct means possible: his bread and butter.

Over the course of the last of our conversations I asked whether he might have left the land as it was previously had he been paid to do so, just as he was now being paid to graze it with cattle. Revealingly, he assured me that he most definitely would, telling me that it had cost him a fortune to hire in the machine, pay for the driver, diesel, plastic drainage pipes and everything else. I also asked him would he be prepared to let this and other land on his farm go back to nature if he received guaranteed payments in the same way as with livestock. His answer was: 'Why not? So long as we can make a living from the land, sure that's all we're trying to do here.' Other farmers might well feel differently and, as I said, that should absolutely be respected. But there has to be an alternative that allows people to make a living while keeping land rich in wildlife, or letting it come back.

Just as devastating are the fires that are regularly set to remove scrub, gorse, and other unwanted vegetation from hillsides. The ubiquitous *fionnán* grass dies away naturally over the winter, drying out to become a beige blanket that, together with dead bracken and gorse, in prolonged dry weather becomes a powder keg of accumulated flammable material. For quite a few years now the climate seems to have adopted a regular pattern of drought in the spring, with sometimes very little or no rain falling for up to six or seven weeks at a time. Throughout this period, in many parts of the country the air is often thick with the acrid smell of smoke from fires, while at night it can look like a scene from Dante's *Inferno*.

Hills are lit up by roaring conflagrations, with flames leaping six metres high or more into the air. People with houses near the frequently burned areas live in dread of this period every year, as homes and other property are regularly incinerated. Countless creatures that are unable to get out of the way are roasted alive, including bird chicks and a host of other smaller animals. Any floral diversity or sapling trees disappear to leave a charred wasteland, which is then recolonised only by grasses.

Setting these fires is illegal from the start of March, but is nonetheless endemic after that date across Ireland every time there's a dry spell. The main reason is the same as that behind the clearances by machine: in order to make land compliant with the GAEC condition laid down for farm payments. That all this destruction is being pushed using the terms 'good environmental condition' is a particularly extreme example of doublespeak.

Our own place in Bofickil is now simply exploding with biodiversity. I have counted well over 100 species of wildflowers, for example (I'm sure a proper botanist would find many more), as well as huge varieties of mosses, ferns, fungi, insects and species of almost every other category. I have seen over 50 species of birds in and around the woods, and they all appear to be getting along just fine without using any of the boxes I had to put up, because they have access to healthy wild natural habitat. And yet none of the areas that harbour all this life are presently classed as eligible for subsidies because they don't comply with the GAEC condition. In short, landowners are being directly incentivised to grub up or burn off any nature-rich pockets that exist on their land, and are therefore doing so on a massive scale.

This scenario is playing out across Ireland, leading to a drastic disappearance of wildlife and the homogenisation of landscapes. Up to 6,000 kilometres of hedgerow, much of it very old, and very often the last refuge for wildlife in an otherwise hostile environment, is ripped out each year to squeeze every last inch of land into production. Perhaps the most grotesque side of it all is that governments (of whatever political make-up) frequently proclaim their deep concern about the plight of nature, while maintaining policies that are actively destroying it.

Farmers depend on their land for a living, and it's pointless blaming them for acting in accordance with decisions made by those who create the rules, whether in Brussels or Dublin. No other sector of society would behave any differently where their basic income – essential for feeding families and paying mortgages – was at stake. But nor is it any wonder that wildlife is collapsing across the board, even if there are plenty of other contributing causes. Such a situation is sheer madness, utterly contradictory and needs immediate reform.

In 2021, the Irish government proposed that up to 30 per cent of a farm holding be able to consist of scrub and other natural habitats, and still all be eligible for payments in the next CAP phase (2023–27). While a very welcome (and long overdue) step in the right direction, it must be extended to encompass *entire farms*, if that is what the farmer wishes.

Are the current farm subsidies eligibility criteria the only reason for the conversion of nature-rich land into lifeless monocultures? Far from it.

In reality this is just another state-incentivised component of the 'Green Revolution', in course since the 1950 and 1960s, which has been so disastrous for the natural world everywhere. And, seen from a longer perspective, that revolution in itself is really nothing more than a logical progression from many hundreds and thousands of years of incremental domestication, just carried to ever further, industrial extremes.

Leaving land in a more productive state than you got it (which generally also means worse for wildlife) is seen by most people as a show of hard graft and enterprising spirit over a lifetime, and the best possible legacy to the next generation. Rather than pushing out nature, it's viewed as rightfully regaining control over something that has been taken from us, as demonstrated in the verb most commonly used to describe it: *reclaiming* land.

Going deeper, it's actually seen as a creative act, in the sense of making something good out of nothingness, from a supposed *terra nullius*, as reflected in another sometimes heard phrase: 'making land where God failed'. That idea surely goes all the way back to the original clearing of wildernesses for cultivation in order to survive. And, down through the millennia, there was seldom any let-up in the grinding struggle to eke out an existence.

People in places like the Aran Islands had to carry baskets of seaweed up from the shore on their backs for mixing with beach sand to bulk soils, where little existed, as a medium in which to grow a few spuds. As literal an instance of 'making land where God failed' as you're likely to find anywhere on Earth. Such hardships, once everyday but now almost inconceivable to us, are the hammer and anvil that forged an outlook that still determines how we relate to the land. Something so long in forming is never going to change easily, but nature will simply continue to fade away if it doesn't. And an essential first step in that direction must be the complete removal of financial penalties to any farmers looking to make such a transformation.

The raft of benefits delivered by wild natural ecosystems such as native woodland are now – or should be – recognised as no less essential to society than food, and that fact must be reflected in how farmers are rewarded for what they do. We need to start giving them another option: that of continuing to receive farm subsidies for *not* farming their land, but for letting wild nature come back instead, if that is what they choose. It's vital to stress that none of this should be mandatory in any way. It should be entirely up to each individual farmer to decide what he or she wants to do – either carry on producing food, allow their land to revert to natural habitat and be custodians of that process, or a combination of the two. But for those looking for alternative possibilities, 'growing' wildlife habitat should be made just as viable an option in terms of state support as growing food.

There would clearly have to be important stipulations in all this. Payment levels for farming and non-farming land would have to be completely equal, and a watertight guarantee given that they would remain so. Similarly, farmers would need just as strong a guarantee that such an initiative wouldn't be yet another transient scheme that would be abandoned after five, ten or twenty years, as they have seen happen with so many others. But neither should farmers be able to just walk away from land and forget about it. For example, monitoring for – and eradication of – invasive non-native species, such as rhododendron, would be essential, and overbrowsing by herbivores like deer prevented if necessary.

Those farmers who prefer to carry on with sheep, or any other type of farming, must be absolutely free to do so, and with all the current financial supports. The latter should be greatly increased in agriculturally marginal, disadvantaged areas like Beara. As things stand, the Common Agricultural Policy is getting the balance very wrong on many levels, and is failing to deliver for either nature *or* people, including most farmers.

Presently, 33 per cent of subsidies go to only 1 per cent of farms. Widening that out, 80 per cent of the money goes to 20 per cent of farms, in both cases generally the wealthiest and least nature-friendly operators. The result is the continuing death of both nature and small family farms. More and more farmers are getting out – 4.2 million across Europe in recent years, an immense social and economic tragedy for rural communities.

Periodically, attempts at meaningful reform are made, most recently in 2020, but are always blocked. Every time, a legion of extremely well-resourced lobbyists for the most industrial sides of farming, and all the vested interests behind them, kick into action. They have privileged access to the politicians deciding how the hundreds of billions of euro in farm subsidies are spent, and ensure that little or nothing changes regarding where the money goes.

The CAP in its present form is, in actuality, a gigantic, taxpayer-funded, nature-killing machine, which does little to help the most deserving, i.e. smaller, farmers. If it cannot be reformed, then popular demands for it to be scrapped will inevitably grow and become unstoppable, as ever more people become aware of its destructive effects, and object to funding that through their hard-earned tax payments. As a very minimum, the cake must be equally shared with smaller farmers, and the GAEC requirement completely removed without delay. Biophilia (affinity with nature) in farmers is currently crushed by a system that does nothing to encourage it, but instead pushes an agenda in which production must always be the main, if not sole, consideration.

None of this is in any way to argue that publicly owned land should be exempt from restoration efforts. On the contrary: for a start, the National Parks and Wildlife Service should be thoroughly reformed, putting people motivated by a genuine love and understanding of ecology into top positions, and funding levels greatly increased. The ecological integrity of Ireland's many national parks and state-owned nature reserves could then be restored according to proper international standards. However, altogether these places constitute only a very small percentage of overall land area, so, while important, the scope of what could be achieved in them is limited.

The semi-state Bord na Móna (peat board), with around 1 per cent of the country, ought to be rewetting *all* their bogs through drain removal, and letting them go wild. Similarly, Coillte, the state-owned forestry body which manages a more substantial 7 per cent of land in Ireland, should be mandated to immediately abandon planting monocultures, and instead move over entirely to continuous cover, naturally regenerated, wild native forests.

Doing so would be much easier than it might sound: take a walk in most clear-felled plantations and you'll find multitudes of self-seeded native tree seedlings coming up, like birch, willow, holly, oak, rowan and hazel. Instead of being obliterated in planting the next crop of alien conifers, these could simply be left to grow to maturity. That would take time, of course, but existing plantations could be used in the interim; we just wouldn't plant any more of them. Timber production doesn't actually need to be based on a perpetual environmental catastrophe; in fact, it could be the exact opposite.

But farmland makes up over 70 per cent of land in Ireland, and therefore farmers must by necessity play a big role in any workable solutions to the present ecological crisis. In order for that to happen, there would very much need to be a fundamental redefinition of what it actually means to be a farmer at all. Instead of being limited to producers of food, it should be extended to encompass the provision of wild natural habitat, and all the essential things that gives to society.

The non-existent antagonism between environmentalists and farmers so constantly hyped by certain sectors also needs rejecting. That notion has no basis in reality: there is a general understanding within environmentalism that winning over farmers and rural communities is critical. Equally, radically widening farmers' options as described above could be a game-changer, empowering them to stay on the land they love, rather than selling up and moving away, as so many have been.

Both farming and environmentalism have nothing to lose, and everything to gain, by rejecting fictional narratives of opposition and seeing each other for what they should be: allies.

Financial measures alone won't be enough, however. The evidence suggests that people are very often prepared to take more affirmative action when they perceive it to be the right thing to do, rather than purely for money. A shift is required among the whole of society, including urban, towards a far greater interest in, and awareness of, how land is used. Farmers – and the communities in which they live – who return land to nature must then be given the full credit that is due. There's no doubt that, were such a movement to really take off among farmers, it would garner enormous kudos and support from everyone.

Very serious and creative consideration must also be given to the enormous potential in establishing community-owned and -run natural forests and other wild habitats. In countries across the world, such as Mexico, Guatemala, Nepal and Namibia, this has been shown to bring extremely positive results for both nature and people. Every possible avenue to increasing wildlands should be explored. While it's essential that agriculture become more nature-friendly, no less important is creating a network of areas in which no food production – or any other extractive activity – takes place, where natural processes can dominate.

We need to turn a large proportion of Ireland entirely back over to nature, and some of the best people to deliver that are those who already know the land most intimately: the farmers themselves. All they need is the proper support from the rest of society.

12

Rewilding the Land

Since its inception in the late 1990s among American conservation biologists Michael Soulé, Reed Noss and others, the concept of rewilding has increasingly been taking the international nature conservation world by storm. In continental Europe, Britain and elsewhere, popular rewilding movements have arisen, injecting much-needed new hope and energy into the fight. Put simply, it means giving areas of land (or sea) back to the wild, but there's much more to it than that.

The primary aim is to allow natural, rather than human-imposed, processes to take the upper hand, making space for the return of ecosystems that are, as much as possible, *functional* again – i.e. that actually work as they should, and are capable of self-regulation. A self-regulating ecosystem is able to operate autonomously, and thus remain healthy and resilient, instead of needing continual management and life-support from people. Remember that *all* ecosystems – and their global sum, the biosphere – did just that perfectly well for hundreds of millions of years before we came on the scene, very recently in ecological terms. So, considered in those terms, there's really nothing very radical at all about the idea.

Rewilding draws from the twin applied sciences of restoration ecology and conservation biology, from which it essentially sprang. But while based on science, it manages to excite and engage people's imagination in a way that the latter generally does not, an enormous bonus in a time of such deep and widespread disconnect from the natural world. The most important thing of all about rewilding, however, is that it has the very real potential to not only stop, but actually reverse, the ongoing death of the living world all around us.

One reason is that it takes account of the fact that nature and species cannot be effectively protected by attempting to statically maintain severely altered and degraded ecosystems that are missing vital species and ecological functions. If that all seems a bit of an earful, think of it along the lines of an old-style mechanical clock: if enough key cogs and wheels are removed, and the face hands are blocked from turning, it ceases to be a working clock. A similar principle applies with ecosystems: in order to survive in a healthy state, they must be whole, and able to flow unimpeded, governed and developing according to their own internal forces. So while the frequent media portrayal of rewilding as being solely about the reintroduction of large native predators is a gross oversimplification, restoring missing keystone species where possible (including predators) is, ultimately, a pivotal element.

A common misconception is that rewilding seeks to return land to an idealised previous ecological state. In reality it would never be possible to go back in time to some arbitrarily chosen baseline – and it would be arbitrary, because healthy living systems are always changing naturally over time, even if that's often difficult for us to perceive. The real objective is not to go back to the past, but *forward*: to complex, vibrant ecosystems that actually work by themselves, and are therefore more resilient in the face of climate breakdown and other shocks coming down the line. As has been said before, the aim of rewilding isn't to turn the ecological clock back in time, but to allow it to actually start ticking again.

That said, the past will certainly always be an essential guide as to which communities of species and ecosystems are most likely to be the richest, and therefore most viable, ecological expressions in any given area. Hence, as with other approaches to nature conservation and restoration, the focus will almost always be on native species that coevolved alongside one another. Another central plank of rewilding is connectivity between core zones of wild natural habitat, in order that species populations can move between them, and thereby lessen or avoid the problems that come with fragmentation.

Fundamentally, to the furthest extent possible within any given set of circumstances, the land itself should determine its own state, rather than that being dictated by us; it thereby becomes what is sometimes described as 'self-willed'. Our task is mainly just to stand back and let that happen: no small thing for a species whose success thus far has been so firmly predicated on the control and manipulation of environments.

Despite the relatively recent origins of rewilding as an idea, there has been substantial (and often heated) debate around its meaning, with quite a few different interpretations now prevalent. While there is probably no harm in a degree of flexibility, it's vital to at least have some basic parameters, or the word risks becoming meaningless. And for me, one of them should be a near total absence of resource extraction by people. So in my view the term rewilding should not be applied where land continues to be farmed, even in a highly nature-friendly way. Whatever form it takes, even at its most ecologically benign, agriculture is at heart undeniably extractive.

That may come as a surprise to many people, who when they think of nature are very likely to envision a largely farmed landscape. But if you actually stop and think about it, there's no escaping the fact that farming entails appropriating, transforming, and utilising the land in order to benefit ourselves, by producing the food and other goods we need or want. There is of course nothing at all wrong with that, at least not if it's carried out in a nature-friendly way. On the contrary, it's essential – after all, we have to eat too. But there should be complete clarity around the fact that farming is not somehow 'natural', unless we are prepared to invert the most commonly accepted definition of the word. (My *Collins English Dictionary*, for example, describes nature as 'the whole system of the existence, forces, and events of all physical life that are not controlled by man'. But more on this later.)

Farming is without exception a human imposition on what was once, at some point in time, wild natural habitat. Wherever it takes place, nature and its ecological processes will always be compromised, to greater or lesser degrees. As such, a separate term should be employed to describe those types of agriculture that seek to find a balance between production and wildlife. Various terms with slightly different meanings are used, including 'agriwilding' and 'farming with nature', but the most common is High Nature Value (HNV) farming.

Both HNV farming and rewilding are essential to tackling the biodiversity crisis: HNV farming for all the species that benefited in the past from man-made farmed landscapes, and rewilding for the many more that struggle or can't survive within them. But while there will usually be some overlap, they are fundamentally different in both conception and ambition, and shouldn't be conflated. An excellent example of how they can share common ground is Knepp Estate, a 3,500-acre farm in West Sussex, England.

Around 20 years ago its pioneering owners, Charlie Burrell and Isabella Tree, took the extremely brave decision to move away from intensive agriculture towards an entirely different, wilder model, with space for natural processes. What they have achieved there in species richness and ecological dynamism is an incredibly successful and exciting demonstration of what can happen when we relax the pressure on nature. However, since fenced-in livestock is still being reared for slaughter, albeit in a much wilder and more nature-friendly way, to my mind Knepp should properly be described as (in this case, very) HNV farming, rather than rewilding.

What rewilding is most definitely *not* about, and this is another oft-heard falsehood, is excluding people in any way: just our extractive and damaging activities – two very different things. Rather than pushing people out, with the exception of some particularly sensitive habitats, rewilded areas should be there for everybody to enjoy respectfully, and rewilding could be just as beneficial for us as it is for nature itself. Aside from the potential economic boost for local communities (which

I'll come back to), it represents a fantastic opportunity to rediscover atrophied parts of who we truly are: those that have become so cut off from the natural world, our first and only real home.

But crucially, and this cannot be overstated, rewilding requires an understanding that being close to nature is not at all the same thing as dominating, controlling, or exploiting it: in fact, it's the very opposite. We need to learn to be able to let go – and then enjoy watching nature come flooding back in and do its thing. Nature has never needed, and generally still doesn't need, human stewardship or management. All that is really required from us is that we sometimes lend a hand by undoing some of the damage we have caused, for example by reintroducing extinct native species, controlling invasives, or blocking up drains. The greatest challenge is then in finding the courage to just let it happen.

The more traditional approach to nature conservation in Ireland and Britain generally seeks to preserve the habitats that suit certain groups of species in a particular ecological state. It tries to hold the clock hands fixed at a certain point in time, which invariably tends to be one that pertained before agriculture became increasingly industrialised over the last half-century or more. Because these past states were themselves the result of human activity, especially farming, this type of conservation often demands a high and continual level of human management. Much of the effort is directed towards trying to keep nature in a given area unchanged, and thus in thwarting the encroachment of what is seen as 'unwanted' nature, such as native tree species in the form of scrub.

Even in terms of its own narrow objectives of saving certain favoured species, in most cases this approach is very unlikely to work in the long term, for a number of reasons. Firstly, everything in an ecosystem is connected, and therefore if important pieces of the equation are missing, others will continue to wither and die. Secondly, all natural ecosystems are in a perpetual state of flux and dynamic evolution. If nature is restricted like a living museum to some human perception of what it should be, the surviving elements – including those whose retention is the main objective – will again continue to wither and die.

Another issue is the very natural human tendency to focus attention on certain types of species – those that are most visible and attractive to our eyes: birds, mammals, butterflies and flowers being the most usual candidates. Where the aim of nature conservation is seen as protecting specific species, the emphasis is invariably on a few of these high-profile elements, rather than, for example, rare mycorrhizal fungi or microscopic invertebrates. Similarly, conservation bodies and specialists are often highly selective regarding which species they especially want to conserve: those that come within their own particular remit.

As an example, I had a memorable exchange several years ago with one (highly knowledgeable) botanist, who argued that Atlantic forests need constant heavy grazing in order to maintain the necessary light levels some rarer woodland lichen types seemingly prefer. (I can't recall which ones now, but it was likely communities of *Lobaria*, including the very impressive tree lungwort.) Strange for me was that it seemed not to count that, over time, this will inevitably cause the lichens' own forest habitat to eventually die off altogether. The further fact that the lichens in question were just some of the many thousands of species within the ecosystem which would be lost as a result, along with all the connections between them, appears to have been equally irrelevant.

Experts in practically every species category tend to prioritise those species they are specialised in, and to view the wider ecosystem through that particular lens. The key point is this, however: for the conservation of almost all species to work, *the whole ecosystem has to work*. Attempting to protect a particular species (or category of species) of concern through continual human intervention may be fine as a short-term, triage-type approach. But it only addresses the symptoms, rather than the core problem, which is loss of overall ecosystem function. Therefore as a long-term strategy it will generally fail.

One UK-based conservationist, Alasdair Cameron, aptly described how the conventional species-centric (as opposed to ecosystem-centred) approach would be likely to play out if applied in a tropical rainforest:

Imagine if UK conservation groups managed a bit of damaged rainforest. It could be the Amazon but I don't want to get bogged down in the biology. The wildflower and owl groups might decide it was dangerously under-grazed and make a deal with local ranchers to bring in cattle to open it up. The bird people would start planting supplementary feeding crops and trapping medium sized predators. The mice and snake people would let the grass grow long and install piles of wood as nesting sites, but would step in to remove scrub every five years. Sport fish groups would moan about the otters. The butterfly organisations might look at the sugar cane plantations and conclude that they needed to be preserved as they were the chief home of the otherwise rare spotted white sugarcane fritillary. The monkey people would plant extra fruit trees, and worry that there were too many large eagles and other predators, and so for years stay relatively quiet about the hunting in their patch. [...] After a while the large animals would vanish, people would forget that they had been there and the groups would settle into micro-managing their patches, raising funds from the public for their chosen species.

100 years later some rewilders might come along and argue that the whole thing was a bit artificial, uninspiring to the human soul, expensive to maintain, and that it wasn't really working anyway because wildlife was still declining. A lot of people in the groups would secretly agree, and accept that things needed to be done differently, but most of the land would remain trapped. Any attempt to change, or reintroduce predators and other missing species, would necessarily threaten the delicate balance that the groups had established, where they could maximise their chosen species within their areas. Each group would conduct monitoring within its own boundaries, and so what would matter most would be what was within their borders. Some would even go so far as to claim that allowing the rainforest to return would be bad for biodiversity, using their chosen species as an example. Agricultural interests would largely back the conservation groups, since the lack of large animals and the widespread use of agricultural practices in conservation suited them pretty well. It was all very controlled, and hugely confusing to the public and policy makers.

Instead of restoring the rich and dynamic tropical rainforest ecosystem, the above would result in a downward spiral of species loss and ecological collapse. Such a scenario might sound ridiculous, but it's actually a pretty accurate portrayal of much of the current conservation thinking in Ireland and Britain today. The scrub that is often vilified as an enemy of biodiversity is nothing other than native forest attempting to return. Medium-sized predators, such as foxes and crows, are commonly trapped or shot for conservation purposes. The potential reintroduction of the larger native predators that would naturally control these overabundant medium-sized predators and deer is seen as a threat, a distraction, or as a misdirection of scarce resources and energy, by many of those involved. Grazing by livestock is often presented as a – or *the* – key conservation tool.

From what I have seen, change is resisted in many quarters. Meanwhile, wildlife continues to decline and disappear at a rate of knots. And though the latter is happening for a wide range of reasons mainly unrelated to conservation, I am convinced that, for the situation to change, a major shift towards thinking in ecosystem terms is essential. Nature is the complex web of interactions between thousands of wild native species, rather than any single one, and that basic underlying fact must inform everything we do to protect it, or all our efforts will be in vain.

Where the more traditional nature conservation methods can be incorporated into HNV farming practices, it makes much sense to do so. And examples of particularly diverse semi-natural habitats, such as wildflower-rich pasture, should continue to be maintained and, indeed, their extent expanded. However, the very best way to allow nature to regain resilience and health, and therefore halt the ongoing collapse of wildlife, is in the form of unrestrained ecosystems that are as big, wild and functional as possible – i.e. rewilding.

An analogous and long-standing debate in the international nature conservation world is the degree to which efforts should be balanced between *land sharing*, on the one hand, and *land sparing* on the other.

Land sharing involves making human landscapes more wildlife-friendly, for example by maintaining unkempt, biodiverse hedgerows between fields, or using less chemicals – or better still, none at all. Transitioning away from intensive chemical-based farming towards nature-friendly, low-impact, organic models – including permaculture and agroforestry – is the most crucial part of that (only a mere 1.7 per cent of Irish agricultural land is presently farmed organically). The 75 per cent collapse in insect numbers in German nature reserves, for example, shows that the effects of insecticides like neonicotinoids go far beyond the areas of application.

Land sparing, though, is about leaving areas entirely to nature. The idea has much in common with rewilding, but with perhaps less focus on such aspects as the reintroduction of missing species and connectivity. While both the sharing and sparing approaches have essential roles to play, the evidence strongly suggests that land sparing produces far better outcomes for the vast majority of wild native species. Yet mainstream conservation in Ireland presently seems to place almost all the emphasis very squarely on land sharing, with little attention given to sparing or rewilding. The reasons for that may well be largely down to the fact that there is essentially no real wild land left on this island, and so perhaps many people have difficulty in making that association.

For example, at the 2019 Irish National Biodiversity Conference there was next to no mention of the land sparing or rewilding sides of the coin. Virtually all the public discussion was focused on how to make human-created environments and activities, especially farming, supposedly more nature-friendly. While it was impossible to be at all the sessions, since three were often taking place simultaneously, others I spoke to who attended experienced exactly the same. Slide presentations showed farmers being paid to remove scrub from their land, and these were unambiguously presented as demonstrations of how biodiversity should be preserved.

The scrub clearance was taking place in certain very particular contexts – the Burren or Aran Islands – where a case can be made for it on a limited scale. The karst limestone pavement of the Burren has a very unique flora that depends on grazing to prevent being taken over by hazel scrub. On the other hand, over time that same hazel scrub develops into one of this island's most species-rich and beautiful habitats in its own right, and a balance ought to be struck between these two perspectives.

However, none of these nuances or specific circumstances was explored, sending the clear signal that scrub removal or control is an important means of tackling the ecological crisis across the board. The undiluted message was that, without human management, biodiversity suffers. (The other key message was that ascribing an economic value to nature is the best way of protecting it, an idea that is also highly problematic and questionable when applied as a general principle.)

Preventing the return of wild nature as a means of conserving ... nature not only struck me as contradictory, it ran entirely counter to everything I had seen over many years in Bofickil, and read on the subject. And I struggled with the notion that nature cannot survive without management by people, when the obvious reality is that its problems only began with our arrival. Across the rest of the world, conservationists seek to preserve and restore wild, unexploited ecosystems as the best way of preventing biodiversity loss. Yet here, at a national conference on that very issue, it was barely even brought up.

There are a great multitude of levels to biodiversity, the most obvious of which is diversity of species. But there's also genetic diversity within species and their populations, the diversity of natural wild habitats, ecosystems and biomes, right up to the whole biosphere. Taking all these and other levels into account is vital, but the question of biodiversity is often approached almost exclusively as if the species level were the only one that counts. This is likely a less positive effect of the elevation of 'biodiversity' to buzzword status in recent years, with a general emphasis on species diversity over and above all the many other ecological metrics.

Equally vital concepts like wildness, wilderness, species interconnection, ecosystem functionality and sheer abundance of life have also frequently been neglected or overlooked in the fervour for the be-all-and-end-all of species lists. By concentrating so overwhelmingly on just one aspect, the big picture can become obscured. As an (admittedly extreme) analogy, a zoo might contain high levels of species diversity in many categories, but it's not an ecosystem, and the species that live in it can't survive without constant human upkeep.

Of course species diversity is hugely important, but it's only one of the many means by which ecosystem health should be gauged.

However, I would be sorry to come across as overly critical of the biodiversity conference, and the wider conservation community in general. My intention is more to offer what I hope will be seen as constructive criticism, which might help in making future direction more evenly rounded, and contribute to the wider discussion that needs to be had. I don't by any means pretend to have the one and only truth in my pocket: like everyone else here, I'm learning all the time too.

The unusual and more isolated avenues by which I came to nature conservation and restoration, together with a self-education through reading, are perhaps partly responsible for my having such a divergent perspective. Presumably most of those involved in organising the conference work at the coalfaces of conservation, and are passionately committed to what they do. And, again, it's understandable that, with the continuing precipitous declines in wildlife all around us, many of them see the most urgent task as stopping that by desperately trying to hang on to what remains as it is. What differentiates our views is that, again, I am convinced that generally won't work.

To illustrate the point, some conservationists see in rewilding a potential threat to already near nationally extinct native ground-nesting birds, like the curlew and corncrake, by creating habitat for predators such as foxes and corvids (crows). But the superabundance of foxes and crows, which are also native, is just another symptom of the fact that ecosystems are not merely dysfunctional, but practically non-existent.

Larger predators don't only regulate herbivores, but other smaller predators also, keeping them in check naturally. When the former are missing, the latter are able to multiply, a phenomenon called 'mesopredator release'. This is one of the main reasons why populations of foxes and crows have been able to explode far beyond naturally occurring densities. (It may well also have been instrumental in the spread of the invasive American mink, which is extremely damaging to native fauna.)

Another decisive factor is the opportunity opened up within relentlessly farmed landscapes to clean up, for example, a constant supply of sheep carcasses on the hills, afterbirth in lambing season and uneaten sheep nuts. Additionally, the annual release of vast numbers of hapless cage-reared pheasants into the countryside for shooting undoubtedly also plays a substantial role in maintaining artificially high numbers of foxes. The latter and crows are among the tiny number of species that have done well out of the dearth of ecological balance that characterises our landscapes.

The science tells us very clearly that the overwhelming bulk of native species will only survive long-term in ecosystems that are as unfragmented, wild, and in which as many natural ecological processes as possible are able to operate. As American wildlife biologist Douglas Chadwick put it:

> The essence of nature is wholeness – a wholeness woven from infinite complexity. Trying to save it piece by piece doesn't really make much sense even if we had all the time in the world, and we most certainly do not.

Rather than approaching conservation issues from the perspective of what might be beneficial for this or that particular species (often those that had gained advantage from artificial landscapes), the thinking needs to be in terms of wild natural ecosystems. That is, allowing nature to independently produce the richest and most functional ecosystems that don't require constant human maintenance. If wildlife is to have any chance at all, society in general, and the conservation sector in particular, needs to be *far* more ambitious, especially regarding land sparing and rewilding. That means looking imaginatively and energetically at how we can go about creating plenty of space just for wild nature.

But as I said, where certain more traditional methods have proved effective in preserving a rare species or semi-natural habitat, there's no reason why those practices shouldn't continue in appropriate places, with rewilding happening elsewhere. There should be enough room for all approaches, with tolerance, humility, coexistence and the sharing of experiences and lessons learned among their various advocates, all of whom seek the same goal, even if by varying avenues.

Soon after myself and Finbarr Caupey reroofed the old Crowley farmhouse and outhouse with corrugated iron for use as a shed, a small group of bats – about 14 initially – started summer roosting in the building. I was delighted to find they were lesser horseshoes, a species whose Irish population of about 14,000 is of international importance, due to decline and regional extinction across most of Europe. When in the shed, I'd see mothers hanging with babies (called pups) by their sides, and over the next few years the colony grew steadily in number, more than tripling in the space of six years.

The bats were, and still are, a bit of a hassle in some respects, for when they are present I always feel the need to avoid going into the shed unless absolutely necessary, and then to minimise any disturbance by creeping about. In addition, while hanging upside down from the rafters and joists all day, they poop out the digested contents of their nightly foraging, sprinkling anything below in tiny (dryish, at least) mouse-like droppings. It's probably fair to say that many people would have been far less welcoming. I tried building them a dedicated bat 'hot box' to live in, placing it in a higher up and less accessible part of the roof, partly in the hope that it might put an end to the fall of mini-craps, but also out of fear that local cats might get in and perpetrate a massacre.

Sparrowhawks, for example, sometimes take bats on the wing, but that's a natural process. The actions of domestic or feral cats, introduced and sponsored by human agency, are very definitely not, and they are responsible for killing astronomical numbers of birds, mammals and other native wildlife wherever they are present. In reality, domestic cats are, in the words of Michael Soulé, 'subsidized recreational hunters' and, as such, the predation they carry out should be seen very simply as just another form of human impact on the wild.

When it came to the 'hot box' though, the bats had their own views on the matter of where they were going to roost (as I suspected would be the case even while dangling precariously high up on a ladder constructing it over the course of two days). They chose to mostly ignore the state-of-the-art residence I had made for them, just like the boxes attached to trees outside, opting instead to stay put in the rafters.

As with the mosquitoes in Italy, a downside of living on the west coast of Ireland, including Bofickil, is the clouds of ferocious biting midges that appear at certain times. When conditions are right (or wrong, rather), which particularly means mild, muggy, and windless mornings and evenings, they can be an absolute maddening nightmare, making going outside extremely unpleasant. Everyone suffers to some degree, but Seánie is like a magnet to them; maybe his fondness for eating anything sweet makes his blood more attractive in some ghoulish sort of way.

In 2010 I spent several months working on the medieval sculpture collection in the gardens of Garinish Island, near Glengarriff on the south side of Beara. The midges there can get so bad that the gardeners have to don all-enclosing headgear and gloves, making them appear equipped almost as if for a biohazard exclusion zone. The only other existing solution, apart from smearing the skin with very nasty and toxic repellents, seemed to be in the form of various devices advertised online. These costly and unconvincing-looking contraptions promised to attract midges by emitting carbon dioxide, in order to then somehow trap and kill them.

But we discovered that the bats brought an enormous and unforeseen benefit. It turned out that midges are among their favourite prey, and woodland their primary habitat for hunting. Each bat can catch 3,000 or more midges per night while active during the warmer months of the year. (They hibernate in caves and other similar cold, damp and dark spots over the winter.) So a quick back-of-an-envelope calculation tells us that the small colony of about 45 or more bats now living in the shed over six months or so could be consuming around 25 million midges per year, their hoovering action radiating out from the vicinity of the house.

That arithmetic may be a bit on the rough and ready side, but what's certain is that midges have never been a problem around the house since the bats moved into the shed. We have effectively exchanged living with frequent crazy-making swarms of biting midges for tiny pellets of their digested remains in the shed – not at all a bad deal in my estimation. And there is also the added great pleasure of seeing the bats flitting about hunting at dusk; silhouetted against the backdrop of a twilit Atlantic, that can make for a *very* evocative scene. The imaginative dimensions of our world have been expanded several increments by having them around.

Going back to the land sharing versus sparing issue: nature definitely needs us to be much more give, and less take, in the artificial environments we have created for ourselves, but that's only part of the answer. Yes, the bats are doing well because I put up with them living in the shed for half the year. But without a healthy native woodland next door providing the right hunting grounds, there would probably be no bats, never mind all the many thousands of other interconnected species that live there.

All of which is perhaps another long-winded way of repeating a central principle that I feel just cannot be stressed enough. What nature really needs most is not only our accommodation in the human sphere, but plenty of big areas of wild natural habitat that we don't exploit in any way, other than as the best insurance policy in existence (see Chapter 17). And as much-needed medicine for the soul.

13

Three Revolutions, Three Extinction Waves

I was lying in the heat of the sun high up on a raised sheet of south-facing exposed bedrock sloping down towards the sea, dreamily drinking in the sublime view of Bantry Bay. My eye registered movement in one of a group of tall pines just over to the left, below me near the water's edge. As I looked over, a large bird was swooping down in take-off in the opposite direction from me, and, being partially obscured by the trees, at first I presumed it to be a heron.

But as it slowly banked around towards me, gaining height with each great, powerful, wing beat to perform a fly-by very close and practically level with where I was by now sitting bolt upright, I could see clearly that this was no heron, but an eagle. The fierce countenance, hooked bill, unmistakable profile and enormous proportions left no doubt: an image of sheer, distilled attitude. The deep swoosh of her wings in the warm air was clearly audible. Electrified, I watched as a couple of hooded crows harried the immense bird, beside which they looked absurdly small. The crows carried on repeatedly dive-bombing the eagle with raucous cries as she flew off west along the edge of the island to my right, until she wheeled about and retraced her flight path, again passing very near to me, as if putting on a repeat show especially for my benefit.

That was the spring of 2013, and I was back working again on the medieval sculptures at Garinish Island. I had gone to eat my packed lunch up on the highest – and one of the least-visited – parts of the island, behind the early nineteenth-century Martello tower. I went back to restoring sculptures on a high, elated by the unexpected experience, which will stay with me for ever.

The white-tailed sea eagle is the largest bird of prey in Europe: females can reach an awe-inspiring wingspan of almost 2.5 metres. The species was once widespread around Ireland, especially along the coasts. However, the clearance of forests by our ancestors in prehistory probably began to impact on populations, due to a consequent lack of nesting sites. Over the centuries, continued habitat destruction, shooting, poisoning and egg-stealing by collectors all took their toll, and the bird disappeared from Beara in 1894, becoming extinct as a breeding species throughout Ireland 15 years later. The slightly smaller golden eagle shared the same fate soon after. Other native Irish birds of prey that were lost in recent centuries were the red kite, osprey, goshawk, marsh harrier and buzzard. Like all predator species, raptors were deemed a menace and ruthlessly eliminated at every opportunity.

Almost a century later, the potential for reintroducing the white-tailed eagle was being actively explored in a joint initiative of the National Parks and Wildlife Service and the

Golden Eagle Trust. Killarney National Park was selected as the most suitable location in which to bring them back. Between 2007 and 2011, a hundred white-tailed eagle chicks were donated to Ireland by Norway, which had a healthy population of the birds. Once reared in very careful conditions to prepare them for living in the wild, the eagles were released from captivity and, by 2012, some of them had settled in Beara. In 2016, 'Eddie' – the first eagle chick to fledge in County Cork in over 100 years – took to the wing in Glengarriff. He was one of seven Irish-bred chicks to do so around the country that year, with seven more in 2017.

At the outset, the eagle reintroduction programme faced suspicion and even outright hostility from some among the farming community, particularly sheep farmers, who feared their livelihoods would suffer through losing lambs to the birds. Other concerns were the obstacles that might arise to wind farm applications, as well as the more general one of just another added layer of bureaucratic difficulties the eagles might bring. A number of public meetings were organised in Kerry by project manager Dr Allan Mee, giving opportunities for everyone to air their views, and the atmosphere at these early events was apparently often fractious and confrontational.

A visit by representatives of the Irish Farmers' Association to Scotland to meet farmers who were used to living alongside white-tailed eagles may have gone some way towards allaying fears among their Irish counterparts. In any case the reintroductions went ahead, despite protests at Kerry airport on the birds' arrival. In the subsequent period up to the start of

2016, at least 33 eagles out of a population of 113, including 13 Irish-bred birds, died, mainly through consuming poisoned carcasses left out for foxes or crows, which accounted for 64 per cent of known causes of death. Other primary factors were collision with wind turbines and shooting.

A consequent government ban on the use of such poisons from 2010 gave a boost not only to eagle survival rates, but also, no doubt, a whole range of other scavengers – nature's 'cleaner-uppers' – like ravens and pine martens, one very positive spin-off of the eagles' return. Equally encouragingly, over time attitudes to the eagles among farmers gradually relaxed to one of general acceptance, and in some cases even warm enthusiasm. Since white-tailed eagles feed on carrion, as well as live prey, they'll eat lambs that have died from natural causes, and on occasion others that are (or whose mothers are) weak or sick. Local sheep farmers have adapted to this through such simple precautions as bringing the weaker of twin lambs inside for better care and protection.

Clare Heardman is the NPWS conservation ranger for the Beara Peninsula, and runs the state-owned Glengarriff Woods Nature Reserve. As such, she has a huge variety of responsibilities, many of which must be difficult and even exasperating at times. However, there are of course also many rewarding sides to her work, and one of the highlights must surely be a deep involvement in the return of this iconic native predator, missing from the Irish landscape for so long. She speaks of several local sheep farmers for whom the presence of the eagles is now a positive and exciting part of daily life, with some of them among the eagles' best champions.

One, whose grandfather remembered having the original eagles around before they became extinct, has a telescope set up in his living room for watching them protectively, and feels real pride that they have chosen his particular valley to come back to. Another sheep farmer a little farther away on the Iveragh Peninsula also found great pleasure in seeing a pair of eagles that were nesting nearby. When he discovered that the female had died, leaving the male to rear a chick alone, he began bringing lambs that had died of natural causes and leaving them near the nest as a way of providing support (all to no avail, sadly, since the chick died).

When Clare is going about her duties as a ranger around Beara and beyond, farmers will often stop to ask how the eagles are doing, whether chicks have fledged or not, and so on. She makes the point that there may well be others less happy about the eagles' presence who are not so inclined to stop for a chat with her, but that they are probably mollified to a great extent by their keener neighbours. The local business community, which relies heavily on tourism for income, is delighted with the publicity and increased visitors the eagles have generated, and one tour boat operator has incorporated the silhouette of an eagle into his company logo. These people are all integral to the local community, working in other fields outside the tourist season, all of which helps to spread and maintain that goodwill.

In short, rather than being seen as an unwanted imposition, thrust upon them by outsiders, the eagles are now generally viewed by the surrounding community as both an asset to the local economy and a source of pride. The same scenario seems to have developed in most of the other areas of the country where the eagles are present, and the initial hostility when the idea of their reintroduction was first raised now seems only a distant memory.

There have been continued setbacks, such as the death of Eddie from unknown causes, or only one chick hatching in the whole country in 2019 as a result of Storm Hannah, which hit the west coast hard that April. Nevertheless the programme seems to be well established at this point, with most of the couple of dozen chicks that have fledged in Ireland still alive. Ten more chicks were brought in from Norway in July 2020, and more will be introduced over the coming years to bolster the slowly growing population.

It would be easy to imagine that having these enormous birds around would be highly noticeable, but, as Clare points out, one of the most surprising aspects of living with such a large predator in your midst is just how little you're actually aware of them. In fact, unless actively looking for the Beara eagles, months or years can pass without catching a glimpse of them, and many people living in the area have still never seen one.

According to the Royal Society for the Protection of Birds, biodiversity directly contributes more than £4.8 *billion* to the UK economy annually. Most of this is attributable to wildlife-based tourism, which brings money into local economies in some of the most remote and struggling regions. The reintroduction of white-tailed eagles to the Isle of Mull in west Scotland, for example, was found to be adding at least £5 million per year to the island economy. The United Nations estimated that 7 per cent of global tourism is wildlife-based, and the proportion is growing at over 3 per cent every year. All around the world, ever more tourists either want to experience wild indigenous nature specific to the places they visit as part of a holiday, or make that the primary reason for travelling in the first place.

So it seems pretty clear that nature does actually have a big role to play in revitalising local economies in many rural areas. Contrary to what I saw in the mountainous regions of Tuscany, the people don't have to leave for nature to return. Quite the reverse: the latter can be a major force in making it possible to stay at home, living in flourishing, sustainable communities, wedded to the local environment.

With it becoming ever harder in many marginal areas of Ireland to sustain a living from farming, many rural communities are struggling to survive. The great risk is that the vacuum will be filled by unending lifeless conifer plantations or other industrial land uses that offer little or nothing to local people. As an alternative, allowing wild nature to come back in a big way could be a powerful antidote to rural decline. Getting farmers onside is vital, and the best means of achieving that is, as discussed earlier, to radically change the farm payments system, giving farmers the voluntary option of 'producing' natural habitat and biodiversity instead of food.

However, I also strongly believe that the principal reasons for allowing nature to come back should not be economic. We need wild, healthy ecosystems because they are crucial not only to the proper functioning of the biosphere we all depend on, but to our own emotional and psychological well-being, whether we realise that or not. It's so easy to get caught up in an artificial world centred entirely around ourselves and other people, as if we somehow exist in a bubble, separate from all other life on the planet. Contact with nature reminds us that, quite the opposite, we are – or at least should strive to be – part of something much bigger than ourselves, an essential exercise in humility that never goes amiss in any one of us.

But beyond what they do for us, wild species and ecosystems quite simply have a right to exist for their own sake, just as we do.

In considering the reintroduction to Ireland of lost native species, it's worth giving some thought to the very definition of what constitutes 'native' in the first place. As things currently stand, that status is usually restricted to those species that can be proved to have been present following the last Ice Age, or else made it, unassisted by people, afterwards. (Though the latter condition is often relaxed where introductions took place a very long time ago.) In my view, this interpretation is far too narrow, and should at least be open to discussion. The reasons why require some delving into the deep ecological past, so please bear with me for a while.

During the Ice Ages, including the last one, all species and ecosystems that require temperate conditions were forced to retreat to glacial refuge areas farther south in Europe, such as the Iberian Peninsula, Italy, Greece and other lands now under the sea. As the climate warmed, causing the ice to gradually recede 17–12,000 years ago, those species and ecosystems that were able then followed back northwards in its wake.

Since much of the planet's water was still locked up in ice, sea levels were much lower than today, so the land masses that are now Ireland and Britain were joined to other areas to the south, allowing species to migrate. The specifics of the routes they took remain unclear, and the dynamics involved were probably complex. However, the Bay of Biscay, and other western intermediate zones since submerged, are likely to have played an especially significant role, both as *refugia*, and as pathways in the biological colonisation of Ireland.

Over time, the melting ice and water expansion due to warming oceans caused sea levels to rise further, flooding these bridging areas. Our islands were thus cut off to all those species that hadn't already made it this far, or were unable to cross the sea barrier by some other means. The connection to Ireland disappeared much earlier than that to Britain: about 16,000 and 8,000 years ago respectively. This, along with the increased remoteness and smaller land area, is among the chief reasons why Ireland has such a reduced native faunal and floral diversity compared to Britain, which in turn is significantly lower than on the continent.

However, there is another decisive factor here that's almost entirely overlooked when it comes to Ireland's biogeography (the natural distribution of species). We know that early humans were present in western Europe for hundreds of thousands of years, with finds from East Anglia dating as far back as around 900,000 years ago, for example. Our *Homo sapiens* ancestors arrived much later, migrating to the areas that are now Britain and Ireland at least 43,000 and 33,000 years ago respectively, according to current evidence.

They were extremely proficient hunters, even more so than the already highly dangerous spear-toting Neanderthals and other humans they replaced across much of Eurasia (though there does seem to have been a little mixing too). The cognitive leap that gave our species the ability to think more creatively led to the development of ever more efficient projectile weapons for hunting (and warfare), above all the bow and arrow and, later, the atlatl (spear-thrower). Such technological advances further augmented the capacity to hunt and kill from a distance, something against which animals had evolved no defence.

Perhaps even more importantly, with complex language modern humans were capable of working in organised groups of dozens or more, planning and carrying out coordinated actions, taking out whole herds in a single hunt. Further, we were (are) highly adaptable opportunists, supplementing meat with a wide range of nuts, berries, roots, insects and other wild foods. And when one quarry species became scarce or died out because of overhunting, we simply moved on to others, progressively working our way through ecosystems.

As we began to spread out of Africa and across the planet around 60,000 years ago, everywhere our ancestors went, including Europe, this powerful combination had a devastating effect on species populations and distributions. The general pattern was to start with those species that gave the best returns in calories for the least amount of effort, and once they were gone to switch to other, less bounteous, sources. That meant commencing with the very biggest animals, especially anything weighing upwards of around 1,000 kilograms. As well as providing enormous quantities of meat, a successful hunt would also have brought great recognition and standing within the tribe, an extremely powerful motivation in a hunting society.

As a result, multitudes of these often gigantic species, which were crucial to ecosystem function, were driven into global extinction. To get an idea of the impacts their loss must have had, just imagine if all the remaining African megafauna disappeared in the wild: elephant, rhino, hippo, lion, buffalo and giraffe, for example. (In fact, most of them are presently heading rapidly in exactly that direction due to human pressures.)

Until relatively recently, there was still much – often acrimonious – debate regarding the primary cause of the megafauna extinction waves, with some palaeoecologists believing that changes in climate were mainly to blame. However, that argument is now essentially over, for several reasons. First, climate change within the late Pleistocene has been shown to be unexceptional, and well within the parameters of dozens of previous glacial and interglacial eras that megafaunas had survived perfectly intact.

Secondly, the many species affected were not limited to those adapted to just one set of climatic conditions: it impacted animals that had evolved for temperate and humid climates no less than cold and dry. The extinction wave was, however, highly selective in another sense, only taking out species with the biggest body mass (although smaller species *were* affected by the fallout). If environmental change had been to blame, the losses would have been much more evenly spread.

But most damningly of all, the chronology of mass extinction invariably coincides everywhere across the planet with the initial period after the arrival of the first *Homo sapiens*. For example, the ancestors of the Aboriginal people got to Australia about 50,000 years ago, and numerous giants all subsequently vanished: marsupial lions and rhinos, flightless birds, monitor lizards, predatory kangaroos, wombats as big as cars, and many others. Within less than a thousand years of the coming of the first people there, 85 per cent of all megafaunal species were extinct.

In New Zealand, exactly the same thing happened, with the great flightless moa birds and 60 per cent of other bird species that inhabited those islands becoming extinct within only a couple of centuries. But here's the thing: the archaeological record shows that there, the extinctions took place only very recently: mostly within the first half of the fourteenth century AD. Why so much later than Australia? For the simple reason that the first human colonists (the Maoris) didn't get there until then. The greatly accelerated time frame in which the New Zealand extinctions were effected relative to Australia would have been due to the continued evolution of hunting over the interim, bringing ever-greater efficacy.

On almost every landmass of the globe, diverse terrestrial megafaunas had developed and survived multiple changes in climate relatively unscathed, often over the course of many millions of years. But, without exception, the arrival of *sapiens* very quickly brought a wipeout. It may seem hard to credit that tiny bands of stone-age hunters could possibly have had such a calamitous impact. But key to understanding the phenomenon is the fact that most big animals reproduce only very slowly. All it would take for populations to decline and eventually die out would be a continual attrition of numbers, at an only slightly faster rate than replacement through the birth of young.

Because of their size, until the arrival of humans many megaherbivores were pretty much immune to predation upon reaching adulthood. They were therefore especially ill-adapted and vulnerable once people turned up with the means to hunt them throughout their life cycles. Predator species, on the other hand, as well as being killed themselves, would have found it increasingly difficult to survive as their prey disappeared. In fact, driving them from their kills may well have been a common human technique for obtaining food, as groups of African Khoisan hunters, for example, did with lion kills into quite recent times.

Over the course of thousands of years in Europe, numbers of sabretooth cat, two species of rhinoceros, straight-tusked elephant, cave bear, Eurasian cave lion, spotted hyena and Eurasian hippopotamus would have become fewer and fewer, until they finally disappeared. These and many other species, as amazingly exotic as they sound, are part of the native European fauna, or at least would be had they not been killed off by people. While the numerous previous interglacial periods were populated by a diverse and fantastic megafauna, this one – the Holocene – is marked by their absence. The loss of such a wide range of keystone species had massively negative impacts on, and greatly simplified down, the ecosystems of which they were a part, with knock-on effects on all other component species.

Hunting wasn't the only means by which we pushed species into extinction and damaged or transformed ecosystems. At least 45,000 years ago (perhaps far earlier), i.e. about the time *sapiens* were spreading into Europe, people began to practise large-scale 'fire agriculture'. Setting fire to landscapes was used to drive and capture game, and to clear unwanted vegetation such as forest or scrub, while at the same time fertilising the ground with ash. (Game aside, these are still the reasons why land is so frequently burned in rural Ireland and elsewhere, with such hugely destructive results for wildlife.)

Fire encouraged grasses and other short vegetation for the grazers we hunted, and made tubers and other underground foods easier to find and dig up. Natural plant communities were drastically affected and altered, along with their associated faunas, causing widespread extinctions and the disappearance of entire ecosystems in many parts of the globe. Crucially for this discussion, the affected areas are known to have included southern Europe, where fire was used extensively as a way of removing forest from large areas, and then keeping them open.

When the first Europeans arrived in Australia, Aboriginal people were still using mass burning to keep the land in the state they wanted, and 'early settlers were all struck by the resemblance of this [resultant] lightly wooded landscape to English parkland'. Whether Aboriginal Australians, English gentry, or whoever else, as E.O. Wilson said, our behaviour was essentially the same everywhere. It seems we set about creating an 'ersatz savanna' wherever we went, doing all in our power to clear forest and other natural ecosystems in order to unknowingly try to recreate our species' East African ancestral habitat.

In a variety of ways, the arrival of humans into landscapes was nothing short of cataclysmic in ecological terms. Here is how Yuval Noah Harari described what befell ecosystems in the Americas after the first Native Americans arrived via Siberia and Alaska some 12,000 years ago:

Within 2,000 years of the Sapiens' arrival, most of these unique species were gone. According to current estimates, within that short interval, North America lost thirty-four out of its forty-seven genera of large mammals. South America lost fifty out of sixty. [Others say 37 and 51 genera were lost respectively.] The sabre-tooth cats, after flourishing for more than 30 million years, disappeared, and so did the giant ground sloths, the oversized lions, native American horses, the giant rodents and the mammoths. Thousands of species of smaller mammals, reptiles, birds, and even insects and parasites also became extinct.

Even places that to our eyes now appear to have largely avoided human impacts, like the Amazon rainforest, have been greatly shaped by the loss of megafauna. The Eurasian continent was no less affected, with 49 genera dying out, although it happened more slowly here, as species had already become wary of pre-*sapiens* humans. It's important to note that the effects went far beyond just the megafauna themselves, and ripped down through practically every level of ecosystems in a cascading effect. That shouldn't be at all surprising, given the degree to which all ecological components are interconnected, and therefore interdependent.

As a species, we really are, as E.O. Wilson described us, the 'planetary killer', and have been for a lot longer than most of us realise, or probably care to. And even if *Homo sapiens* is especially adept at causing ecological mayhem, earlier hominids weren't lacking in their ability to do so either. But it must be remembered that, until relatively recently, people had little way of realising the scale of the destruction they were causing. The shortness of the human lifespan (and it was much shorter in the past) compared to the time-scales involved, together with the previously mentioned shifting baseline syndrome, would have made it impossible. Our ancestors were, in that sense, mostly blameless; but that no longer holds true for the accelerating wave of extinction and other huge harms we are now perpetrating.

It is no coincidence that most of the remaining planetary

megafauna is now in Africa, the continent where our species originated (elsewhere, mostly only in parts of Asia did some megafauna like elephants, rhinos and tigers escape oblivion). African species coevolved with early humans, and therefore had some chance of developing an instinctual awareness that this insignificant and puny-looking, largely hairless primate was in fact the most dangerous of all, before it was too late. Even there, however, 29 genera were made extinct.

Those on other continents, which hadn't evolved to be cautious of humans, and met with us only when hunting techniques had been further honed to perfection, had little hope. The idea that we lived in harmony or balance with nature until relatively recently is, sadly, a myth. Furthermore, we haven't done so for a *very* long time, probably since our pre-*sapiens* ancestors moved towards a more meat-based diet, around 2 million years ago.

Harari calls this the 'first wave extinction', which was due to a cognitive revolution among humans. Likely the result of a long interplay of genetic mutation and cultural change that proved evolutionarily advantageous, it allowed ever more complex and abstract thought. A later second wave extinction resulted from the agricultural revolution and the spread of farming across much of the globe from around 10,000 years ago, rendering wilderness into human-engineered landscapes. The third wave extinction, brought on by the scientific/ industrial revolution, is still happening all around us, and at an ever-accelerating pace. The present wave is also the first to seriously affect marine ecosystems, which have been devastated.

Hence, what we are living through today should really be considered the third of three major human-induced extinction pulses, each caused by a revolution in our ability to impact on our biophysical environment. But, rather than distinct events, they can also very arguably be considered collectively as a single drawn-out, but exponentially quickening, process, lasting from the Pleistocene all the way through to this moment. Either way, the effects have been cumulative: the second wave annihilated species and ecosystems that had survived the first, while the present one is now finishing off many of those that somehow managed to get through the first two.

It's almost impossible now to imagine the magnitude of biological abundance, diversity and wonder this planet contained before our ancestors began to demolish it. It's estimated that the total global biomass of wild animals today is only around 15 per cent of what it was in the Pleistocene, while that of wild terrestrial vegetation worldwide has been reduced by half. One study, specific to the eastern Mediterranean region, found that the average body mass of animals hunted by people there 10,500 years ago was only a minuscule 1.7 per cent of what it had been 1.5 million years before. The cause was categorically found not to be climate change, or any other natural factor, but human 'overkill'.

An essential difference with more traditional conservation approaches is that rewilding seeks to be mindful of all three extinction waves and associated devastation, rather than just the present one which started with the Industrial Age. Of course, there is obviously little or nothing that can be done to reverse global extinctions that have taken place at any point in time. But only an awareness of the full extent of the destruction, rather than just the most recent phase, gives a true picture of how we operate as a species, the present situation, and how ecosystems might be repaired in ways that really work.

And if the first wave extinction seems too far back in time to be relevant now, remember that these were species and ecosystems that in many cases coevolved in tandem over *tens of millions* of years. Seen in those terms, even the most distant human-caused extinctions in the Pleistocene were actually only recent. That deeper past informs the ecological present no less than the more immediately obvious losses that have taken place in the modern era, and are still ongoing.

So what, if anything, does all this have to do with how we define a native Irish species? Quite simply, the first wave extinction and other associated ecological damage were also occurring in the very southern European refuges in which temperate species and ecosystems were waiting out the last Ice Age. And it was happening over the course of around 30,000 years *before* the receding ice allowed them to begin migrating north, and ultimately colonise what is now Ireland. Moreover, that takes account only of *Homo sapiens*: earlier humans were around long before.

To what degree were many species – or whole communities of species – unable to arrive because of extinction (local or global), drastic population reduction, ecosystem collapse, or other negative effects of hunting and other human actions in those refuges, rather than for natural reasons? For specific species it's impossible to say now, but it must have been a *hugely* significant factor overall, given an ecological onslaught that went on for so long, and which must have left almost nothing untouched.

Against this background, is it logical to consider the extremely limited assemblage of species on the island of Ireland in the Holocene as somehow a 'natural' state regardless? In my view, it very much is not, and the current definition of native species in Ireland seems far too simplistic, as if none of the huge human-caused destruction of nature in the Pleistocene had even occurred at all, or was somehow irrelevant.

On a more practical level, it's extremely limiting ecologically, given the enormous benefits that many of those excluded species would undoubtedly bring to our trashed ecosystems. Reflect, for example, on the beaver. Their natural distribution includes almost the entire northern hemisphere, but not, as far as we yet know, Holocene Ireland. (Worth bearing in mind here, though, is the old adage that absence of evidence isn't evidence of absence). Does it make sense to preclude even exploring the idea of their (re)introduction, despite all the above, along with the fact that they hugely enrich aquatic ecosystems everywhere they are found, and would provide a fantastic boost to tourism?

Not in my opinion. Beavers are a classic example of what are called 'ecosystem engineers'. By damming rivers, they shape environments, creating the extremely dynamic conditions for a vast suite of native species to thrive. Their dams also filter pollutants from the water, and, given that the number of 'pristine' rivers in Ireland has fallen from 500 in the 1980s to a mere 20, this couldn't be more badly needed. The presence of these strict vegetarians (the mistaken belief that beavers eat fish is common) also greatly reduces flooding downstream, a factor that will become ever more important as climate breakdown worsens.

It's true that to acknowledge the palaeoecological facts

outlined in this chapter inevitably brings up a great many complex conundrums – a veritable 'can of worms', given where things are at now. And I'm certainly not advocating an irresponsible, haphazard approach. Nor am I for a moment arguing that the whole issue of non-native invasive species shouldn't be treated with the utmost seriousness it deserves. As shown in Chapter 5, invasives constitute one of the main threats to native wildlife and ecosystems in Ireland, as elsewhere. (Remember, however, that being very definitely non-native has never presented any obstacle to the continual mass introduction of sitka spruce, pheasants, and a whole raft of other alien species that are *known* to be highly damaging.)

Any interventions should be evidence-based, with full consideration given in advance to all the potential consequences, either positive or negative, of introducing species, followed by scientific trials. But in my opinion there is a need for *far* greater open-mindedness, imagination and elasticity in considering what species might have occurred here but for such severe and extended human impacts prior to the biological colonisation of this island. And consequently, how we might make our native ecosystems as rich, functional, and resilient as possible in the future.

As a last thought on the subject, consider this. Going by the current definition, there is significant doubt surrounding the native Irish status of such widely occurring European species as the red fox, badger, pine marten, red squirrel, hedgehog, pygmy shrew and wolf. In fact, aside from bats, one authoritative source lists only three mammals still found in Ireland as definitely native: mountain hare, stoat and otter.

Food for thought, perhaps?

14

Beara Rainforest

When we came to Bofickil, there was an electricity line running right across the woods from near the old farmhouse. Although decidedly in the 'first world problem' category, it always grated on me. A pair of heavy steel cables arced between regularly spaced and very artificial massive creosoted timber poles, each bearing multiple bright yellow metal warning signs with flashing lightning symbols. For me, all this clashed with, and detracted from, the otherwise natural surroundings, but I accepted it as one of those things in life that nothing can be done about.

That is until seven or eight years later, when an Electricity Supply Board (ESB) employee called to the house to inform me that at least one of the poles was rotten, and so they would need to be replaced. To carry out the work, they would have to bring in a variety of heavy tracked machinery to bore holes in the ground, carry in and erect the new poles, and raise their operatives to the necessary height to disconnect and then reattach the lines. To gain access for all this industrial plant, they would need to clear a wide track through the woods. My mind pictured a scene of utter devastation.

After considering the direction of the electricity line on both sides of the woods, I came up with a possible alternative route, by running the poles along the road. As well as facilitating any future repair work, it would actually straighten and shorten the line, while avoiding damage to the woods and removing the necessity to have any poles in there at all. Once I pointed out the advantages to the ESB area manager during a site visit, it was agreed to reroute the line. Several months later the new poles were duly installed along the road, but it then transpired that there was another major problem.

Even though the new poles were by the road, from there one section of the line would still have to be suspended across a jutting corner of the woods to an older pole. In order to raise the line between the poles, a path would have to be cut through the trees underneath, an area full of particularly beautiful old oaks and mixed other species. (Though in truth, I'd feel much the same about any other patch.) The thought of a trail of destruction was again difficult to bear, and once more the thinking cap went on, searching for an alternative solution.

The ESB man told me that if there was even a light rope between the pole tops, they could use that to draw their heavy cable over the trees without cutting them. The problem was they had no way of getting a rope across in the first place. Without saying anything to him, over that weekend Seánie and I set to work experimenting with various devices, and, by trial and error, we found a combination of methods that worked. Tying a long length of builder's twine to a heavy steel threaded nut or, according to circumstances, the back of an arrow, we fired the line over the trees in stages with Seánie's catapult and bow. A six-metre length of timber roofing lath with a notch cut in the top also came in handy: if we climbed into the trees, it proved invaluable for pushing up through the branches to free the string when entangled.

After many hours of failures, frustrations and struggles, we finally managed to get the twine all the way across, and, using a ladder, pulled it up taut and tied the end to the upper section of the second pole (we'd fixed it to the first one at the outset). When I rang the ESB man the following Monday to tell him the line was in place, he seemed taken aback, and even put out (maybe it went against regulations for customers to do such things), but didn't ask how we had done it. The electricity line now runs along the road, and the trees are untouched. The poles are gone from the woods, with no signs of where the line once passed through: you'd never even know it had been there at all. It's surprising what you'll come up with if you're determined enough, and put your mind to it.

My hope is that these sorts of experiences, and more generally growing up beside a wild rainforest, will have helped expand the lads' horizons regarding the planet we live on, and the possibilities in relating to it. Over the years, I have taught them to identify most of the trees and plants growing in the woods, and we often discuss various aspects of how nature works. I have probably learned as much from these interactions as they have. Both have a keen eye for the many things I overlook, such as the fact that hollies seem to be adorned with far more spiders' webs than other tree species. (Our agreed guess is that the spiders instinctually see hollies, being evergreen, as a better bet for going to all the trouble of building onto.)

I suspect that, at some level, the boys probably think their dad a bit odd, focusing so much time, energy and passion on that one aspect of life – the natural world – that often seems to barely register for so many people. But I can live with that; as much as we can, I think it's essential that we be true to ourselves, and to those we love. My endeavours haven't been entirely in vain either, and one of my dearest hopes is that my sons' individual relationships with nature will grow ever stronger as they get older. Perhaps that will happen as they tire of the ephemeral, empty delights that come from shiny man-made things, and begin to yearn for deeper meaning and connection. But of course they have their own journeys to make, and only time and their own choices will decide what directions those take.

As for me, at this stage I'm better placed to understand that I am indeed unusual in respects (though not in any scary or unpleasant sense, I don't think), and why. My earlier years were tough, marked by profound loss, real poverty, and an unbroken succession of grim, cramped, rented flats and bedsits that often meant moving area. That gave rise to a burning need for a place of my own as something anchored, solid, and a pretty steely determination to make it happen, whatever the obstacles.

Might there even have been some sort of atavistic Irish 'land hunger' element to it? (In Beara, I've heard it said that 'land is like a religion for some people'. As set out in previous chapters, there are very real historical reasons for a frequently obsessive relationship with land in Ireland, passed down over generations.) Who knows, but that single-mindedness of purpose can't have made me always the easiest person in the world to get along with.

One thing is certain though: I never would have ended up helping bring life back to a piece of Irish Atlantic rainforest, with all the richness of experience and learning that has entailed, had I not been so hell-bent for years. And I believe I've reached a contented peace with it all, including the harder stuff that played a part in shaping who I am; and that there has also been a mellowing, bestowed by the passing of time, and the great joys that have come my way.

Mike Caupey was repeatedly slapping the table and roaring 'Eileen Crowley's woods is going to be called the "Beara Rainforest"! If only she could hear it!' The hilarity he manages to catch in situations – and his total enjoyment of a good belly laugh – is always infectious, and I too found myself doubled over as his howls of practically tearful laughter echoed around my kitchen.

The question of how the Bofickil woods might act like a pebble thrown into a pool, rippling out awareness of the incredible beauty and uniqueness of our native rainforests, had long been on my mind. Several years ago, that thought spurred me to look into setting up a low-key tourism enterprise. The idea was to bring small groups of visitors for tours in the woods, during which we would have an interactive, *in situ*, discussion of forest ecology, conservation, and other related issues. An additional hope was that helping attract visitors into the area would allow the woods to be seen as contributing to the local economy, and thereby help promote a wider appreciation of the importance of such places.

With all that in mind, in early 2017 my friend Owen helped set up a website spelling out the restoration work I had been carrying out, and offering visits to anyone interested. I called it 'Beara Rainforest', provoking Michael's uproarious outburst when he heard about the plan. Unfortunately, insurance and other costs turned out to be much higher than I had anticipated. My sculpture business also entered another particularly busy period, and so the project was shelved (though the website remains). Perhaps this book will go some way towards helping spread the word.

I was, however, bringing large groups of visitors into the woods every summer as part of the local Eyeries Family Festival, calling the event 'A Walk on the Wild Side'. Without exception, these occasions went down very well, with people delighted to experience an Irish rainforest in the raw, and learn a little about the ecology. Also, students from third to sixth classes in the local primary school (including my own two lads when they were that age) were coming for organised trips in the woods every year. Again, this was as much a learning process for me as I hope it was for the kids themselves.

I made the major error of conducting the first visit as though they were adults. We stood in the woods in a big group and I asked the children what they knew about biodiversity, photosynthesis, food webs, and so forth, before giving them a spiel on each subject and the general importance of the natural world in our lives. Liam took me aside a few days before the following year's visit, told me that his friends had found this boring, and suggested that the best thing would be to send them off looking for bugs and other interesting things in the woods.

So I went to the chemist in town and bought a number of small sample jars in clear plastic. When the schoolchildren arrived, I asked them to divide into groups of three or four, each of which was given a jar. After just a few words from me, they were all sent off looking for insects, spiders, fallen tree leaves, and any other items of note they might manage to turn up. This approach proved infinitely more successful, with the kids excitedly running about the woods trying to outdo one another in their discoveries.

At the end we all got together again to examine everyone's finds, from fearsome-looking devil's coach-horse beetles and multicoloured caterpillars to the most spectacular variety of spiders imaginable. Following a general inspection and discussion of what each of the specimens might be, all the living things were brought back to the same spots where they had been found, and we started making our way back up towards the school bus. In subsequent years we kept to that same procedure.

The hope is that seeds have been planted in a few young minds, which may germinate over time into a deeper awareness, and love, of nature.

Looking around, two sharply contrasting trends are apparent. On the one hand, there is a very necessary growing shift towards a greater appreciation of the natural world. Ever more people are coming to a more profound understanding of our total dependence on it, and that nothing else in life compares to connecting with the living manifestations of our unique planet, the 'pale blue dot', as seen from space. But there is also a growing distancing from all forms of reality, interfacing with the world more and more through the screen of a computer or smartphone. This enormous change has been accelerating at a bewildering pace over recent years. It affects all ages, but has progressively more hold over the young, who have never known life without an online dimension.

On the positive side, the internet does make information about what's happening easily accessible, whether it's the threat to wild orang-utan populations from expanding palm oil plantations in South-East Asia, or other developments closer to home. And it has undoubtedly played a pivotal role in the groundswell of young people campaigning on environmental issues over recent years, largely inspired by the brilliant Greta Thunberg. It's essential that younger generations give value to the living world if we are to change our current calamitous trajectory. They are the future, and will determine the extent to which we either manage to find ways of living with our planet less destructively, or fail – with disastrous consequences for all remaining life, including our own.

But it's hard not to also see a deeply disturbing side to spending so much time engaging with artificial realities that are expertly engineered to cultivate a psychological dependence on constant and instant dopamine hits. As I have found, there is an immeasurable satisfaction in life that comes from having a distant – maybe seemingly almost unattainable – dream, and beavering away at it for weeks, months or years until it begins to reach fruition. Such choices often involve hard work, sacrifice, discomfort, danger and having to wait patiently before the reward comes, if it comes at all. How can kids ever experience that, when easy, risk-free, immediate and guaranteed pleasures are always on standby as alternatives?

Nor is it ever possible to disconnect: the gadgets are always on, continually bleeping as new messages or notifications are received. I have seen the effects on my own two lads, and at times it truly breaks my heart. We live in a place that would have been the most wondrous playground imaginable to me as a child, and yet now the phones or computer games always hold the strongest attraction. It's next to impossible to ban them when their use is so widely accepted by society, and that may not be the right way to go anyway: this is very new territory for all of us, and none of it is easy. Ultimately, workable solutions probably only really exist at societal and systemic, rather than individual, levels.

Throughout their childhood and youth, I have done my utmost to encourage my sons to share the deep love I feel for the natural world. Those efforts may in fact even have been counterproductive to some degree, and over time I changed tack, leaving the door to nature open but studiously avoiding anything that might be perceived as overt pushing. Together we built what we call a treehouse, but it's actually just a raised platform with side rails but no roof or walls, and a rope ladder for access, all constructed of (theoretically) rot-resistant larch.

We positioned it about five metres high up in a middling-sized oak deep in the woods, without cutting, drilling, or fixing into the tree in any way. While we were at it, we also hung a long swinging rope with a wooden seat from the same tree. Ever since, spending time there has become a regular and very pleasant part of being in the woods, whether alone or in company. Clambering up the rope ladder takes some getting used to, the sensation being very different from the fixed structures to which we are accustomed. Feet and legs tend to push forward a little crazily, with the result that until you haul yourself onto the platform you're leaning back diagonally.

But it's very much worth the effort. Standing or sitting on the deck with your legs dangling over the side, and arms resting on the first horizontal timber rail, or leaning your back against one of the three moss-clad mini-trunks that emerge through the centre of the platform, can be bliss. There is no more comfortable and relaxing way of letting the sights, sounds and energies all around – the music of the woods – flow over and into you.

On more windless days the babble of a nearby stream is audible, while in autumn there is the occasional dry thud of a fat, freefalling acorn striking the leaf litter below. Right alongside is another particularly large and majestic old oak, with thickly woven mats of mosses profusely embellished with polypody fern and lichens throughout its powerfully muscular, twisting limbs, all growing near eye level when you're up in the treehouse. Early on, Liam noticed a fairly large epiphytic birch tree growing from a debris-filled void about four metres up in the oak, left where a branch had died and rotted away.

On the far side of the platform, several old birches are equally richly festooned with epiphytes. But here the assemblage is very different, dominated by a variety of *Cladonia* lichens, such as mealy pixie-cup, whose outlandishly bizarre forms have to be seen with binoculars to be fully appreciated. Viewed in detail, they can resemble a multitude of imaginary minaret-like towers in the futuristic cityscape of another planet.

These species seem more attracted to the surface chemistry and, no doubt, other characteristics of birch bark, since there are none on any of the oaks. Perhaps the birch's mostly smoother bark is simply more conducive to lichens, which are less affected by drought than mosses. The delicate birch twigs are also draped in one of the most glorious and fuzzy opulences of old man's beard lichen to be found anywhere in the woods, as if the trees had been doused all over in fluff. The mosses and polypody are there lower down too, but far less abundantly so than on the oak. Here, lichens rule the epiphyte world.

The immobile nature of the treehouse renders more easily perceptible the slow life-and-death transformations that have continued to take place in the woods all around since we put it up in the summer of 2016. A nearby middle-aged birch tree that was visibly poorly, slowly dying of some undiagnosed ailment, has been gradually collapsing back down towards, and more recently into, the ground. Bracket fungi have erupted from many parts of the smooth-lenticelled amalgam of grey, white and purple-brown that is the skin of its ruined carcass, also populated by a host of other woodland waste disposal agents. In a few more years it will have vanished almost entirely, subsumed along with all its accumulated stores of sun-energy back into the living earth that gave it life.

In contrast, all around it are naturally regenerating young oak, rowan, holly, hazel, sally and birch, all benefiting from the burst of light levels with the gap in the canopy above created by the fallen birch. And what was previously a small, barely noticeable shrub of a holly almost underneath the treehouse has now grown well above the deck. Similarly, a nearby 'island' of wettish open ground surrounded by trees, once a meadow where hay was harvested, and which the Crowleys called Gloun (we still do, as with all the other old place-names), is being rapidly colonised by trees. Many of them are now also as high as, or higher than, the treehouse.

When wanting to get seriously relaxed up in the treehouse, a folded welly boot serves as an amazingly comfortable pillow, turning it into an ideal spot for an aerial afternoon snooze. Or else to just lie there, dreamily gazing skyward through the dappled sunlight, feeling the gentle swaying and occasional creaking of the supporting tree in the breeze. Cumulus or cirrus puffs sail through a sea of cerulean blue, their tracking framed by rustling clumps of leathery oak leaves in the branches above, reaching up like raggedy outstretched fingers.

Under the influence of such kinetic visions, time loses any meaning, and the mind enters a state of reverie, interpreting the passing clouds as the Earth spinning on its axis, while tracing an orbit through the cosmos. The tree platform thus becomes a fantastical magic vessel, with the power to teleport occupants away on a voyage of discovery to other spatial and temporal dimensions.

Soon after coming to live in Beara, an acquaintance remarked that allowing dead trees and branches to rot away in the Bofickil woods was a 'criminal waste', a choice of words I found revealing, and which I never forgot. They capture the essence of an urge that seems hardwired into us all: to relentlessly use everything we possibly can, and to obsessively 'tidy' land up, rather than ever just leave it do its thing.

This innate attitude is no doubt borne of the struggle for survival that was our ancestors' daily existence over aeons, and which often ended badly if their approach to it wasn't pretty single-minded. The need to maximise any potential benefits that might broaden the chances of living for another day, week, month, or year – for ourselves and our loved ones – must have been a huge factor in our evolution, at both genetic and cultural levels. And it's still there, in us, driving our behaviour. Indeed, many people seem to perceive using everything possible ourselves as a moral issue, much akin to not wasting good food (as do I, but in reverse).

As I travel all around the country working on sculpture

projects, I never cease to be struck by how in Ireland this approach is carried to an absolutely chronic extreme. Almost every last piece of the countryside has been, and continues to be, thoroughly tamed and exploited in some way, whether for increasingly industrialised farming or growing lifeless monocultures of alien trees. Elsewhere the land is locked down under roads, buildings and car parks, in a million-fold, and (literally) concrete expression of Joni Mitchell's still piercing lines from 'Big Yellow Taxi' about paving paradise with parking lots.

Even our national parks and other state-run supposed wildlife refuges are mostly grazed to the bone, apart from rampaging invasive plants. Places like Killarney National Park seem to be valued by authorities purely for the tourism revenue they bring in, with the merest lip service paid to their role as biological sanctuaries. Meanwhile marine ecosystems continue to be ripped apart by heavy overfishing, and the sea beds by bottom-trawling and dredging, to a point where total ecological collapse has either already occurred or isn't far off.

To put it bluntly, almost nowhere is nature allowed free rein, except by temporary oversight, and that mindset is killing it. The largely unquestioned idea that the land and seas serve one purpose only – to supply food, lumber, or other things we require – is simply wrong. They are the space needed by the wild ecosystems that produce clean air and water, healthy soils, and a stable climate; ecosystems that are a living matrix for the millions of species with whom we ought to be sharing the planet.

So my own philosophy with regard to the woods is quite the opposite. From the beginning, it has always been one of not exploiting them in an extractive way. In sparing the land, I have tried to make a tiny exception to that land- and seascape of scarcely interrupted ecological wreckage and desolation: an enclave in which another writ holds sway, at least on my watch. In my mind, it's an unspoken (until writing these words) joint protest on the part of myself, the land, and everything in it – living or otherwise – against a near ubiquitous and fast-worsening monotonous sterility. In my mind, it's a handkerchief-scale revolt against the very Anthropocene – the 'Age of Humans' – itself, the present epoch in which the human stamp on the planet has become so overwhelming and dominant as to be nothing less than a geological force.

These aren't mere abstract ideals either. For example, strange as it might seem, decaying wood is actually just as important to a natural forest ecosystem as the living trees, so removing dead timber leaves a great ecological void. On one occasion in the woods with Seánie, he borrowed the billhook slung from my belt and started using it to tear into the trunk of a fallen, rotting tree to see what was inside. I probably tend to be a little overprecious in my approach to the woods, preferring to leave things just as they are unless absolutely necessary, and so had never engaged in such vandal behaviour. But I was delighted he brought his hands-on curiosity to bear, because the variety of creatures he uncovered was simply astounding. We spent ages digging through the decomposing wood, seeing ever more amazing minuscule beasts emerge as we went.

In a wild forest, trees both young and old die from a variety of causes, and then rot away over time. But our mania for managing every last piece of land, even places that are supposed to be natural, and our phobia of anything dead that might form a reservoir of disease and spread to the living, has left native forests largely bereft of decaying wood. This deprives an enormous suite of living things of their natural habitat. Collectively known as saproxylics, they include species that live off dead wood, those that live off them, and those for whom dead wood plays an important role in their existence in some other way.

By George Peterken's estimate, around a fifth of all species that originally lived in forests were dependent on dead or slowly dying wood, or the fungi that inhabit them. Many of these species have difficulty migrating across land that contains no old forest, and since patches of forest are now unexceptionally small and fragmented, once the saproxylics are gone, many of them are unable to return. What Seánie exposed while digging into that rotting trunk was a whole mini-ecosystem of life, with tiny invertebrate 'grazers' feeding on the dead wood, other species preying on them, and so on, almost like a hidden miniature Serengeti.

Dead wood is an essential part of the life cycles of a whole raft of forest dwellers, with the specialist fungi, bacteria, beetles and larvae that help break it down feeding all its contained reserves back into the living ecosystem. Deceased trees are also important nesting sites for many species of solitary bee, for example. And all the saproxylic species are intimately integrated with, and essential to, other forest inhabitants and energy cycles. So I never take dead wood from the forest, but leave it instead to gradually rot away as nature intended.

For me, one of the absolute star inhabitants of the woods is a small, fairly inconspicuous mousy-brown bird called the treecreeper. They feed by scuttling up the trunks of trees in a spiral from the base searching for invertebrates, which they are able to pick from fissures in the bark with their long, thin, curved beak. When they reach a certain height in the tree, they flutter down to the base of another and start winding their way back up again, in this manner working slowly through the woods. Treecreepers are in some respects like mini-woodpeckers, sharing a number of characteristics. Both have stiff tail feathers to prop themselves up while clinging to tree trunks, often upside down, and frequently use large dead trees – known as 'snags' – for nesting and other important activities.

The great spotted woodpecker is a beautifully marked and coloured native bird that, like so many other species, was driven into extinction as Ireland lost almost all its remaining forest habitats in the seventeenth and eighteenth centuries. But over the last decade they have been naturally spreading back across the island, initially from Wales, in one of the most uplifting stories in recent times for all those of us who care about wild nature.

As well as often using standing dead trees for excavating their nest holes, woodpeckers drum on dead wood to call to each other and to repeatedly stake out their territories. In America, one species has even been found to carry in their beaks the spores of fungi that break down wood, making it easier to tunnel into (and symbiotically spreading the fungus), and it wouldn't be at all surprising to learn that ours do likewise. When they make it down to Bofickil, they should find things to their liking, and, given they were spotted in Glengarriff Nature Reserve in May 2021, it's likely they'll get here soon enough.

The winter of 2013–14 was one of exceptionally savage and continual storms and gales, and some of the more powerful of them brought quite a few big veteran trees crashing down in the woods. This happened especially when the ground was already saturated with accumulated rainwater, weakening the strength of the soil to which their roots cling. In many cases large sheets of naked underlying bedrock were revealed in this way, the sandstone shining silver-grey or pink-purplish clean with every trace of soil stripped away by the fallen tree's mesh of root filaments.

Over the following weeks and months there was the constant rasping whine of chainsaws up and down the country, as people cut up the trees that had fallen on their land for firewood, and to clear them away. I didn't touch those that came down in the Bofickil woods, and what I found was that, in almost all cases, only the branches that ended up near the ground died away, decommissioned due to the lack of light. In the spring, these trees simply started putting their energy into the newly established vertical axis, adaptation to windthrow obviously being something they have evolved to take in their stride. Existing branches that were previously lateral but now pointed skywards went on to became primary stems. And a profusion of new growth also sprang from the now uppermost sides of trunks, boughs and upturned rootplates, shooting up towards the light.

Fallen individuals that adopt this pattern are exquisitely termed 'phoenix trees', after the Greek mythological bird that regenerates from the ashes of the fire in which it dies. Although a natural reaction to having a big old tree come crashing down can be one of sadness, the phenomenon creates some of the most spectacularly structurally diverse, tangled and rich woodland habitat of all.

We tend to have a very regimented stereotype of what a tree should look like: a single straight, upright trunk carrying a 'nice', evenly rounded crown. E.O. Wilson noted that, as a

A large fern growing from a tree as an epiphyte in the woods.
Anywhere in the world you find significant numbers of
epiphytes in a forest, you're in a rainforest.

Our forest with the sea beyond, all shrouded in thick mist: just the sort of conditions temperate rainforest thrives in.

A river running through the Knysna forest, one of the many temperate and subtropical rainforests I explored in my mother's homeland of South Africa.

A hairy dragonfly (*Brachytron pratense*) on gorse in one of the woodland glades at Bofickil. Dragonflies prey on flying insects like midges, taking them in midair.

The crumbing ruin of an old cabin on our land, now immersed in rainforest. Between 50 and 75 per cent of people in our area died or emigrated during the Famine or soon after. Despite its immense beauty, this is a post-apocalyptic landscape.

A view down onto the canopy of the forest, including an oak 'snag' (standing dead tree). Great spotted woodpeckers will love this habitat when they finally make it down this far, which hopefully should be soon.

Charlie, our collie dog, standing atop a rock outcrop up towards the commonage, with a multitude of self-seeded native trees below. Give it a decade or so, and this will all be wild, highly diverse rainforest.

An absolute star inhabitant of the woo the treecreeper. They feed by scuttlin up the trunks of trees in a spiral from the base searching for invertebrates which they are able to pick from fissur in the bark with their long, thin, curved b

A lone whitethorn (hawthorn) on the mountain commonage. As with most other Irish uplands, were it not for overgrazing, the entire mountain would, in time, revert naturally to wild, native rainforest.

An oak and a *leath-ceann* (windswept) birch, surrounded by their young progeny up towards the commonage. Again, in a decade or so, all this will be wild forest, and not a thing was planted here.

The renowned ecologist, conservationist and founder of the Scottish charity Trees for Life, Alan Watson Featherstone, in our rainforest, one of many such visitors over the years from all over Ireland and beyond.

A green world: the magical interior of our rainforest ecosystem. Once, much of Ireland would have looked something like this.

The lifeless interior of a plantation of alien conifers. These dead zones already make up almost 90 per cent of Irish 'forest' cover (10 per cent of the land), and there are plans to hugely increase that. They shouldn't be referred to as 'forests' at all: they're nothing of the sort.

A flooded part of one of the streams through the forest. Wherever there is unpolluted water, there is life.

Uragh Wood, an ancient (pre-1660) and very precious tract of rainforest by the shores of Lough Inchiquin, Beara. Its name comes from *An Iúrach* – 'The Place of the Yews'.

Me stretching out on the tree platform in our woods. There is no more comfortable and relaxing way of letting the sights, sounds and energies all around – the music of the woods – flow over and into you.

When I first came to live in Beara, at times I'd waken at night to see the moon cast a long, gently rippling wedge of reflected silvery light towards me across the sea, and wonder whether I was still dreaming. More than twelve years on, I still do.

species, we are drawn towards a very particular aesthetic when it comes to trees, showing a clear preference in psychological tests for forms resembling the lone acacias that occur on the African savannah. For him, this was just another indication of how our evolutionary origins still inform who we are.

In any case, anything that deviates from that ideal is often likely to be singled out for elimination, whether dead trees, fallen trees, or the great variety of irregular shapes that living wild trees naturally assume. That is a desperate pity, for the greater the diversity of forms and stages of life or death, the more niches for wildlife, and hence the more ecologically rich a habitat becomes. We must learn to embrace that.

I am sometimes asked whether I go foraging in the woods for edible fungi and whatnot, but, to my mind, exactly the same principle applies: I prefer to just leave it all alone. We are not living in hunter-gatherer times, when tiny bands of people roamed vast, barely touched, landscapes; totally the opposite. To repeat, we have transformed almost every last scrap of land into artificial states designed to provide maximum benefit to one species alone – ourselves – with wild nature pushed out to the very utmost degree. Seen in that light, rather than being 'close to nature', taking from the last vestiges of semi-wild habitat is just another human impact on what little remains of the natural sphere.

Which brings us back, yet again, to a core point: what nature needs most, both on land and at sea, is plenty of large, and strictly observed, no-take zones where no human extractive activity whatsoever takes place. To make that possible, we need to learn the extremely difficult – perhaps *the* most difficult, for us humans – ability to let go, and just leave things be.

15

Fleeting Shadows

It would be easy to think of a natural forest as just a big bunch of trees, but nothing could be further from the truth.

There are instead a great array of components, the most obvious of which are the living, or biotic, ones: the trees themselves in all shapes and sizes, fungi, flowers, invertebrates, birds, mammals, soil microbes, and so on. Then there are all those that are non-living (at least not in the conventional sense), or abiotic, such as sunlight, water, rock, air and dead organic matter. All these, and many other elements, are the essential building blocks of a woodland ecosystem.

But the mortar that binds it all together and makes it work – and the really fascinating part – is the seemingly almost infinite complex connections, or ecological interactions, between all these things. Indeed, the more we come to understand the wider living world, the more we realise that its core essence is *relationship*.

One manifestation is the common sight in the Bofickil woods of a scattered trail of feathers leading across the ground to a larger patch of feathers, perhaps over a low and horizontal moss-covered bough. Sometimes there are also a few other remains of a dead bird, such as a beak, or a spindly leg and foot or two. These are the telltale signs that a sparrowhawk has used the spot as a plucking post for one of its kills. And one of the most electrifying experiences is to see a sparrowhawk actually swooping through the trees, often close to the ground, seeking to surprise a blackbird, wood pigeon, or other unlucky member of the woodland avifauna in mid-flight.

Predation is one of many essential ecological processes in any natural ecosystem – which can be seen as flows of energy and nutrients in manifold, but essentially cyclical, directions. In the alchemy that is photosynthesis, trees and other plants combine carbon dioxide and water with the primary energy in the form of the light that their outstretched leaves receive from the sun to make carbohydrates, which are their food. This chemical reaction powers all life in the woods (on Earth, practically), and all the other organisms have evolved to take advantage of its bonanza in some way, such as the caterpillars that come to feed on the leaves, or the jays that eat acorns.

The caterpillars also make tasty morsels for a wide range of small birds, such as the long-tailed and other tits that perform the most amazing acrobatics upside down while picking twigs and leaves clean, thereby providing a service to the tree. The jays and other ground feeders take care of the many caterpillars that fall from the canopy above. The tits, jays, and other bird species are in turn preyed upon by the sparrowhawks and other predators. This is called a 'food (or trophic) web'. Throughout the process, whenever any of the organisms involved poops or dies, for example, that material enriches the soil in which the trees and other plants grow, returning the favour in some of the myriad feedback loops. (This is all to greatly oversimplify things of course, but that's the gist of it.)

Unfortunately, predators are invariably the first category of species in line to get it in the neck from us people, since they're seen as a threat to our interests, which always come first. Their absence is highly damaging to the proper functioning of an ecosystem, throwing it entirely out of whack. Every missing component inevitably leaves behind an 'ecological ghost', like removing one of the cogwheels from a clock, to repeat that analogy. And the effect is cumulative, with every further cog that's taken out making the whole mechanism increasingly less able to operate as it should, and thus less able to resist invasive species, for example. Caroline Fraser relates this concept very well (the emphases are hers):

> Why do species matter? Why worry if some go missing? Part of the answer lies in the relationships coming to light between creatures like the canyon coyotes and the chaparral birds. After the nineteenth century's great age of biological collecting, when collectors filled museums to bursting with stuffed birds and pinned beetles, the twentieth and twenty-first centuries have proved to be an age of *connecting*. Biologists have begun to understand that nature is a chain of dominoes: If you pull one piece out, the whole thing falls down. Lose the animals, lose the ecosystems. Lose the ecosystems, game over.
>
> Put another way, in this era of connection, we have learned that everything is interdependent. There are no spare parts. Predators regulate a constellation of other predators and prey;

grazing animals regulate grasslands; grasslands and forests regulate climate. The physical world is like a big organic machine, an old car, for example, composed of interconnecting moving parts. Eco*systems*. You can lose inessential cosmetic elements, the bumper, the hubcaps, and it will still run, for a while. But eventually, if you lose enough critical parts, the machine will fail. When parts of an ecosystem are lost – predators, grazers, pollinators – the machine starts stalling, stuttering, failing. The processes of life grind to a halt.

A good illustration is the dynamic that has been playing out in Ireland between three species: red and grey squirrels, and the pine marten. A few American grey squirrels were famously brought to County Longford in 1911 (as a wedding present!), and began spreading inexorably across the country from there. Upon arrival in an area, they would initially coexist with the smaller native red squirrel, but after a few years the reds disappeared. The reasons appear to be multiple, and include a disease that the greys carry but are immune to themselves, while the reds are not. Grey squirrels can be extremely damaging to native woodlands, because they have a habit of stripping the bark from around the bases of young trees, thereby killing them, just as the goats and sika deer had been doing in the Bofickil woods.

In England and Wales, where grey squirrels had been introduced even earlier, the reds had to all intents and purposes been wiped out by the start of this century. (There is a population still hanging on in the Isle of Wight, protected by the sea barrier.) Here in Ireland the outlook was looking pretty bleak for the reds too, with a 2007 survey showing greys to be present throughout the entire east and north. But researchers Emma Sheehy and Colin Lawton of the National University of Ireland Galway also found the first fascinating evidence of a dramatic turnaround in the situation.

The pine marten is a very beautiful native mustelid (i.e. member of the weasel family, so related to badgers, stoats and otters), about the size of a small domestic cat, but with a longer and much bushier tail. They have a dark-chocolate-coloured coat, apart from a creamy patch to the chest and neck. Once common, the species was driven almost to extinction in Ireland, as it was hunted for its fur and seen as a threat to poultry and game birds. The disappearance of its forest habitat also played a major role in the decline, as well as consumption of poisoned carrion left out for foxes. By the 1970s, pine martens were found in only a handful of enclaves in Ireland, principally the Burren in County Clare, and a few other counties including Kerry. Largely owing to legal protection introduced in 1976, the species then began to make a gradual recovery, slowly spreading back across its former range.

Although martens prey on red squirrels, they do so far less than on the non-native greys (in natural woodland, that is; in alien conifer plantations the opposite is true). Grey squirrels spend more time feeding on the ground and, being heavier and less nimble, are also much easier to catch in the trees than the reds, which are frustratingly (for martens) able to run out to the tips of branches. As pine martens spread back across the country, grey squirrel populations in those areas were found to crash, with red squirrels soon returning in their wake.

Ecologists and conservationists in Britain were hugely excited by the Irish findings because, as with red squirrels, martens too had become effectively non-existent in England and Wales. Several reintroductions have since taken place from a healthy population in Scotland, from where they are also spreading naturally south of the border into England, and it appears that they are having the same effect on grey squirrels there as their Irish cousins.

Along with the pine marten, other missing native species would have contributed to stopping the grey squirrel problem dead in its tracks: wildcat, lynx, goshawk (grey squirrels can make up 95 per cent of goshawk prey in the UK), and no doubt others. We remain surrounded by the ecological phantoms of a great variety of species that we have killed off, breaking a vast multitude of ecosystem interconnections that still flap in the wind.

One example that will resonate with every gardener is the robin redbreast, and how when you start digging one of them very often instantly appears, watching intently for the opportunity to fly in and snatch an unearthed worm or insect. When I'm walking in the woods, at some point the same thing invariably happens, with one of them following me closely. If I have a robin in tow, I'll sometimes scrape the surface of the woodland floor with the heel of my boot, pushing away the top layer of leaf litter and twigs. It's a joy to watch as he becomes visibly excited, cocking his head this way and that to get a better look at what I'm doing, and moving in as close as he dares. As soon as I distance myself a little, he'll flutter down to the agitated patch to investigate for any invertebrate pickings.

Robins clearly evolved a relationship with ground-disturbing megafauna, following along behind and grabbing anything tasty that came to light, just as I saw Cape starlings do with rhinos in Africa. Although there are no longer any such wild megafauna that fulfil that role in Ireland, robins are still instinctually driven to hang around any large animals (which is really all we are in their eyes) they see disturbing the ground. The return of native wild boar, which spend most of their time rooting about, would go some way towards filling that gap, and would probably reconnect many of the other loose ecological wires also.

By rummaging the soil, they create exactly the right conditions for the seeds of tree species like oak to germinate. Boars love acorns, and woody habitats generally, so helping grow new forests works very much in their own favour – another example of the mutually beneficial arrangements that have developed through coevolution. By digging out and eating the underground rhizomes, they also help to repress bracken, which can take over in dryer land that has been overgrazed for long periods by livestock, especially sheep. That facilitates the natural regeneration of woodland and other species-rich natural habitats, which is seriously inhibited by very dense bracken.

There's good evidence to suggest that boar would even help control new infestation by rhododendron, which was naturally present in Ireland during the last interglacial period, the Eemian. Their tamed descendants, domestic pigs, certainly seem to do so quite effectively. As with grey squirrels and most other invasive species, it's likely that the problem isn't so much the actual rhododendron at all, but the fact that other ecosystem components which would keep it in check are absent as a result of human activities.

What all this demonstrates once again is the much greater resilience of healthy, intact ecosystems, replete with as many of their constituent parts and wild processes as possible. They are in a far better place to defend themselves against non-native invasive species than heavily compromised ones, in which important species are missing or other serious damage has been inflicted. A helpful way of thinking about it is in terms of your own body's immune system: if it has all the right antibodies and other defences in place, it has more chance of keeping itself healthy. But if these are weakened or absent, you're much more prone to attack by infection and disease. It's essentially the same for ecosystems that have lost many of their pivotal species, as ours have.

Ultimately, the best solution to invasive species – as well as unnaturally overabundant native species like crows, foxes and bracken – will in most cases be to allow wild native ecosystems to return to as complete a form as possible (although human intervention will usually continue to be required in the meantime). If we are at all serious about arresting the ongoing collapse of nature in Ireland, that's the direction we need to be going in as rapidly, and on as great a scale, as we can.

The dire state in which I found the Bofickil woods when I first arrived in Beara was due to a similar absence of cogs from the ecological clock mechanism. It was being grazed and browsed to death because the large native predators that would naturally regulate the numbers and behaviour of herbivores in a functioning ecosystem were missing, as they are everywhere else in Ireland, and many other parts of the globe.

Ecologists now have a better understanding of the crucial

role predators play within ecosystems, instigating what is called a 'trophic cascade' of effects throughout. Probably the best-known illustration of what happens when they're no longer present is how things spiralled downhill at Yellowstone National Park in the United States in the decades after the elimination of wolves there. Hunting by people was insufficient to keep the deer population in check, and numbers continually rose until the natural vegetation of the park, including forests, could no longer regenerate, causing it to die off.

The reintroduction of several wolf packs in the 1990s has since brought about the most spectacular recovery in the park's ecological health. That process was compellingly recounted in the YouTube video *How Wolves Change Rivers*, narrated by environmental activist, writer and journalist George Monbiot. Released in 2014, it very quickly went viral, with well over 43 million views at the time of writing.

The island of Ireland once had several such species that would have fulfilled that ecological role in various ways: primarily wolves, but also brown bears and lynx. As discussed earlier, there would almost certainly have been others, such as lions and hyenas, but for the massive human-induced extinction wave, and related ecological devastation, in southern Europe before the Holocene. All around the country, most of the few remaining patches of native forest are in the same decrepit, slowly dying condition as the Bofickil woods were when we first arrived in 2009. Natural regeneration of trees is prevented by overpopulated deer and other browsers, native ground flora is stripped out, and invasive plant species are able to take over.

Beyond the ecological impact, other negative effects of a superabundance of grazers like deer include a high incidence of traffic accidents. Driving around dawn or dusk is especially dangerous, for deer often appear out of the undergrowth at the last moment, and can come crashing up onto the bonnet and in through car windscreens. If I have to travel at dawn for work reasons, I'll often have to dodge up to a dozen sika on just the 30-minute drive between Bofickil and Kenmare. Deer-related accidents are common, and people have been killed in the wider vicinity.

The highly debilitating Lyme disease is another huge problem in many areas, as deer and feral goats spread the parasitic ticks that can carry it. For the first 18 months after coming to Beara, every time I was in the Bofickil woods I would find a half-dozen or more *sceartáin* (as ticks are still called locally) afterwards crawling up my trouser legs, necessitating a full strip and search when I got home. Within a couple of years of the deer fence going up, they had virtually disappeared, because the larger hosts that are crucial to their life cycle were gone.

For so many reasons, there is clearly a very real need for solutions to overly high densities of deer, but what are they? Contraception is impractical, and, even if it could somehow be done, it wouldn't prevent continuing damage over the remainder of a deer's lifetime – about 15 years for sika, for example. Fencing or culling (shooting) can act as partial stopgaps, but there are major drawbacks to both.

Fencing is extremely expensive, unsightly, needs frequent monitoring and maintenance, has a fairly short lifespan in Irish conditions, and can act as a barrier to non-target species. And by preventing any browsing aside from smaller species, it replaces one unnatural situation – overbrowsing – with another (albeit preferable) one: an almost complete absence of herbivory. Controlling herbivore numbers by culling avoids these issues, but entails others that are equally problematic. First, it can be very difficult to effectively reduce densities down to levels that allow natural regeneration of native trees and flora, especially in rough country. Sika, for example, are notoriously secretive and tough to hunt, even more so after the first few have been taken.

Culling is also controversial with the public, which is largely unaware of the ecological devastation wrought by artificially high numbers of deer, or the fact that the deer themselves suffer desperately from starvation as a result. Ironically, many nature lovers and animal rights enthusiasts are often among the first to object. Even hunting organisations oppose culls such as those sometimes carried out by the National Parks and Wildlife Service in Killarney National Park, presumably wishing to maintain 'target-rich environments' for their sport.

But above all, culling is not natural, and doesn't replicate most of the ecological effects of wild native predators. Even more important than bringing down numbers, the latter change the way herbivores behave, by creating what ecologists call a 'landscape of fear'. In the presence of predators, deer are aware they continually risk ambush or being chased down. As a result they are much more skittish, and avoid certain areas where instinct tells them that is more likely to happen, allowing patchworks of native vegetation to flourish. While potentially helping lower numbers, shooting does nothing to reproduce any of these effects.

Additionally, natural predators zone in on more vulnerable prey, such as the weak or sick, thereby keeping herds healthy and maintaining evolutionary processes. By contrast, hunters often tend to seek out very different characteristics, such as big stags with the largest antlers that will make the most impressive trophies. Hence shooting is a form of very *un*natural selection, forcing evolution in artificial directions. And again: predators don't only regulate herbivore prey, but, vitally, smaller predators too. On so many levels ecologically, culling is a highly inadequate substitute for natural predation.

But in the absence of any alternative – i.e. the present situation in Ireland – fencing or culling are certainly far better than nothing: without them, the country's precious few remaining patches of native forest will continue to decline and disappear.

Ultimately, the reintroduction of our lost native carnivores presents the only really viable long-term solution. There have been calls to consider bringing back wolves, most notably by Pádraic Fogarty in his book *Whittled Away: Ireland's Vanishing Nature*. The last Irish wolf was likely shot in County Carlow in 1786, but in Cork and Kerry they were gone by about 1710. As Pádraic pointed out, the contention that Ireland doesn't have the right, or sufficient, habitat to support them now is quite simply mistaken. Wolves have spread back naturally to practically every country in mainland Europe, including far more densely populated and built-up countries like Germany, the Netherlands, Denmark and Belgium, and are doing just fine.

Fears about potential threats to human safety from wolves are also unfounded. As a rule they studiously avoid any contact with humans, and attacks are so rare that people living in wolf country are more likely to be killed by lightning or a bee sting than they are to be even injured by wolves. Indeed, their presence would probably actually save human lives by reducing deer–vehicle collisions (DVC) and Lyme disease. A 2019 study carried out by two American universities found that each wolf in a dispersal area reduced the average annual costs associated with DVC by \$160,000–354,000, and described them as 'a cost-effective biological control'.

Studies have also shown that wolf predation of livestock is usually very low, since they tend to prefer hunting the same (or similar) wild prey species with which they co-evolved. Losses can be reduced still further by protective measures, such as traditional livestock guardian dog breeds. These have been used effectively for millennia in Italy and other parts of Europe where coexistence with predators, rather than extermination, has been the objective.

However, as someone living in a rural community where pastoral farming continues to be the primary land use, I am all too acutely aware of the degree of apprehension any plans to reintroduce wolves would be likely to arouse. These concerns are only natural given the place larger predators hold deep within the human psyche. And they are reinforced on a generational basis in the storybooks we give our children, for example, painting them as a mortally dangerous threat to people and domestic animals. The message that wolves and other keystone predators like sharks are a sort of demonic evil also continues to be widely and continually propagated by the mass media, particularly Hollywood.

Such portrayals play on deep-seated ancestral memories that still reside within all of us, of having to be constantly alert to the possibility of ending up as something's dinner. The fact that wolves are pack animals doesn't help, nor a general disconnect from nature that pervades most sections of society. Consequently, there is a way to go before their reintroduction is likely to be accepted in Ireland, although that's a conversation we definitely ought to be having. There is, however, another contender that merits serious consideration in the short term.

The European lynx is an exquisitely handsome medium-sized forest-dwelling cat, about 1.3 metres long, with a spotted coat, long legs, pointed tufts at the tips of its ears and a short, stubby tail. They are extremely shy, solitary animals, and are almost never actually seen in the territories they inhabit. Although an 8,875-year-old lynx femur bone was discovered in Kilgreany Cave in County Waterford, that hasn't been generally accepted as sufficient evidence to allow the conferral of native Irish status. To my mind, that seems far too cautious: in fact, there may be more evidence for lynx being native than such species as badger, fox and red squirrel; as I asked in Chapter 13, should we discount them too?

In any case, as a result of this strange ambiguity there has been almost no discussion of their possible reintroduction. An exception is *Whittled Away,* which is refreshingly clear on both the lynx's native status, and that they should be brought back. In my view, though, the question of whether lynx can be considered native or not isn't central, for the same reasons already outlined with regard to the beaver. That is, they occur naturally across practically the entire northern hemisphere, are highly beneficial to ecosystems everywhere, and there really should be some flexibility regarding the whole issue of native Irish species anyway.

Lynx are ambush hunters, and would prey on overpopulated deer – especially their young, as well as rabbits, hares, foxes, squirrels, and other smaller mammals and birds. It's probable that, like pine martens, they would take far more grey squirrels than red, contributing to the red squirrel's comeback. By killing and repressing overabundant foxes, lynx would also potentially ease the mesopredator release that is so problematic for native ground-nesting birds and other species. On so many levels, they would help restore a desperately needed level of equilibrium to dysfunctional Irish ecosystems.

Lastly, lynx pose no threat whatsoever to people, and only very rarely take sheep or lambs, which would likely be more than offset by a reduction in fox numbers. Regardless, an easy-access compensation scheme would need to be set in place for any losses to farmers. But much more than that: increased farm payments for any land known to be part of a lynx territory (much like the present hen harrier and freshwater pearl mussel schemes) would be highly conducive to creating a climate of positivity among the farming community.

Throughout mainland Europe, native terrestrial mammals, including predators such as lynx, wolves and bears, can and are returning naturally to territories that were once part of their natural range. On these islands, however, the sea barrier makes that impossible, and so we'll have to be more proactive if we want to see our own ecosystems similarly regain some of their lost richness and functionality.

Plans for the reintroduction of the lynx in Britain, where they were driven to extinction around the eighth century AD, are at an advanced stage, if not quite realised yet. As with the beaver, which has already been returned to many parts of that island, there is no reason why we shouldn't be looking very seriously at their reintroduction in Ireland too. Of course, no action should be taken without a reasonable level of buy-in from local communities, and the process should be as democratic, transparent, and inclusive as possible throughout.

If lynx were brought back, the gains wouldn't be solely ecological, or in the practical benefits of helping native forests return, or reductions in deer-related accidents and Lyme. Imagine the thrill of being able to walk in Killarney National Park, or other pieces of native woodland elsewhere in the country, with the knowledge that such a largish wild cat may have passed that way earlier, even if the chances of seeing one were almost non-existent. Imagine the great boost it would bring to the tourism industry – their release in just one place, the Harz Mountains in northern Germany in 2009, has been estimated to add £12.5 million sterling to the local economy annually. Imagine the statement that allowing their return would make to the world regarding our maturity and confidence as a nation, one that is willing to take the leap and share the land once more with such a beautiful wild creature.

That last point raises another crucial aspect. None of us would like to see such fabulous, but far bigger and more dangerous, species as elephants, tigers, rhino, buffalo, or lions die out in the parts of Africa and Asia they still naturally inhabit. Our world would be so much poorer and more dismal without the knowledge that they live, somewhere, in the wild, even if we might never actually get to see them there ourselves. But how can we seriously expect the people who live alongside these much more threatening animals to continue to tolerate their presence, if we can't find it within ourselves to accept the return of a species so innocuous that we'd hardly even know it was there at all?

What are we afraid of – fleeting shadows?

16

More Complex
Than We *Can* Think

There was a loping flash of dark brown along the low horizontal branch of a big old oak, before vanishing behind the thickly moss-wadded tree trunk. I blinked, rooted to the spot, wondering if I was seeing things. Moments later she reappeared with lithe, perky movements on a stone wall at the base of the tree, momentarily standing up on her hind legs to check me out inquisitively. Plainly visible were the acutely intelligent little face, creamy yellow bib covering the chest and throat, and long, flowing bushy tail that, taken together, means only one thing: *an cat crainn* – the tree cat, in Irish. Then she was gone.

I remained motionless for some time afterwards, quietly savouring the wave of warm delight that was breaking over and inside me. During the previous months I had come across scats in the woods, similar to those that I had first seen in some of the Burren hazel woods in County Clare during a bioblitz in 2013. Mammal expert Chris Barron, who was at the bioblitz too, taught me to recognise the sometimes almost 'hazelnut whirl' shape as the deposits of pine marten. So the suspicion that they had taken up residence in the Bofickil woods was already there; but this sighting in early 2020 was for me the first definite evidence of the return of Ireland's rarest native mammal.

I have since caught a few more glimpses of them in and around the woods (including once from the kitchen window), attesting to the presence of a small but apparently healthy local population. The European pine marten, to give its full name, is without doubt one of the most beautiful and ecologically important members of our native woodland fauna. A generalist omnivore, they predate on insects, small rodents, rabbits, squirrels, birds and their eggs, frogs, lizards, and so on, as well as feeding on fruit, nuts and carrion. They therefore perform key roles in the ecosystems they inhabit, facilitating many ecological processes.

On another more recent occasion, not far from one of the streams around dusk, I was standing quite still for perhaps a quarter of an hour or so, as I often do. My attention was drawn to a large pool in the stream, and I looked over in time to see the wet outline of an otter – *madra uisce* (water dog) – which then gracefully slipped back into the water. Again, that delicious feeling. I had seen them previously along the nearby seashore, but never imagined they would actually venture upstream into the woods. Otters now show up regularly on a camera trap set by the same stream, likely drawn in by frogs, brown trout, eels and other prey.

Other creatures have revealed their presence in the woods by more unique avenues. A patch of large feathers turned out to be those of barn owl, and all the indications were that this nocturnal predator had itself been predated while perched on the tree branch overhead. Barn owls tend to hunt along woodland margins and other more open areas, rather than within forests, and the bird may well have been asleep when it was taken, almost certainly by an opportunistic pine marten, going by the fresh scats I found nearby.

The appearance of such charismatic hunters as lesser horseshoe bats, pine martens, otters and barn owls in Bofickil has been an indescribable thrill and joy to me, even if they seldom show themselves in the woods. The mere knowledge that they are there at all, and seeing their occasional signs as a reminder that it isn't all just my imagination, is enough. Walking in the woods feels different, and further enriched, by that knowledge. And these are certain to be only some of the ecosystem components that have been moving back in, with many other species also taking up residence or passing through. Just as each one is an indication of the increased ecological health and functionality that has been flowing back into the woods, so will they each play a role in further promoting that health and functionality.

As I had seen at the Wrights' place near Skibbereen almost two decades ago, if the natural habitat is there, along with adequate protection, the wild will return, weaving new webs of life. It might not be the elephants, leopards and baboons of the Knysna forest, but for me it has been no less exciting. And its return is but one aspect of a much wider process, in which *Badh Fiadh-Choille* – Recess of the Wild Wood – has been moving ever closer back to living up to its name.

Over the years, my relationship with the land and woods has grown ever more intimate, as I have come to know practically every nook and cranny. And gaining an awareness of how wondrously complex a healthy native woodland is in ecological terms has heightened enormously the pleasure that comes from being in there.

Yet at the same time all the more primal emotions and experiences remain undiminished, and I have never forced myself to study the science beyond what might interest me at any given moment. I don't, for example, feel the need to be able to identify every insect I encounter, realising how unrealistic that would be with possibly upwards of 16,000 species in Ireland. The same goes for the bryophytes (around 835 species, subspecies and varieties), and lichens (almost 1,200 species).

But it goes beyond that. In a sense, I actually enjoy seeing all sorts of far-fetched creatures go buzzing past my face without knowing exactly what they are. I find it adds to the mystery and wonder that are vital aspects of my own personal experience and enjoyment of nature, which is every bit as much about deeply feeling its essence as being au fait with the science.

For that reason I usually stop for some contemplative silence during the course of a ramble in the woods, whether alone or with visitors, in order to take a moment to truly absorb their sounds, smells and rhythms. Doing so can often bring encounters that would almost certainly otherwise be missed, as with the otter. (I also usually make a point of doing the same when visiting any other forest.) A receptivity to bird song, humming insects, the flow of wind through leaves and branches, the gurgling of a stream, the rich leafy perfumes of the woods after rain: all this, and so much more, is just as indispensable as the more cerebral sides in attempting a deeper comprehension. I find it's as important to *feel it*, as it is to reason it.

If at some point, for example, I come across a particular unfamiliar species that I'd like to be able to name and know more about, then I look into it. Ditto if there's something that I feel might represent a potential threat to the woods' ecological health, such as an unidentified exotic-looking plant that could be a non-native invasive species. It sometimes happens that well-informed visitors, usually someone who is well-versed in one of the relevant life sciences, enlightens me on some aspect of the woods I was previously unaware of, which is always a welcome pleasure. Otherwise, at this stage I'm mostly happy to just enjoy the life pulsating all around me, in the knowledge that it's doing relatively fine. But having some basic understanding of the mechanics behind it all, i.e. the ecology, greatly enriches the emotional enchantment, and vice versa.

Those charting the human relationship with nature pinpoint the hugely revolutionary thinking of seventeenth-century French philosopher René Descartes as having been pivotal in bringing the process of separation between us to its present extreme. His ideas were, and have remained, so profoundly influential that they are now practically taken for granted as self-evident truths, and still underpin our intensely dysfunctional and destructive approach towards the natural world. Here is Jeremy Lent outlining how so in his wonderful book *The Patterning Instinct*:

In Descartes's own words: 'I do not recognize any difference between the machines made by craftsmen and the various bodies that nature alone composes.'

With this step, Descartes completed the process, begun by monotheism, that eliminated any intrinsic value from the natural world. With nothing sacred about nature, it became available for the human intellect to use remorselessly for its own purposes. The scientific project, just getting off the ground in the seventeenth century, would henceforth view every aspect of the material world as free game for inquiry, investigation, and exploitation.

To me, following a Cartesian interpretation of nature as just machine, separate from us, and to be studied detachedly, wouldn't be merely uninspiring, insipid and dull. It would miss so much of what a living system is, and so much of the potential joy in interacting with one. In my experience, both ways of perceiving and relating to the woods – i.e. intellectually *and* intuitively/sensorially – are essential, greatly overlap, and are mutually reinforcing.

One of the greatest benefits of allowing nature to just do its own thing, i.e. rewilding, is that, once issues such as invasive species have been taken in hand, not a whole lot more input is required. Other than to take pleasure by spending time in its midst, of course, which I feel duty-bound to indulge in on an almost daily basis when possible. In the woods, other than perhaps the sound of a car passing on the nearest road, there is nothing obvious to indicate that you're not in the middle of a boundless wilderness, stretching from one coast to another. There are very few places on this island that allow some such idea of how primeval Ireland might have felt before human impacts.

There is, though, one job that never ends: seeking out rhododendron, for which winter and early spring are the best times. Being evergreen, its distinctive glossy leaves stand out much more clearly when most of the native vegetation has lost its leaves or died back during the colder months. Whenever I'm in the woods, a small segment of my mind is constantly on the lookout for rhododendron and other invasive plants like Chilean myrtle.

There's always a great sense of satisfaction in finding one and rooting it out, which sometimes requires going back to the shed for a telescopic ladder if the plant is growing from the side of a cliff. I usually hang invasives upside down from an adjacent tree, often tucked in behind an ivy stem, so the roots dry out and die. The shrivelled remains then serve as a sort of totemic trophy that endures into the future: an ecologically positive – and far less grisly – version of the stuffed and mounted animal heads you sometimes see hung on walls.

Every successive year, there are always fewer rhodos to be pulled out, but it's unlikely there will ever come a point when there are none. And, in truth, even if that did come to pass, a part of me would be almost sorry in an entirely irrational and selfish sort of way. Apart from the contentment that comes from discovering one and getting rid of it, hunting them down is always a good excuse to go clambering through the more far-flung and less accessible corners of the land that, for a spell, have been left unvisited. That helps me keep up to speed on how the whole place is developing, rather than just the more well-trodden sections.

It also often causes me to see wildlife that normally goes unobserved, perhaps a faintly ridiculously bobbing woodcock, perfectly camouflaged among the leaf litter under newly formed scrub. And I've made some exciting new discoveries while poking around for invasives – colonies of Killarney fern I was previously unaware of, for example.

The only other activity I sometimes engage in is keeping the briars from taking over. A native plant, brambles are fantastically beneficial to wildlife. The flowers are a great source of nectar for pollinators, the berries are food for birds and other animals, and the tangled stems and leaves give cover. Plenty of insects and other herbivores, ranging in size up to deer, also love devouring the leaves, and they are often one of the first plants to be eaten, despite the protective thorns. Perhaps in part as an evolved strategy owing to their high palatability, brambles grow very aggressively in the complete absence of any browsing, which for the moment is the situation that pertains in the Bofickil woods.

Just as predation is an essential ecological process in any natural system, so is herbivory. The problem is that we humans have engineered things in such a way that there is no let-up from grazing and browsing almost anywhere, while the counterweight of larger predators has been totally eliminated. The deer fence brings some semblance of balance back, since it allows the native plants and trees to start growing again. But, of course, in the longer term no browsing at all is just as unnatural as no predation. At present, however, there is no other option. I see it as a question of trying to steer a course that brings the best ecological outcomes, but within a context that is wholly artificial and out of equilibrium, and will remain so as long as there continues to be no natural predation of deer. There are no perfect choices.

The fence is already showing signs of being well past its best, however, and whole sections will soon begin to fail, making attempts at repair increasingly impractical. When that happens, sika will begin to venture back onto the land, returning a degree of grazing and browsing to the equation. My hope is that local hunters will continue to keep deer densities at a reasonably balanced level that allows natural regeneration of the trees and other native plants to continue, and avoids a return to the wrecked state I found here on arrival.

In the meantime, with no browsing there is a risk that the briars will dominate. That's fine to some extent, but would be harmful if they took over completely, since it would severely reduce diversity among the ground flora as well as the natural regeneration of trees, and make the woods impossible to walk through. Inaccessibility wouldn't just prevent me from enjoying the place; it would also greatly reduce its potential for showcasing how incredibly lovely, rich and worth bringing back our lost rainforests are, which I see as a primary function. (There has been a steady stream of visiting ecologists and conservationists, from Ireland and abroad, especially since I set up the Beara Rainforest website in early 2017.) In addition, it would become next to impossible to find and remove rhododendron and other invasive plant species, risking reinfestation.

So on some days when walking through the woods I bring my billhook, which is perfect for cutting briars at the base, because you can reach in and curl the hook around the stem and pull, slicing through. But I do this work in a relaxed way, and only when the fancy takes me, just to keep the briars somewhat in check. Again, the plant is a hugely important one to a lot of wildlife, and there's no shortage of it around the land, despite my occasional labours.

Other than removing invasive plants when I find them, checking (and sometimes fixing) the fence after storms, and occasionally cutting a few briars, I don't manage the land or its inhabitants in any way. As much as possible in the existing circumstances, the land is deciding what *it* wants. It is difficult to adequately convey the pleasure that comes from seeing that process unfold, and it's never possible to anticipate how it will go: no one spot ever develops the same as any other.

It is immensely exciting, in an understated way, to see pioneer seedlings of wild birch, sally, oak, hazel and all the other tree species appear, and then grow, in an area where there is little but *fionnán* grass and some furze or heather. The presence of mature woodland nearby further enhances the gratification, by providing a constant reminder of the potential of such an initially modest-looking development. Seedlings become saplings, then develop into young adults, and light levels begin to fall away underneath. The *fionnán* that covered the ground in a thick, knee to waist-high bristle the colour of hay gets ever thinner, leaving only the tussock cores marooned in leaf-littered, but otherwise largely bare, ground. As the trees overhead thicken, the grasses often die off completely, with perhaps only a few mosses remaining.

Interestingly, in wetter areas the lower trunks of young trees – usually, but not always, birch – are frequently divided into multiple 'stilt roots', mangrove-like, as though the ground had dropped away by about 20 centimetres or so to reveal the upper roots. This is generally not the case with adjacent, more water-loving sally saplings, for example. It happens when trees germinate higher up within the *fionnán* tussocks, taking advantage of the relative dryness before later shading out the grasses below, causing the death of their hosts in a low-key version of strangler fig behaviour.

Birch and other tree species can grow in a similar, but even more spectacular, manner, if their seeds germinate on a decaying log. Over time the log rots away, leaving the trunk of the new tree suspended above ground on its stilt roots, which have penetrated down through the log and into the ground. My guess is that the stilt roots of the trees that adopt the mangrove-like approach merge as they grow, perhaps contributing to the formation of buttress-style flanges at their bases.

The falling leaves that cover the now naked floor begin to build up soil levels and fertility, as well as altering its chemistry and making it more conducive to colonisation by other tree, and lesser plant, species. The first members of the woodland ground flora may start to appear very soon, with perhaps herb Robert creeping in here and there, or mats of opposite-leaved golden saxifrage in marshier areas. Elsewhere, electric yellow, blue-mauve and brilliant white bursts of celandine, dog violet and wood sorrel are often the first to arrive.

Although this process can be slow beneath trees that establish themselves away from existing woodland, if there is older forest close by with a varied flora, it can follow more quickly. This is just another of a great many reasons why expansion of existing pockets of wild native woodland in Ireland through natural regeneration should be prioritised over planting isolated sites. Colonisation of adjacent land by not only the trees themselves, but by all the other wild floral and faunal ingredients of an ecosystem, will always happen far more rapidly.

In drier spots, the heathers and gorse might stubbornly persist for quite a time, a hangover from the previous non-woodland state, and can become surprisingly tall while trying to compete with the trees coming up all around. It's a race their evolutionary heritage doesn't equip them to win, however, and eventually they resign themselves to the inevitable and pass into oblivion, just as with the *fionnán*. Where succession is more rapid, a decade or less can suffice for a piece of land to go from highly ecologically impoverished grassland to ever more biodiverse closed-canopy woodland. And the longer the process continues, the more complex and cumulatively richer it becomes, as more species arrive and further myriad interactions between them form.

Nor is it a process destined to ever really reach a final state either. Contrary to what ecologists once thought, there is no such thing as 'climax' natural forest, at least not in the sense that the ecosystem reaches a sort of peak, at which it remains in pretty much perpetually static equilibrium thereafter. A more accurate way of thinking about it would be in terms of an ever-fluctuating 'shifting-mosaic steady state': the ancient Greek philosopher Heraclitus's observation that 'the only constant in life is change' applies perfectly to forest ecosystems. They never stop transforming, even if those transformations may often be too gradual to be perceptible to the human mind. For me, understandings like this make an interest in ecology, as well as spending time in the woods, so much more profoundly stimulating and rewarding.

Natural – or ecological – succession, which has already been mentioned several times, is the proper scientific term for the process by which land spontaneously transitions from one ecological state to another. It usually comes into play when an area is reverting to a richer state in the aftermath of 'disturbance'. (Another ecological term, generally meaning an externally induced change away from more normally prevailing conditions; it can be natural, such as that caused by a storm or volcano, or otherwise, for example a forest being cleared by human activity.) The natural regeneration of trees often plays a large part in succession in Ireland because the forests that once covered most of the island were removed by people, so that's the state to which nature generally tries to return if allowed. However, the two terms are not synonymous.

One of the most beautiful aspects of natural succession is the sheer magnitude of its regenerative power, bringing both inspiration and reason for great hope. It shows that nature can largely heal itself, if we only remove some of the impediments we generally keep firmly and relentlessly in its way, the imposition of artificial grazing regimes being by far the most widespread and significant.

In the late summer of 2020 I sold off all our 34 sheep, mostly at Kenmare mart, the rest to neighbours. Three of the small and hardy variety of cattle known as Dexters, which come with an either black or ginger red coat, then arrived to take their place; two of them turned out to be in calf, quickly almost doubling numbers. Originally bred in the eighteenth century from local mountain cattle in the southwest of Ireland, and probably not dissimilar to the first bovines brought to Ireland by Neolithic farmers, they are well adapted to rough ground and harsh Atlantic weather.

Before ever getting the sheep, my first preference had been Galloway cattle, a long-haired Scottish breed that's also perfectly at home in mountainous ground. Mike Caupey had suggested going for sheep instead, and, knowing little or nothing at the time about livestock, I followed his advice, but the idea never went away. Periodically, whenever the sheep were causing me particularly extreme levels of grief, by breaking into neighbouring mountain commonages, for example, in desperation my mind would start plotting a switch to cattle.

These thoughts were usually short-lived, given the trouble and expense of establishing a herd, and learning the ropes of something new. However, one day while having to carry a very weak ewe down off the mountain on my back, over the roughest of ground with deep *fionnán*, any remaining resistance gave way. I had plenty of cause to seriously question my own sanity as I repeatedly stumbled and fell under her dead weight. (Happily, she revived soon after; it took me a good while longer.)

There are also very sound ecological motives for replacing sheep with tough mountain cattle like Dexters and, thinking back, I now realise that these, even more so than the hassle, were the main reason why I never took to sheep farming. In all my dealings with the sheep, at the back of my mind there was always an acute awareness of how damaging they are to natural ecosystems, and of how that contradicted everything else I was trying to do (even if they were on the commonage, which would remain overgrazed by other shareholders' sheep whether my few were there or not). That served to put a constant damper on any enthusiasm there might otherwise have been, with the result that I never put the required time and effort into properly training the dog, for example, making everything far more difficult. A well-trained working dog is essential with mountain sheep.

Being non-selective browsers, if only allowed periodic access to ground and kept in low enough densities, cattle are far more likely to allow the recovery of a patchwork of natural habitats, including native forest and wildflower meadows. (Although *any* herbivores, including cattle, will graze land to the quick if overstocked.) The high levels of ground disturbance their hooves create in more trampled spots provide opportunities for native tree seeds and insect-eating birds. If organic, as ours are, the absence of biocidal chemicals, like avermectins in cattle dung, also helps promote a range of ecologically important invertebrates, such as dung beetles.

Maggie, Gertrude, Amber, Nelly and Minnie mostly alternate between the mountain commonage in summer and the 8.5-acre piece of ground above the road in winter. By then, the deciduous tree saplings coming up everywhere have dropped their leaves, and are therefore left undamaged by browsing. In effect, it's combining High Nature Value farming with something akin to the age-old traditional practice of seasonal grazing called booleying, which survived in folk memory in the Eyeries district until at least the 1950s.

As things progress, it will be exciting, and hopefully instructive also, to compare and contrast that with the ongoing rewilding of the other 21.5 acres, where wild sika will begin to sometimes pass through as the deer fence deteriorates. (I also experimented with putting the Dexters in for a few weeks in early 2022 to increase disturbance levels.) Whatever the divergences, both areas will be unequivocally continuing in the direction of augmented wildness and species diversity.

For me, the aim is finding workable compromises between making a partial living from the land within the present agricultural framework, while at the same time trying to achieve the best possible outcomes for wild nature.

Another of the ecological concepts that describes what I have experienced partaking in, and watching, the return to health of the Bofickil woods is hinted at above, and captured in the greatly underrated word 'stochasticity'.

Maybe a good way to explain what it means is to start by naming its opposite: determinism, i.e. when a result is predetermined by existing factors. Stochasticity, on the other hand, is where the range of variables influencing the outcome, and how they interact, is so broad as to make it impossible to anticipate what the exact result will be. From what I have seen, natural succession is a pretty stochastic process; indeed, the natural world as a whole operates in a non-linear, even chaotically harmonious, way.

It's true that the onset of natural regeneration once the deer fence went up was largely predictable, determined by the presence of mature trees as seed sources, and suitable conditions for local wild trees and other plants to germinate and grow. But what can never be foreseen is the form it will take in any one part of the land, with regard to species composition, density, rate of change, the arrival of ground flora, and so on. The spectrum of factors deciding how any particular patch will end up are extremely diverse, and the interplay between them makes for a practically endless variety of unpredictable results.

How could it be known beforehand that a jay will bury an acorn in a particular spot, or whether that spot will have the right conditions for germination, or to carry on to maturity even if it does? Or that an unseasonably violent storm will come slamming in from the Atlantic in late spring when most of the trees are already in leaf, tearing some of them down and opening gaps in the canopy, allowing light to flood in and give life to an oak seedling waiting patiently below? Multiply that basic concept to almost infinity, and you begin to see how marvellously non-deterministic is the living world. And wouldn't it all be so much less wonderful and fascinating were it otherwise?

There are areas of very vigorous natural regeneration here on open ground where it seems clear enough what's going on. As I said earlier, perhaps the spot is relatively sheltered from the prevailing southwesterly wind, or it never completely dries out, even in summer droughts. Or maybe the soil was laid bare by machinery during the erection of the deer fence, recreating the disturbed conditions that pioneering birch and sally seeds evolved to take advantage of (following in the wake of retreating glaciers after an ice age, for example).

But there are also plenty of patches that defy any such obvious explanations as to why the process is taking place especially quickly, or slowly, or in a particular way. And the more I have seen of natural succession in Bofickil, and learned of woodland ecology, the more I am convinced that often the principal factor at work is a mostly invisible one. That is, the presence, or otherwise, of a fungal network underground.

Some of the relatively recent (and still rapidly unfolding) advances in forest ecology would be dismissed as crazed science-fiction fantasies were they not now well established as scientific fact. And the most mind-bending of all may well be those relating to the complex and crucial symbiotic relationships between mycorrhizal (fungal) networks and trees.

The Bofickil woods in autumn present spectacular displays of fungi of all shapes, sizes and colours. They include the tiniest, most delicate, often semi-translucent little growths, which you would never notice at all if you didn't put your face right down to the leaf litter, or a moss-covered bank. Others approach the dimensions of dinner plates, with every size in between. Colours range from subdued variations of brown, grey and cream, to bright yellow, purple, white, orange, pink, black and red with white spots – the poisonous fly agaric so familiar from fairytale book illustrations.

Even among those with the more classic mushroom shape of cap and stalk, the latter often decorated with a frilly ring or two part ways up, there is great variation, from dainty and ethereal to stout and beefy. Then there is a bewildering assortment of fantastical other forms, such as puffballs, which, when mature, spontaneously peel open to reveal a hollow inside, and emit a cloud of dust-like spores if they receive a knock. To walk in the woods in fungi season is to enter another, magical world.

There are about 5,500 known species of fungi in Ireland,

but the real number is estimated to be way higher, at around 9,000. And if distinguishing them wasn't already challenging enough, the same species can look radically different through the various stages of its development. As with the invertebrates, bryophytes and lichens, I therefore never seriously attempted to identify the fungi in the woods beyond the more obvious or striking ones: again, I'm happy to simply enjoy the visual show every autumn.

However, extremely beautiful and fascinating as they are in their own right, the fungi that appear in the woods are merely the transient fruiting bodies of a huge and ever-present underground web. Ecologist Anja Murray described that relationship perfectly in an episode of her wonderful 'Nature File' on Lyric FM radio: what we see above ground is similar to the fruit that appears on an apple tree in the autumn, except the tree that produces them is invisible, hidden beneath the ground under our feet.

One of the most important things that can happen in the life of a tree seedling struggling to survive and grow is that its roots connect early on with an already existing mycorrhizal network, or mycelium, in the surrounding soil. With no leaves or chlorophyll, fungi can't photosynthesise, and therefore have no means of making food for themselves as plants do. One way of getting around that is to simply take the nutrients they need from either living or dead and decomposing organic matter such as wood, feeding on them as herbivorous animals do on leaves and grass. (So when old bread in your cupboard goes mouldy, it's just fungi doing their job.)

Another is to create a partnership with plants, in which they provide each other with essential services they need to live. The vast majority of land plants are largely dependent on just such an association with fungi, and trees are no exception. The microscopic filaments of the fungi surround or even tap into the roots of a tree, becoming a sort of extension of the root that exponentially increases its abilities to access water, minerals, and other things the tree requires from the soil. In return, the tree provides the mycorrhiza with some of the proceeds of the food production that it's able to carry out in its leaves. Some species of fungi are host-specific, preferring to work only with one or a few specific plant species, while others are more easy-going regarding who they hook up with – the libertines of the mycorrhizal community.

But the benefits to the arboreal party to the bargain go way further. The mycelial network links the trees of the forest together, acting as a means by which the trees help each other out, and even communicate. Water, food in the form of carbohydrates, and other essential resources are sent via the fungi from mature trees to seedlings struggling to get established. Old dying trees similarly use them as pathways for bequeathing their accumulated reserves to the healthy trees around them.

Based on many years of research in the temperate rainforests of western North America, forest ecologist Professor Suzanne Simard estimated that connecting with a fungal web increases a seedling's chances of survival *fourfold*. That might explain why, in the open areas around the margins of the Bofickil woods, it's common to find a cluster of naturally regenerated saplings – often of different species – growing together, but with no others anywhere around for quite a distance. Maybe they got lucky, and germinated in the vicinity of a mycorrhiza.

Trees also use these underground networks as a means by

which to 'speak' to one another – not in the way we do of course, but by using chemical, hormonal and electrical signals to pass on useful information. For example, an oak at one end of a forest might find itself under heavy attack from a certain species of caterpillar (it can tell which one by their salival secretions). It will then pass on that information, giving the other trees time to prepare their defences by increasing levels of the chemical tannin in their leaves, or even emitting scent that summons parasites to attack the caterpillars. Trees also communicate with one another by releasing into the air a variety of pheromones that convey certain messages.

One of the most amazing aspects of the association between trees and these fungal circuits is that the actions they facilitate transcend some surprising boundaries. Trees don't only pass excess resources on to, or communicate with, their own specific offspring (although they *are* able to distinguish, and do favour, these), or even just other individuals of their own species. They actually do so *between* species as well, acting together like members of a sort of local community self-help group. And it makes total sense: trees do so much better in a diverse, multilayered, forest environment – where they can create together the conditions that are to their liking, i.e. mild, moist and stable – than when isolated and vulnerable.

I see the evidence of that everywhere in and around the Bofickil woods: lone trees struggle to survive and are more prone to suffer or die in long droughts, for example, while those that grow together are far more resilient and likely to flourish. It was similarly noted that elm trees in woodland had better rates of survival during the Dutch elm disease epidemic in the 1970s and 1980s than those growing alone or in hedgerows. The reasons for this were probably various, but trees generally prosper to a far greater degree when part of a woodland community, which is by and large their natural habitat. Like ourselves, they are mostly highly social creatures.

A single myco-net can extend over many acres, and numerous such overlapping and interconnected webs allow the whole forest to work together, making it a real 'super-organism'. Here, the idea of clearly distinct individual organisms – and even of separate species – becomes blurred. Darwin's theory of evolution, which was so revolutionary in advancing an evidence-based comprehension of how life on our planet works, held that it's all about ceaselessly intense competition, with every individual struggling to survive in an adversarial 'red in tooth and claw' world. And that certainly is a big part of the equation: trees in a forest compete vigorously with their neighbours for the resources they need, such as space, light, water and minerals in the soil.

But there's clearly another side to the coin of life too: one of close, at times symbiotic, cooperation among separate organisms and different species, of working together with one another for the common good. Nor is there any shortage of other examples of such mutualism in the workings of natural systems generally: quite the contrary. In fact, evolutionary biologist Lynn Margulis posited that symbiosis, rather than competition, between species is actually the primary driving force behind evolution itself. As she put it: 'Life did not take over the globe by combat, but by networking.'

Rather than opposites, however, the reality is probably closer to their being, again, two sides of the same coin, with an infinity of incessant interplays between.

The American plant ecologist Frank Egler really did nail it when he said: 'Not only are ecosystems more complex than we think, they are more complex than we *can* think.' For Professor Simard, the symbiosis between trees and mycorrhizae shares much in common with the human brain:

> I've used the word intelligence in my writing because I think that scientifically we attribute intelligence to certain structures and functions. When we dissect a plant and the forest and look at those things – Does it have a neural network? Is there communication? Is there perception and reception of messages? Will you change behaviors depending on what you're perceiving? Do you remember things? Do you learn things? Would you do something differently if you had experienced something in the past? – those are all hallmarks of intelligence. Plants do have intelligence. They have all the structures. They have all the functions. They have the behaviors.

None of this should be misinterpreted, for example by thinking of trees along the lines of the 'ents' in Tolkien's fantasy *The Lord of the Rings*. The intelligence Simard speaks of is a very different one to our own, or that of other animals. As the journalist Brandon Keim put it while interviewing Simard:

Are there things we're missing in plants because our concepts of intelligence are drawn from humans and from animals? There could be whole ways of being we don't even have words for.

Keim's last sentence hints at one of the great obstacles to our trying to conceive of the natural world in non-human terms: the limitations of language itself, and therefore in our ability to place ourselves beyond our own restricted vision of things. Like many other aspects of life on our astonishing planet, the fungi–trees partnership stretches those mental frontiers in no small way. In a somewhat ironic imitation of our online 'world wide web', this linked-up ecological community is sometimes referred to as the 'wood wide web'. (Ironic because mycorrhizal networks were, after all, around for hundreds of millions of years before us.)

Again, it's perhaps wise to be a little cautious in conceiving of wild species and ecosystems in overly human terms – an approach called anthropomorphising, which can risk diminishing real understanding. But some use of metaphorical language is probably also harmless, and even beneficial, if it helps convey the truth that there are many more layers of complexity and meaning to healthy native forests and other natural ecosystems than meet the eye.

And it might also help bring home another, equally vital, truth: rather than being merely standing pillars of timber or carbon, wild native trees are deserving of deep respect as fellow citizens of the planet we all share. Indeed, the same thought should apply to all components, both living and non-living, of all natural ecosystems, from the apparently insignificant to the most magnificent.

To the whole biosphere itself.

17

The Narrow Strip
of Earth/Air/Water

Seánie had an early-afternoon dental appointment in Kenmare, and the two of us made a deal that, rather than him going to school for the morning, we'd cheekily spend it together revisiting Uragh Woods by the shores of Lough Inchiquin on the way.

We found the 200-acre NPWS-managed forest in exactly the same desperately wrecked state as it had been for years, stripped bare by sika deer, feral goats, sheep and now even cattle. The fence erected to keep them out had long ago collapsed in many places, and the only natural regeneration of trees was in the very few spots inaccessible to herbivores: in the crevices of sheer rock faces, or at the top of the upturned rootplates of storm-blown trees.

Though there was still no sign of any rhododendron, it had extended its range on the other side of the lake, and it was purely a question of time before the tiny seeds would blow across into the woods. They would then find the denuded woodland floor ideal for germination and rapid spread. In the sheep-shorn grasslands all around the forest were the remains of ancient tree stumps exposed in the peat, a vision of the destiny facing the woods on their current trajectory.

By now I was more fully aware of the fact that Uragh (from *An Iúrach* – 'Place of the Yew Trees') was one of the very few fragments of forest in Beara to have escaped the seventeenth- and eighteenth-century clearances. It is thus among the less than 0.1 per cent of Ireland still covered by ancient, i.e. pre-1660, woodland. (Think about that for a moment: *less than a tenth of 1 per cent*, none of which has itself escaped the severe impacts of thousands of years of human activities.)

Uragh is home to numerous massive old oaks, as well as aspen, rowan, holly, hazel, willow, alder and other tree species, all thickly draped in epiphytes, leaving no room for doubt that this is full-blown rainforest. As we walked through the woods, their upper reaches shrouded in thick billowing mists, we saw signs of pine marten, and heard the shrill, haunting cries of a peregrine falcon high overhead; despite the neglect, the area was still rich in fauna. As ever, it struck me as yet another measure of just how little importance is given to natural heritage in Ireland, that even these last surviving biological treasure houses are just being left to languish and die. If we're incapable of even protecting such tiny but priceless remnants, what hope is there for the rest of nature in Ireland? I decided there and then to try to raise awareness of Uragh's dire condition.

Using images taken with my phone, I put together an illustrated narrative for my Twitter account (@IrishRainforest) relating the situation at Uragh. From the moment the 'thread' went live there was a flood of reaction, not only in Ireland but far beyond, with many thousands of 'retweets' and 'likes'. Everywhere, there was outrage that such a rare and exquisite habitat could be simply abandoned to slow decline, an indication of just how strong a connection people feel with our vanished – and still vanishing – rainforests. For many, the discovery that Irish rainforests are even a thing at all arouses immense surprise and curiosity.

Within less than a week, the issue was being raised in the Dáil by TD Neasa Hourigan. She obtained an assurance from the minister responsible, Malcolm Noonan, that a new deer fence would be erected around Uragh the following year, and other measures put in place to preserve and revitalise its ecology. Thanks to the support that thread received from people far and wide, Uragh and all the life it contains should finally get the protection they so deserve, at least for a while.

But it's no more than a drop in the ocean of what needs to be done. Killarney National Park, and most other vestiges of temperate rainforest, the incredibly rich natural biome of much of this island, remain firmly on the path to ecological oblivion.

'The narrow strip of earth/air/water on our planet which constitutes the biosphere', as my dad described it in his letter to *The Irish Times* over half a century ago, rarely enters our consciousness. It shouldn't be that way. It is our beautiful and precious living home, and, being realistic, is more than likely to remain the only one we'll ever have.

As the relatively thin zone in which all life exists, the biosphere is composed of the sum of all the planet's interconnected ecosystems, which work together as a sort of 'super-ecosystem'. Apart from radiation arriving from the sun and space, and heat from the Earth's core, it's essentially a closed system, its energies endlessly circulating within. It is also now generally accepted to be self-regulating, meaning that it generates and maintains the relatively stable conditions that promote the very life it contains. Just as our bodies regulate their own temperatures and chemistry, for example, so does the biosphere make and keep the planet habitable through natural ecosystem processes.

The concept of a self-regulating Earth was explored by a variety of belief systems and individual thinkers in the past. The previously mentioned Aldo Leopold, for example, discussed the possibilities in his 1923 essay 'Some Fundamentals of Conservation in the Southwest'. However, the first to begin to set out the scientific basis for the idea was James Lovelock, the same independent British scientist who found that naturally regenerated wild trees had fared so much better than those he had planted on his land in Devon.

More famously, in the 1950s Lovelock had invented the electron capture detector, which revealed the terrible damage that widely used pesticides, above all dichloro-diphenyl-trichloroethane (DDT), were causing to ecosystems. A deathly silence had fallen over much of the countryside, as songbird populations disappeared due to eating poisoned invertebrates. Toxin levels became ever more concentrated as DDT worked its way up to the top of the food chain, almost wiping out peregrine falcons and other predators.

The results led to biologist Rachel Carson's seminal work on the subject, *Silent Spring*, published in 1962. Vicious attacks and attempts at suppression from the chemical industry lobby at the time largely failed, and the book brought about a mass awakening of ecological consciousness, practically launching the modern environmental movement. In many countries bans were imposed on DDT for most applications in the 1970s and '80s, and worldwide from 2004, bringing a rebound among affected species.

Through his electron capture detector, Lovelock was also the first to discover the presence of ozone-depleting chlorofluorocarbons (CFCs) in the atmosphere. Consequently, their production was ultimately phased out globally, allowing a gradual recovery of the ozone layer, which is essential in shielding the Earth from the sun's harmful ultraviolet radiation.

Lovelock's 'eureka moment' in viewing Earth as a self-regulating system came in late 1965, while working for NASA in a laboratory in California. He had been asked by the space institute to devise a means for detecting possible signs of life on Mars from afar, causing him to consider how that might be done if one were looking at Earth instead. He soon realised that the clearest giveaway would be in the respective atmospheres.

While that of Mars was only 0.17 per cent oxygen, but nearly 95 per cent carbon dioxide (CO_2), by contrast ours consisted of 21 per cent oxygen and only 0.032 per cent CO_2 (in 1965: it has greatly increased since then). The *only* way oxygen is produced naturally on Earth is through photosynthesis – by either land plants or marine phytoplankton. Before the appearance of life on Earth some 3.5 billion years ago, there was virtually no free oxygen in the atmosphere, but levels have remained constantly within the narrow parameters required by life itself ever since.

So the biosphere has effectively been maintaining the gaseous mix it needs for all that time. Seeing things from this perspective caused Lovelock to start looking holistically at other ways in which Earth's natural ecosystems create the planetary conditions conducive to life, and to develop his ideas into a scientific hypothesis. He later named it after Gaia, the ancient Greek Earth mother goddess, as suggested to him in conversation by friend and fellow scientist, the well-known writer William Golding (author of *Lord of the Flies* and other books).

Throughout this period, i.e. the 1960s and 1970s, Lovelock and his family were spending much of the year in a house they had bought west of Adrigole, on the south coast of the Beara Peninsula.

There he established an onsite atmospheric monitoring station, which played a primary role in revealing the global CFC problem. With a large veranda overlooking Bantry Bay, Sheep's Head and Roancarrigmore Island lighthouse, *Ard Carrig* still sits at the very base of Hungry Hill, whose image had first drawn my attention to the area over two decades ago. Lovelock described it as a 'dream place', and he wrote his first book on Gaia there:

> I used to sit on my favourite slab of rock overlooking Bantry Bay and the broad Atlantic. Here I would think through scientific problems that were my life's work and here I composed my first book, *Gaia: A New Look at Life on Earth*. I wrote it almost entirely in the cottage below.
>
> As I sat in the warm sun on my ledge, high up on the

sandstone slabs of Hungry Hill, it was not easy to think about the Earth in any way except romantically. I composed the book as if I were writing a long love letter to a woman I had never met. I saw her as someone intelligent, lively, and full of fun, but not as a scientist.

It is clear from his autobiography that Lovelock and his family fell utterly in love with Beara – both the landscape and the people. He wrote that they would have made the peninsula their permanent all-year-round home, but for the fact that the isolated location would have made it very difficult to remain at the cutting edge of modern science, especially in those pre-internet times. It's tempting to consider the possibility that passing so much happy time in such a wild and beautiful spot on the edge of the Atlantic might, in some way, have contributed to the conception of the Gaia hypothesis. And the way in which the place clearly coloured Lovelock's thoughts while writing his book on the subject almost seems to hint that there may have been something of that at play.

In reality, however, its genesis of course lay purely in scientific reason and evidence, rather than any sort of 'feel-good factor'. But I'm probably incapable of objectivity on this, given the degree to which my own personal relationship with, and perception of, our living planet has been so thoroughly transformed since moving to Beara. So there may well be a risk of fanciful thinking on my part; it really is an extremely special part of the world.

As the wider scientific community became more aware of Gaia into the late 1970s, the idea began to arouse a fair degree of controversy, and was far from universally accepted. There were several criticisms, perhaps the principal one relating to the fact that it seemed to many to be suggesting that the Earth was somehow a form of living being and, crucially, that it was able to act with intent or purpose. Another was the issue of what mechanism could possibly have given rise to the Earth becoming self-regulating, since it couldn't have come about via evolution by natural selection, responsible for all actual organisms.

A further major problem was the highly cross-disciplinary nature of the theory, because science had become increasingly reductionist, with specialist practitioners unwilling or unable to grapple with matters outside their own narrow field of expertise. Despite its origin as a primordial goddess in Greek mythology, even the choice of name – Gaia – attracted hostility, seeming to smack of new-agey, cult-like beliefs, rather than actual science.

However, things have since moved on, and these objections largely resolved. Lovelock and his principal collaborator, Lynn Margulis, were consistent throughout in denying claims that there is any intentionality implied in the process of self-regulation. He also pointed out that, just as with most other new scientific theories, there are aspects that still remain to be understood, such as how self-regulation might have come about. Importantly, Lovelock realised and admitted an initial inherent mistake: '... my error [was in] writing "life regulates the Earth". I should have said Gaia is made of living organisms and the material Earth and she regulates herself.' A subtle, but vital, difference: just as any ecosystem is composed of a great variety of closely integrated elements, whose nature is both living and non-living, so is our biosphere.

In the meantime, the scientific evidence to back up the fundamental veracity of Gaia theory has also been steadily accumulating from ever more quarters, as we reach deeper understandings of how our home planet works. This has been paralleled by analogous advances in thinking around systems theory, which finds that interconnectivity and complexity are fundamental to the coherence of all systems, not least natural ones. As described by Jeremy Lent (the italics are mine):

> The systems perspective offers important insights into the nature of reality that upend many assumptions forming the basis of the predominant [reductionist] worldview. It tells us that *the relationship between things is frequently more important than the things themselves*. It emphasizes that everything in the natural world is dynamic rather than static and that biological phenomena can't be predicted with precision: instead of fixed laws, we therefore need to search for the underlying organizing principles of nature. These principles, it reveals, occur across widely different domains, from heart rhythms to climate variations and from lake ecologies to internet social media connections. It also shows how self-organized systems are fractally embedded within one another: a cell may be part of an organism, which is part of a community, which is nested within an ecosystem, which in turn is part of Gaia.

Thus an essential prerequisite to any real understanding of an ecosystem, ranging in scale from a rock pool to a fragment of Irish Atlantic rainforest in Bofickil, from the Amazon to the biosphere itself, is to see it as far more than the sum of its parts. Systems theory also further corroborates the crucial point that ecosystem function and resilience depend on having as many component parts present as possible. As regards the name Gaia, less offensive alternative options along the lines of 'earth system science' or 'geophysiology' have been suggested, including by Lovelock himself. But Gaia seems to resonate with people, and has stuck.

The single most important message to take from Gaian science is that our planet is only inhabitable for one sole reason: its wild, natural ecosystems make it so.

The word 'ecosystem', an amalgam of 'ecological system', was first made known in 1935 by the British ecologist Arthur Tansley. For me, its meaning was superbly captured in a couple of almost throwaway lines written by Susan Wright and Peter Cairns: '... a forest, a wetland, a peatland or a river is less of a physical entity and more a set of dynamic processes with no pre-determined end point.'

The concept of ecosystem has been a central theme throughout this book, and not without reason. The more I have thought – and learned from those much wiser and more knowledgeable than me – about the natural world and our planet, the more it has become apparent that everything depends utterly on healthily functioning wild natural ecosystems. That might appear to be stating the blindingly obvious, but a quick look at the way societies across the globe are trying to confront the rapidly unfolding perfect storm of environmental meltdown very much suggests otherwise.

To give one example close to home: in 2019 the Irish government announced plans to plant 22 million trees per year for the next two decades, a total of 440 million. This is being trumpeted as an ambitious means of combating possibly the greatest existential threat we have ever faced: climate breakdown. On the face of it, such a major tree-planting project seems like a very positive development. As mentioned above, in 1965 CO_2 levels in the Earth's atmosphere were at 0.032 per cent, already significantly elevated due to human activities relative to the approximately 0.028 per cent at which they had stabilised for the previous 10,000 years. But in May 2019 they reached nearly 0.042 per cent, the highest in the last *15 million years*. And emissions are still continually rising, with a record-smashing 36.3 billion tons loaded into the atmosphere in 2021 alone.

Scientists are now as unanimously agreed as ever happens on the correlation between rises or falls in atmospheric CO_2 levels and global temperatures (albeit with a time lag, one of the most unfortunate and problematic aspects of our predicament). In effect, the gas acts as a pretty precise 'control lever' on planetary heat levels. Every country has a deep responsibility to do all it can to reverse the dangerous trend of rapidly rising levels, particularly in wealthy parts of the world like Ireland, where per capita emissions are by far the highest – both historically and to the present day. So efforts at mitigation through forest creation should normally be welcomed; but not in this case.

It turns out that 70 per cent of the proposed new trees will be plantations of non-native sitka spruce conifers and suchlike, while the rest will be 'broadleaf', presumably native, but again largely in monocultures. The forestry industry and relevant authorities will claim that trees of any sort suck CO_2 down out of the atmosphere, and that when they are then cut down and made into things we need, carbon is locked up for a lengthy period. But that reasoning is false, for it ignores a range of issues, and not only will it not work, it will actually make things worse. To illustrate, researchers recently found that a 10 per cent increase in European 'forest' cover between 1750 and 2010 (an extra 200,000 square kilometres of trees) had led to a counterintuitive temperature *rise* of around 0.12 degrees across the region. The reason why is that the trees were mostly non-native conifers.

Forests don't only help regulate the climate by absorbing CO_2. In a process called transpiration, they release vast quantities of water through their leaves as part of the hydrological cycle, creating clouds that reflect solar radiation back into space. The Amazon alone, for example, releases 20 billion tons of water into the atmosphere every single day. But conifers like sitka have water-retaining needles rather than leaves, and are therefore far less effective in that role. Compared to most native trees in temperate regions like Ireland, they are also very dark, and dark surfaces absorb heat, rather than reflect it as lighter ones do (this is known as the 'albedo effect'), thereby raising temperatures.

But even as regards carbon sequestration and storage, non-native conifer plantations fail miserably. Almost 75 per cent of the carbon storage potential of temperate forests is in the soil, rather than the actual trees themselves. In a natural forest, most of the carbon drawn from the atmosphere and stored in the trees' trunks, branches, leaves and roots remains in the ecosystem. In the stable cool and moist conditions of the woodland floor, the constant fall of dead woody material is converted into humus (the organic part of soil) by the actions of an army of bacteria, invertebrates and fungi, thereby indefinitely locking up the carbon they contain. The longer natural forests are allowed to age gracefully, not only is their ecological value continually enhanced, but also the more carbon they are able to store.

Plantations, on the other hand, are regularly thinned, clear-felled and then replanted, all of which disturbs the soil and releases carbon. In Ireland, they're generally sited on agriculturally marginal land or peat, and vast quantities of carbon are lost from such soils over the course of planting and harvesting. The result is that, on balance, carbon is actually *emitted*, rather than captured. Nor should plantation monocultures of broadleaf – including native – species be considered much better: they are not natural or functioning ecological systems. A recent report published in *Nature* magazine concluded that natural forests in the tropics store *40 times* more carbon than plantations in the same zones.

There is no reason to believe that the ratio between natural forests and plantations in Ireland is any less; in fact, it's likely to be far more. According to some, temperate rainforests accumulate 'more organic matter than any other forest ecosystem on Earth'. Many other undisturbed wild natural ecosystems, such as mangrove swamps, salt marsh, kelp forests and seagrass beds are also excellent at locking down CO_2. Among the best of them are peat bogs, which can sequester 0.7 tons of carbon per hectare per year. As with all other natural ecosystems, the restoration of Irish bogs through rewetting should be urgently prioritised; generally all it takes is to block up the drains that were dug to dry them out.

Even more important, in my view, than their capacity to stabilise the climate, natural ecosystems like wild native forests are of course also essential habitats for collapsing wildlife populations. Ecological breakdown, the other existential environmental crisis, is already occurring on a massive scale across the planet. We continue to ruthlessly erase wild habitat – primarily for agriculture – and empty the world of wildlife of every type, from elephants and lions down to the tiniest insects and beyond.

Many people, myself included, believe this to be an, if anything, even more pressing issue than climate breakdown, though both problems are of course inextricably linked, and exacerbate each other greatly. Yet the ecological catastrophe receives only a small fraction of the (already grossly inadequate) media attention given to the climate. As a consequence, the general public is either largely unaware of it, or of how bad the situation really is.

The protection and restoration of what remains of natural ecosystems, and allowing them to return where they have been destroyed in the past, is the most effective, tried-and-tested solution to the death of nature, and also an essential weapon against climate breakdown. Monoculture plantations, even of native trees, are a disaster for wildlife, the climate and local communities, and the idea that increasing their area can in any way constitute a valid response to the present situation defies all logic and reason. So why do governments in Ireland and across the world continue down the senseless path of plantations? And there's no end of other instances of similarly myopic actions, which dispense with natural ecosystems for short-term, and usually illusory, gain.

Local to Beara, in 2014 a licence was granted to industrially extract 1,860 acres of wild native kelp forest from Bantry Bay, mainly for use as animal feed additives. Kelp forests, like coral reefs often described as 'the rainforests of the sea', are extremely rich habitats, providing food, shelter and spawning grounds for a great plethora of marine life. They're also highly effective as carbon sinks, and at buffering coasts from storm surges: extremely important considerations as climate breakdown worsens. Several applications have been filed to machine-cut wild kelp forests in other localities on the west coast, and the stiff resistance mounted by the local community of Bantry Bay is probably the only thing blocking a bigger roll-out for now.

Across much of Europe and the world, there's a drive to build hydroelectric dams as a means of producing 'clean, renewable' energy, disregarding the fact that they necessitate drowning large areas of habitat, and prevent river ecosystems from functioning. Using the same 'clean, green' rationale, some of the most biodiverse old-growth forests on the planet are being razed on a vast scale to produce millions of tons of 'biomass' every year for burning in Europe's electricity plants.

The list of examples of such obtuse thinking goes on and on. And as has been pointed out, 'A bulldozer run on hydrogen produced from a wind farm can still decimate a tropical rain forest.' The question isn't just how we produce energy: equally important is what we then do with it. Genuinely clean, renewable energy is definitely the direction we need to be heading in as rapidly as possible, but *not* where it comes at the expense of natural ecosystems. They must be paramount, a message that's just not getting through.

Are we completely mad? Any objective analysis (and there's plenty of it) shows unequivocally that, as a species, we are behaving as if we were. But rather than madness, the principal driver is now very clearly a ferociously aggressive economic system – capitalism – and associated culture that places greatest value on all the wrong things. Endless hyper-consumption, mostly of throwaway tat, to facilitate equally endless wealth accumulation by a tiny few, is given precedence over living systems, people, and all else.

All too often, there's a total absence of understanding as to the centrality of wild natural ecosystems in the healthy functioning of our environment, and therefore every aspect of human society. We carry on as if the constructs we've created existed autonomously from nature, despite all scientific evidence and reason telling us the very opposite is true. The human economy is always placed first in our order of priorities ('after all, it's the bottom line'), while the natural world is actually treated as expendable – an 'externality', to use the language of economics. It should be the diametric opposite: the economy is wholly dependent on the natural sphere in every way. Where does that 'bottom line' fit on a dying planet?

The only *real* bottom lines are biophysical and ecological ones. The present economic framework demands perpetual growth, an ecocidal – and therefore suicidal – approach on what is very definitely a finite world. As David Attenborough put it: 'Anyone who thinks you can have infinite growth in a finite environment is either a madman or an economist.' Yet that model is almost never challenged by mainstream parties from across the political spectrum, either on the right *or* left.

Quite the opposite: economic growth is still generally seen as the primary measure of societal well-being, the main point of disagreement revolving around how fairly the proceeds of plundering the natural world should be shared out. I'm very firmly with the left here: people must all be treated equally, but other species and the ecosystems of which they're a part have to have rights too. And it needs to be clearly understood that all growth inevitably *does* come at the expense of the living world: the idea that it can somehow be 'decoupled' from environmental destruction is a complete fallacy, cynically used to justify a business-as-usual approach.

All the deforestation, overfishing, strip mining, liquidation of wild ecosystems, pollution of skies, seas, land, rivers and other life-killing activities currently taking place on such a huge scale: all these directly contribute to gross domestic product (GDP). On the other hand, setting a natural forest, or any other life-giving system, aside from exploitation does nothing to add to GDP, and is therefore ascribed zero worth, platitudes aside. Increased GDP and economic growth in general is always unquestioningly celebrated as somehow 'a good thing' – in the news, by politicians, and by 'economics experts'.

It really is as if selling our own, or our children's, body parts on a continual basis were universally accepted as positive, just because someone was making money from it. Somehow we have managed to create a parallel universe for ourselves, in which the illusions we've built are given more weight than actual physical realities. But of course physical realities never allow themselves to be brushed aside for ever: they always come back to bite in the end. That moment is upon us.

Just as with climate and ecological breakdown, the scientific consensus on the question of growth is overwhelming.

A joint statement by over 11,000 scientists in November 2019 included the following: 'Our goals need to shift from GDP growth and the pursuit of affluence toward sustaining ecosystems and improving human well-being.' In May 2019 the government of New Zealand announced that it is moving away from the use of GDP as the main indicator of national well-being towards a more balanced model. This and other examples from around the world show that a change in direction *is* possible.

Unfortunately, however, our problems go much deeper than just economics. Aside from small numbers of people in some surviving tribal cultures, as a species we appear to have learned some profoundly mistaken lessons from the path that has taken us to where we are now. Namely, that nature is something to be overcome, subdued and dominated, as though an enemy. That we are smarter than it. That we can always use our intellect and technologies to both manipulate the environment to obtain the results we want, and to then fix any issues arising from that.

Such an approach generally worked well enough for us in the past, with our impacts mostly limited to a local or regional level. Even then, the consequences could often be disastrous within a specific area, the evidence of what happened in Beara down through the ages just one among countless examples. Throughout human history, myriad societies have self-destructed largely because of overexploitation of their local environments. It's worth pondering one of the many stark observations Jared Diamond makes towards the end of his book on precisely that subject, *Collapse* (the emphasis is his): 'Deforestation was a or *the* major factor in all the collapses of past societies described in this book.'

At least when things went wrong in the more distant past, however, there was usually somewhere else less affected where people could move on to and start afresh. Unless, that is, they were living on a very remote island, or were surrounded by hostile neighbouring groups. But that situation has now changed radically: ecosystems – whole biomes, even – that affect the proper functioning of the entire planet are now dying, or at serious risk of doing so.

The coral reefs are rapidly being killed due to a range of human-induced factors, including warming and acidifying seas as a result of climate breakdown. And global deforestation has accelerated at a terrifying velocity, now equal to the entire land area of Britain (64 million acres) every single year, the vast majority of which is tropical rainforest, the oldest and richest repositories of biodiversity on Earth.

18

Sharing Our Earth
with Other Creatures

The 15 or so tree species in the 30 acres of the Bofickil woods is fairly diverse by Irish standards, especially for a tract of that limited size. But it pales utterly in comparison to the 600 that can be found in just one hectare (2.5 acres) of some tropical rainforests. Similarly off-the-scale levels of biological diversity are found in most other species categories in tropical forests, with as many as 60,000 different species of insects in a hectare, for example. In fact, in some of these places it's possible to stand in a single mountain spot and have an astounding one in nine of all bird species on the entire planet living within your field of vision.

But biologists consider those species of all types that we know of to be only a small fraction of what exists, with vast numbers still undiscovered. An incredible 86 per cent or more of the planet's species are estimated to remain unknown to science, and new ones continue to be found on a regular basis, often in equatorial forests. Most of these places figure among the world's 'biodiversity hotspots': areas in which the biosphere's variety of life is overwhelmingly concentrated. What accounts for the huge disparity in species richness between the tropics and temperate zones like Ireland?

There are several explanations, but antiquity is primary among them. The northern latitudes have been subject to intervals of dramatic natural climate change for millions of years (*not* to be confused with the present, human-induced and far more rapidly unfolding episode). The result has been a long succession of ice ages and brief warm interglacial periods, with, as already discussed, each ice age pushing all temperate species down into southern regions. That has allowed little time for species to diversify, which mostly happens through local populations adapting in different ways to variations in local environments over lengthy periods, a process called adaptive radiation. (The process is a two-way street, in that communities of coevolving organisms collectively shape their environments also.)

Isolated for long enough, these evolved divergences give rise to separate species, usually defined as such when they are no longer able to reproduce viably between the different populations. The negligible time opportunities for this process to take place in Europe is yet another reason why Ireland has such a reduced species range compared to other parts of the world. In stark contrast, the climate in many parts of the tropics has remained remarkably constant, often for tens of millions of years. Such enduring stability has given life the time required to evolve into mind-bogglingly diverse forms, in the most wonderfully specialised and complex relationships imaginable.

However, rather than showing any signs of relenting,

tropical deforestation continues to ramp up. Even where trees remain uncut, very often there has been a steady process of defaunation in which all the large animals have been hunted out, leading to what is termed 'empty forest syndrome'. Again, a forest isn't just trees: the animals and other elements are critical to its proper functioning, and their loss leaves it eviscerated. Like crazed pyromaniacs, we humans are burning down the most immense warehouses of planetary richness in existence, with only a very partial knowledge of what they even contain. E.O. Wilson put it thus: 'It has always been clear that the struggle to save biological diversity will be won or lost in the forests.'

In Brazil, for example, the rate of forest clearance in the Amazon to open up more land for agriculture, principally beef production, has soared dramatically to 13,235 square kilometres in the year to July 2021 alone. The cause is the government under President Bolsonaro, which came to power in January 2019 and has been actively slashing restrictions ever since. The Amazon is the planet's largest terrestrial carbon sink, and creates its own weather systems that give rise to the wet conditions the forest itself needs, as well as bringing regular and necessary rainfall to the inhabitants of the region and their farms. It also plays an indispensable role in regulating the global climate.

But scientists such as Thomas Lovejoy, who was the first to coin the term 'biological diversity' and who studied the forest from 1965 until passing away in late 2021, warn that the Amazon is reaching a long-predicted tipping point. This means that its ability to continue generating the present hydrological cycle will be so severely impaired that an enormous dieback or transformation of currently intact forest will follow. If that happens – and there's strong evidence to suggest that it has started already – vast quantities of carbon will be released into the atmosphere, with extremely grave consequences for all life on the planet, including our own.

Responding to any criticism of their actions, the governments of Brazil and other countries behaving similarly are invariably quick to point out that we in Europe destroyed most of our own natural forests long ago. (And remember: Ireland now has practically the lowest native forest cover of all.) Although a deeply dishonest argument – at this stage there is *zero* justification for destroying native, especially primary, forest anywhere – the basic truth behind it is irrefutable. The fact that Irish rainforests were cancelled from the land much earlier in time is a pretty weak defence, especially given how relentlessly we continue to prevent them from returning. In this part of the world, we are just at a far more advanced stage in the removal and suppression of original natural habitats, for the simple reason that we got out of the starting blocks much sooner.

It's often said, including by many – perhaps most – environmentalists, that 'people are part of nature too'. The truth of that is worth pondering, since where we fit, or don't fit, with nature is clearly at the core of our burgeoning problems.

For me at least, it's not quite so simple. Sure, our origins are obviously biological, in that we evolved through natural selection, and are, in that sense, just as much 'of this planet' as any other species. The whole biosphere, including us, is related, connected, born of the same stuff; and biophilia – the innate love of wild nature – seems hardwired into all of us, even if evidently closer to the surface in some than others. Above all, it's an undeniable fact that our existence depends entirely on natural processes, at every level. So we're definitely not separate from nature, despite often thinking and behaving as though we were.

Yet, as noted in Chapter 12, the dictionary on my shelf defines nature as 'the whole system of the existence, forces, and events of all physical life that are not controlled by man', which very plainly includes neither us, nor our activities. So people are only 'part of nature' if that commonly understood meaning of the word is negated. Though it's true there are other definitions more inclusive of people, if we and everything we do are part of nature, what sense can such terms as 'artificial' or 'non-natural' then have?

It would be ludicrous to claim, for example, that the Alberta tar sands oil-extraction operations, which have created ponds of toxic sludge covering 220 square kilometres, were somehow a natural phenomenon. Ditto for nuclear weapons, the highest levels of climate breakdown-causing CO_2 in the atmosphere for the last 15 million years, catastrophic levels of forest and other habitat destruction, and countless other severe human impacts on the biosphere.

Biologists are generally agreed that we are now in the midst of a mass extinction event, the sixth in the history of the planet, the last one having taken out the dinosaurs around 66 million years ago. Evidence for the present mass extinction is there all around us, especially to anyone who has 'taken the red pill'. Global populations of wild vertebrates like mammals, birds and reptiles plummeted by an average of 68 per cent in the years 1970–2016 alone, for example, just one among legions of mind-numbing statistics of this type.

The previous five mass extinctions, in each of which around 70–95 per cent of global species were killed off, were all caused by natural events. But it's not asteroid strikes or volcanic activity that are to blame this time: our species is fully responsible for what is now befalling all non-human life on Earth. And the human-caused extinction waves and erasure of natural ecosystems didn't begin any time recently either. As discussed in Chapter 13, they have been ongoing for a couple of million years, albeit gathering speed and momentum throughout, slowly building up to the current maelstrom of violence towards the living world. So we can't just pass them off as purely the product of our present form of economic system, technological capabilities, or dominant culture, however much these may have exponentially supercharged impacts – as they most certainly have.

Can a species *really* be said to still be 'part of nature', though actively and rapidly wiping it out on a planetary scale? And, if we are to fully accept that argument, how then to counter those who take it to a logical extreme, claiming we needn't worry too much about all the destruction, since everything people do is 'part of nature' anyhow? Whole books could be written on this, but the answers are obviously far from straightforward.

An easier question is why our behaviour is so hugely damaging, compared to all other species. From a purely ecological perspective, it seems clear that the kernel of the problem lies in our evolutionary past, and stems from the very characteristic that most defines us. Essentially, the cognitive breakthroughs we achieved that ultimately make us human began a slow process of release from the ecological constraints that govern all other species, and keep them in balance with their environments. It was this declaration of 'independence from biology', as Yuval Noah Harari put it, which allowed our 'breakout' from east Africa, along with subsequent expansion across, and eventual domination of, the entire planet.

Hence becoming human unwittingly entailed gradually setting ourselves apart from the rest of nature, with the gap growing progressively wider ever since – the real Exile from Eden. That process has been greatly exacerbated and accelerated over time by the collective adoption of increasingly anthropocentric worldviews that place people and the natural world in separate spheres, with us at the centre and the latter as mere 'stuff' for our use.

We don't trash wild nature because we are somehow innately 'bad', however. Rather, we do so simply because we see the results as beneficial to ourselves in the immediate term, and above all because we can, having figured out how, unlike any other species. Correspondingly, the consequences for wild species and ecosystems are given too little consideration or importance: throughout our evolution, doing otherwise was rarely a prerequisite for survival, so it doesn't come easily to us now.

But we are not mindless automatons, programmed like daleks to exterminate. The very cognitive capacities that brought us such 'success' as a species can be used to start putting things right. In fact, our best grounds for optimism may very well turn out to be *the* defining human trait stemming from those capacities: an extreme ability, demonstrated time and time again, to rapidly and radically reconfigure how we live in relation to each other, and our environment. When it comes to cultural, societal, economic and political norms, what appears an interminable stasis today can be – and very often is – swept away tomorrow.

However, even more than intelligence, it will require real *wisdom*. Just as humans are the cause of the extinction crisis, so can we be the solution, by giving back to nature the space it needs to live, abundantly blended with the other vital ingredient: the long periods of time natural ecosystems need. The greatest challenge of our era is to begin narrowing the gap between ourselves and the living world again, changing 'the role of *Homo sapiens* from conqueror of the land-community to plain member and citizen of it', as Leopold so presciently wrote.

That doesn't mean trying to make the impossible journey back to some halcyon state of harmony with nature that in reality hasn't existed for aeons, but rather going forward to something new, in which both people and nature are able to prosper. Our relationship with nature is a broken one, but it can be repaired. True healing will require complete honesty about both the degree and longevity of the dysfunction that exists within that relationship. That heightened self-awareness must then be channelled into real restorative action on vast scales.

No matter how bad things are, or how much worse they might get in the future, there will still always be a living world of beauty, complexity, and wonder remaining that is absolutely worth fighting for; tooth and nail. And there are a multitude of success stories from all around the globe to show that, when given a chance to recover, nature can do just that, often spectacularly. By working together *with*, instead of against, nature, we can fix this.

On 1 March 2019, the United Nations declared the ten years up to 2030 as the 'UN Decade on Ecosystem Restoration', reflecting an increasing awareness of how essential healthy ecosystems are to our existence, at every level. While a positive step, it must be reflected in real, decisive action on the ground. And even then, in reality a decade will be nowhere near enough: the rest of this century – at least – needs to be one of restoring ecosystems.

The key to success or failure in bringing back the wild will be how we produce our food, the main human activity responsible for damaging and displacing natural ecosystems, both terrestrial and marine. On land, moving towards farming practices that are at once far more nature-friendly on actual farmland itself, but crucially also free up large areas for rewilding, has the real potential to reverse the decline of nature.

The latter can be achieved by a mass shift in the direction of more plant-based diets, which require only a very small fraction of the land area to produce the same amount of calories as animal-based foods. Doing so could make 3.1 billion hectares (76 per cent of global farmland) available for reversion to natural habitat. Similarly, large no-take zones could turn around the continuing collapse of ecosystems at sea. Our future depends on it.

Recent analysis has found that 37 per cent of the greenhouse gas (GHG) mitigation required to have a chance of remaining below 2°C of global heating from pre-industrial levels by 2030 could come from natural climate solutions, i.e. natural forest regeneration, and so forth. To take just one example: allowing whale populations to return to what they were before whaling began could draw down an astounding 1.7 billion tons of CO_2 annually, almost 4 per cent of current human emissions.

Such nature-based solutions mean, again, working with ecosystems, and treating them with the respect deserving of the wondrous life-supporting complexes they are. Phasing out use of fossil fuels and other greenhouse-gas-emitting activities at breakneck speed will always remain beyond vital of course, and nothing must ever be used as a substitute for that. But we know for certain now that this won't be nearly enough by itself: some means of taking CO_2 out of the air in vast quantities will be essential too. Restoring nature is the fastest, most sure-fire, and cheapest way to do that, and will also be essential in the at least equally as important task of preserving remaining biodiversity. Aside from the practical aspects, at heart it's also fundamentally a question of ethics.

Quite simply, it is profoundly immoral for us to think and act as if the entire planet were ours alone, and that we don't have to leave enough wild spaces for the millions of other species that have just as much right to exist as we do.

Almost every tree planted on the whole estate, very possibly the most hard-core of all the social housing complexes in 1980s and 1990s Dublin, had been demolished, one by one – hacked, broken, crushed, mangled, poisoned.

But for years a single individual survived against all the odds, a large cherry outside the windows of our second-floor flat. A blaze of white blossom in springtime, the tree stood out defiantly as a symbol of beauty, life and hope against an otherwise desolate backdrop of grimy concrete, strewn rubbish, smashed glass, urine, burned-out stolen cars and hypodermic syringes. (Giving you, the reader, a fuller picture of the extremity of the contrast between Beara and previous life episodes, and why I will remain so intensely grateful, to the end of my days, every time I walk in the Bofickil woods, or look out over the Atlantic.)

One day I was drawn to peer out the window by my mother's despairing words 'What's *wrong* with them?' The local kids were piling up pallets and other timber scraps high around the trunk, and soon the tree was again ablaze, this time for real. And so died the last tree of St Michael's Estate, roasted alive on a funeral pyre for no other reason than an afternoon's soon-forgotten entertainment. The sight of its still-smoking, charred skeleton has lingered in my memory as another potent symbol: of the depth of self-destructive madness and violence that pervades so much of human behaviour towards the other life forms with whom we share this planet. (And each other, at times.) I still sometimes think of that cherry now, especially when the wild apple trees are in flower in the woods.

Living there throughout my teens, the abject, multi-generational poverty and social dysfunction all around were hand in glove with a particularly extreme detachment from, and corresponding lack of empathy and concern for, the natural world. Or much of anything at all, for that matter. How many people across the planet now live in conditions similar to, or far worse than, those I witnessed daily in my own youth? According to the United Nations, in 2020 at least 1.3 billion people were living in poverty, half of them children. For many, that means a life of trawling rubbish tips, or working for near nothing in the most hazardous and toxic conditions imaginable, prostituting their bodies, or other soul-killing ways of existing. For all, it means shorter, crueller, partially wasted lives.

As with climate and ecological breakdown, all this is part and parcel of the current economic, social and political order; an inevitable consequence, rather than an unfortunate, unintended side-effect. And when life is nothing more than a relentless struggle to scrape by, with no hope on the horizon that things will ever improve, there just isn't the scope, energy or will to care about much beyond that. Under such circumstances, issues like the death of nature or a collapsing stable climate can be very abstract, if you're even aware of them at all. Social justice must be understood as indispensable to ecological justice, *and vice versa*.

Several years ago, E.O. Wilson laid out what it will take to safeguard most – not all, around 85 per cent – of the remaining species on Earth: setting aside at least half of global land and seas for wild nature. The proposal would mean refraining from exploiting those areas, and instead conserving and restoring natural ecosystems of every type within. The remaining, human-dominated parts of the planet would also need to be managed in a far more nature-friendly manner than at present, with High Nature Value farming replacing the present industrial models, for example.

Something similar is in fact envisaged by the year 2050 (with an intermediate 30 per cent by 2030) in the 'Global Deal for Nature' drawn up under the UN Convention on Biological

Diversity, but still to be agreed on by the international community. Unfortunately however, we know all too well from experience that, even if passed, global environmental resolutions almost always remain just that: fine words, with little or no action.

When global targets for preserving biodiversity were agreed in Aichi (Japan) in 2010, for example, they were subsequently largely ignored; and the same is true of a total of 26 international climate conferences to date. Even if agreed and *binding*, which areas are designated, and the degree of actual sanctuary afforded to them, will also be critical. There are already plenty of existing 'paper parks' around the world, where protective measures go unenforced and nature continues to disappear.

There must be no question of people being put out of Half-Earth: only the industrial extraction of resources, or other large-scale activities that seriously harm wild nature, should be excluded. Indeed, Wilson rightly identified indigenous communities as 'often the best protectors' of their own lands. There would be plenty of roles created as custodians of wild ecosystems, both those already present, and others that will develop. Just as with moves specifically to tackle climate breakdown, complete equity and inclusivity for everybody – a just transition – is essential in such a tectonic directional shift.

To succeed, it will have to not only be aligned with, but also play a key role in, redressing the crushing levels of poverty, violence, inequity and discrimination that are such stark and universal features of society everywhere. And nowhere more so than in the global south, looted and polluted by the rich world in a pillage of astronomical proportions that began centuries ago, and still goes on. Half-Earth must be wholly integrated with ending, and making amends for, that too.

As a solution, putting half of the globe beyond the reach of human exploitation will seem exaggerated to many. But according to the very best science, that is the minimum required to protect most life on the planet (to repeat: not all, only about 85 per cent of currently surviving species), and therefore our own. For that reason it's ultimately very much a question of social, as well as ecological, justice – not only for people living now, but for future generations also. Viewed in that light, doing anything less can be seen for what it is: wildly irresponsible.

Again, it's the idea that the whole planet can be appropriated for the almost exclusive use of one species only, and that only small, compromised and dwindling scraps can be left for the many millions of others, that is exaggerated and needs leaving behind. Places like Costa Rica, which has already marked 30 per cent of its territory for conservation, and returned 50 per cent to rainforest from a low of 21 per cent, show it *can* be done in a way that is fair for all.·

As pinpointed so neatly by Rachel Carson, at the heart of it all lies 'the problem of sharing our earth with other creatures'.

So what might genuinely 'sharing our earth with other creatures' look like in an Irish context? Well, that should really be for nature to decide, rather than us. But with ecosystems so drastically altered, for so long, and with so many species artificially absent, it's an unavoidable fact that the degree of ecological integrity attained will be largely dependent on human decisions. It will be up to us how far we are prepared to go, regarding the extent of land and sea set aside from exploitation, as well as restorative actions like bringing back missing species.

Ideally, there would have to be an opening of minds as to what could have been here had human impacts not occurred not only in the Holocene, but the Pleistocene also. Only in that way could something approaching the full biological potential that this particular corner of the planet holds truly be realised. But it's worth reflecting that those same human pressures in prehistory likely helped give rise to the almost continuous forests that swathed Ireland after the last Ice Age. How so?

Well, the megaherbivores like straight-tusked elephants that, to some extent, shape and counterbalance the formation of forests didn't get here to exert their influence, as they would have in previous interglacial epochs. However, while the coast-to-coast forest that once existed here should probably not be considered an entirely natural state, the present landscape, with only around 1 per cent of mostly highly degraded native forest cover, is obviously far, far less so.

What, then, is this island's natural condition? The last interglacial era, the Eemian (about 130,000–115,000 years ago), gives the best idea, since the climate was relatively similar to the Holocene, but global human impacts were still negligible (though by no means non-existent). However, the key question we really need to be asking ourselves at this point is another. What combination of ecological states would provide all our native wildlife with the conditions it needs to survive, and thrive, in abundance, as parts of healthy, resilient, self-regulating ecosystems? Ultimately, a dynamic, unfettered, continually evolving rich tapestry of natural ecosystems is the only way.

These would largely consist of native forests of every sort and density, ranging from thick, closed-canopy rainforest to patchy montane scrub: forest was the predominant vegetation type in northwestern Europe during previous interglacials (despite the best efforts of elephants). They would be interspersed with all shades of wildflower-rich grassland, wetland, bog, floodplain and other wild, biodiverse habitats and their ecotones (transition zones), all merging in and out of one another in deliciously chaotic and messy fashion. And the wildness would flow unimpeded down to the shore and beyond, into the sea, with all our marine ecosystems and species able to recover and flourish in strictly observed no-take marine protected areas.

There would of course have to be discussion as to how we create the conditions for all that to come about, and function, by itself. And we would then need to resist the ever-present temptation to interfere, manage, or direct outcomes, as well as the yet much stronger urge to exploit these areas, however 'sustainably'. Just as important as rewilding, farming would have to be transformed in such a way as to become really compatible with nature, as well as giving up space for those large areas that would need to be totally free of extractive activities.

All this might seem a preposterously unrealistic, unachievable prospect, given the abysmal and worsening lack of ecological integrity that exists on our island today. But it needs to be looked at from another, entirely different perspective. Quite simply, it will take nothing less to stop the continuing death of nature in Ireland, or for us to start pulling our weight in helping to stabilise the global climate through the restoration of functional natural ecosystems.

Arguments continue to rage over which societal sectors should cut their greenhouse gas emissions by how much, or make other 'sacrifices', and there looks to be no end to the debates. But if your family home were on fire, would it make sense to stand around endlessly contesting who should fill or carry buckets of water, try to get the garden hose going, call the fire brigade, or run inside to grab the baby? Would each household member put their energies into coming up with, and listing off, the reasons why they shouldn't have to do this or that, or practically anything at all? Or why they in particular should be allowed to continue spraying petrol on the flames instead of water? No, of course not: everyone would immediately throw themselves fully into doing whatever was required to put out the fire.

The point is that we now know for sure that our home *is*, very much, on fire. We are in a dire ecological and climate emergency, and as Greta Thunberg so rightly says, an emergency requires that we act like it. It requires that, instead of approaching ballooning problems with what is, or is not, 'politically feasible, acceptable, or realistic' to the fore, we come at it from the very opposite direction. We sit down, as if in a state of war, and work out exactly what needs to be done to avert disaster, how we achieve that in a fair manner, and then put in place everything necessary to make it happen. The first bit is pretty well sorted by now: the science is quite clear on what needs to be done; we just have to actually start doing it.

There is no shortage of examples demonstrating the vast

majority of people's capacity to act collectively in a brave and decisive way when the circumstances are widely understood to call for it. And there has never, *ever*, been a greater need for that than now. It's time for every one of us to stand up for our living world, and make ourselves count, individually and together. Once we reach a critical mass, change becomes unstoppable.

There are so many real bright sides to all this, if we only open our eyes to them. The potential gains from seeking a radically redefined relationship with the natural world through ecosystem restoration on a mass scale go far beyond just the essential and the pragmatic. It wouldn't only help prevent ecological and climate breakdown, as well as reviving rural communities, and so on.

Playing a role in the return of vitality to, and spontaneous expansion of, a wild native rainforest in Beara has unquestionably been the most deeply fulfilling and meaningful thing I have ever undertaken. Witnessing at first hand the fabric of life's incredible reweaving in and around the Bofickil woods has given me so much grounds for optimism: it's yet another demonstration of the raw power of nature to heal itself, if only permitted to do so.

I sincerely hope the journey I have been sharing with this at times searingly beautiful piece of land and forest, now so teeming with diverse life, still has a long way to go. Living with it has been a passionate love affair from the beginning, an 'astonishing time of gifts', to steal the words of Robert Macfarlane. Rather than owning it, if anything it owns me

– heart and mind, body and soul. In the same spirit, what a wonderfully exciting and joyful future awaits us, if we can only find it within ourselves to fully absorb Ed Wilson's profound truth that *'The biosphere does not belong to us; we belong to it.'*

All we then need is the collective vision and courage to put that ethos into action.

Now I never wake in the morning to the sound of monkeys whooping crazily in the distance, but frequently instead to bright liquid birdsong in the wild woods just outside. Other days – much more often than in the Kilmainham cottage – conditions are misty and still. On such occasions I sometimes open the roof light window of my upstairs bedroom and spend some time looking out, the bottom of the window just the right height to place my arms on comfortably and rest the chin.

With the canopy of trees shrouded in mist to the visible horizon, and no sound other than that of fat drops of water constantly dripping from the leaves all around, in those moments there is the even now very surreal certainty of actually being in a wild rainforest.

An Irish Atlantic rainforest.

Endnotes

CHAPTER 1: RAINFOREST IN THE CITY

11 **'Chapel of Maighneann'**: Colum Kenny, *Kilmainham: The History of a Settlement Older Than Dublin* (Dublin, 1995), 7, 10–12.

13 **Inventory of Architectural Heritage**: https://www.buildingsofireland.ie/buildings-search/building/50080168/dublin-city

CHAPTER 2: *SOGGIORNO ITALIANO*

23 **Italy's regional parks**: These are similar to national parks. Sadly, however, this designation did little to protect the landscape from the quarrying or its damaging effects, with 70 quarries remaining active within the park. The huge profits being made by a very few, but powerful, people have meant that local politicians, of whatever leaning, do nothing to change things.

24 **little that isn't natural**: At least not in appearance, but in reality the Apuan region has been heavily altered by human activity for millennia.

27 **an incredible inspiration**: Ian and Lynn played a fundamental role in establishing another native woodland project on a 320-acre estate at Manch, near Enniskeane in west Cork, and are also involved in an ecology programme in Tobago, in the Caribbean. Although I only ever met them that once, calling them inspirational doesn't go nearly far enough.

CHAPTER 4: A NEW LIFE DOWN SOUTH

39 **Michael Harrington (Caupey)**: There are about two dozen branches of Harringtons, each of which is distinguished by an added appellation, such as Caupey, Causkey, Bawrs, Bawn, and so on. A similar situation exists with O'Sullivan, the second most common surname in Beara.

40 **Bofickil in 1863**: Riobard O'Dwyer, *Who Were My Ancestors? Genealogy of the Eyeries Parish*, Castletownbere, Co. Cork, Ireland (1986), 129.

42 **millennia in Beara**: William O'Brien, *Early Settlement Landscapes and Upland Farming in South-West Ireland* (Cork, 2009), 342.

43   **role in its demise:** Martin Verling (ed.), 'The Decline of Irish in Kilcatherine Parish', in *Beara Woman Talking: Folklore from the Beara Peninsula* (Cork, 2003), 152–65.

43   **'ecosystem of spiritual possibilities':** Robert Macfarlane, *Landmarks* (London, 2015), 10.

43   **closure around that time:** Alan Williams, *The Berehaven Copper Mines* (Sheffield, 1991), 176–7.

44   **book of old photographs:** *Beara's Pictorial Past: Volume 2*, produced by the Beara Historical Society (Castletownbere, 2003), fig. 50.

45   **Bofickil (and Faunkill) woods:** I'll refer to them as simply the Bofickil woods from here on for the sake of brevity, but they are roughly equally divided between Bofickil and the next townland, Faunkill and The Woods, across the main stream that flows through the land.

45   **They are tamed, cultivated:** See Oliver Rackham, *Woodlands* (London, 2006), ch. 13.

54   *Memories of Knysna*: Sue Allanson et al. (eds), *Memories of Knysna* (Knysna, 1993).

CHAPTER 5: A DYING FOREST

57   **began domesticating goats:** Jared Diamond, *Guns, Germs and Steel: A Short History of Everybody for the Last 13,000 Years* (London, 1997), 167.

57   **'desert makers':** Donald Henry *et al.*, 'Blame it on the Goats? Desertification in the Near East during the Holocene', *The Holocene* (1 September 2016).

58   **conservation measures:** J.B. MacKinnon, *The Once and Future World: Nature As It Was, As It Is, And As It Could Be* (New York, 2013), 146–51.

58   **'Immense herds' of goats:** Eugene Costello, 'Hill Farmers, Habitats and Time: The Potential of Historical Ecology in Upland Management and Conservation', *Landscape Research* (30 August 2020).

58   **Sika deer, on the other hand:** Paddy Sleeman *et al.* (eds), 'Mind the Gap II: New Insights into the Irish Postglacial', *Irish Naturalist's Journal* (Belfast, 2014), 14.

59   **generally considered native:** *ibid.*, 14.

60   **bark is the living section:** Fritjof Capra, *The Web of Life: A New Scientific Understanding of Living Systems* (New York, 1997), 214.

60   **overgrazing and browsing:** Grazing is where herbivores eat plants like grasses at ground level, while browsing is feeding on those higher up, such as bushes and trees. For simplicity, I'll generally just use 'grazing' to refer to both.

61   **dense and toxic layer:** Clifton Bain, *The Rainforests of Britain and Ireland: A Traveller's Guide* (Dingwall, 2015), 45.

62 **squandering of decades**: My understanding of what transpired between Groundwork and the park authorities is largely based on conversations with a range of people who were involved in running the work camps. See also Paddy Woodworth, 'Rhododendron: An Ecological Disaster in Killarney National Park', *The Irish Times* (18 May 2019).

62 **quite unfathomable**: I have been reliably told that, before the Killarney district started to become more affluent in the 1970s, many people regularly poached (illegally hunted) deer, keeping numbers low enough for the natural regeneration of trees to take place. If true, it's quite bizarre to think that unlawful activity was for a long time the ecological saviour of the oakwoods. (Which is not, of course, in any way to condone such activity.)

63 **recognised as serious problems**: J.R. Cross, 'Rhododendron Ponticum L.', *Journal of Ecology* (March 1975); J.R. Cross, 'The Establishment of Rhododendron Ponticum in the Killarney Oakwoods, S.W. Ireland', *Journal of Ecology* (November 1981).

63 **perfect for invasion**: While rhododendron thrives in the acid and acid-neutral soils of the west, farther east it 'passes the baton' to another remarkably similar invasive plant: cherry laurel, which prefers soils with a more basic pH. Woodlands in the crossover zone between rhododendron and laurel will often have both present.

63 **19 per cent of Atlantic**: Bain, *The Rainforests of Britain and Ireland*, 51.

63 **that once covered**: Fraser Mitchell, 'How Open Were European Primeval Forests? Hypothesis Testing Using Palaeoecological Data', *Journal of Ecology* (21 December 2004).

64 **native to Asia**: Tim Blackburn and Kevin Gaston, 'Abundance, Biomass and Energy Use of Native and Alien Breeding Birds in Britain', *Biological Invasions* (11 July 2018).

64 **imminent local extinction**: Nicholas Milton, 'Game Birds "Could Wipe out Adders in Most of Britain within 12 Years"', *Guardian* (1 October 2020).

65 **the second biggest driver**: Céline Bellard et al., 'Alien Species as a Driver of Recent Extinctions', *Biology Letters* (1 February 2016); Peter Stoett et al., 'Invasive Alien Species and Planetary and Global Health Policy', *The Lancet Planetary Health* (1 October 2019).

65 **Sessile oak, for example**: Edward Milner, *The Tree Book: The Indispensable Guide to Tree Facts, Crafts, and Lore* (London, 1992), 18, 32, 68.

65 **insectivorous bird species**: Janet Marinelli, 'How Non-Native Plants are Contributing to a Global Insect Decline', *YaleEnvironment360* (8 December 2020).

66 **red fox and domestic cat**: Mindy Weisberger, 'Cats in Australia Kill over 2 Billion Wild Animals Each Year', *Live Science* (11 July 2019).

67 **exclude native plants**: Edward O. Wilson, *The Future of Life* (London, 2002), 73.

69   'conservation has failed': Oliver Rackham, *The History of the Countryside: The Classic History of Britain's Landscape, Flora and Fauna* (London, 1986), 29.

71   **Years later he wrote:** James Lovelock, *The Vanishing Face of Gaia: A Final Warning* (London, 2009), 19.

CHAPTER 6: REACHING THROUGH TIME

74   **'only an effing Dublin jackeen':** As all Irish people will know, 'craic' roughly means fun, while 'jackeen' is what Dubliners are called in some parts of the countryside, and 'culchie' is a Dublin term for a country person. Ironically, the origin of the word culchie possibly lies in 'coilteach' – Irish for 'man of the woods'. If true, that would make it more than just a little rich for me to be calling anyone else a culchie. Kenneth Nicholls, 'Woodland Cover in pre-Modern Ireland', in P.J. Duffy et al. (eds), *Gaelic Ireland c. 1250 – c. 1650: Land, Lordship and Settlement* (Dublin, 2001), 182, n. 5.

77   **'does Joxer want to know?':** The lines of poetry are from Ó Direáin's poem 'Iascairí an Chladaigh'; no recognised translation has ever been made that I know of. Whether my dad ever finished his letter, or submitted it to *The Irish Times*, I don't know, but I wasn't able to find any record of it having been published.

79   **copper mine, a *lios*:** Denis Power *et al.*, *Archaeological Inventory of County Cork, Volume 1: West Cork* (Dublin, 1992), 15, 73, 112, 125, 222, 242.

80   **as well as slurry:** Slurry is semi-liquid fermented cow manure, which collects in a pit under the floors of slatted units (large sheds where cattle are housed over the winter months and fed on silage, hay, and cattle nuts), and is then mechanically macerated before spreading with another tractor-pulled machine.

81   **it was a catastrophe:** John McNeill, *Something New Under the Sun: An Environmental History of the Twentieth Century* (London, 2000), 219–26.

84   **a unique subspecies:** A subspecies develops where a population has been isolated from other members of the same species for a sufficiently long period to evolve distinct characteristics as a result of differences in its environment. If the process continues for enough time, it can lead to a new species altogether.

84   **a passing 'flocking':** Not dissimilar to the shoaling of fish, some bird species engage in this behaviour, especially in winter, mainly for the increased protection it affords against predation, as the numerous pairs of eyes increase the odds of spotting in time a hunting sparrowhawk, for example.

86   **sublime poem:** Wendell Berry, *Collected Poems 1957–1982* (New York, 1985), 69.

86   **accumulating weight of evidence:** Wilson, *The Future of Life*, 139–41.

87   **Studies conducted in hospitals:** Deborah Franklin, 'How Hospital Gardens Help Patients Heal', *Scientific American* (1 March 2012).

Endnotes

87 **increasingly accepted as fact:** Harriet Sherwood, 'Getting Back to Nature: How Forest Bathing Can Make Us Feel Better', *Guardian* (8 June 2019).

88 *Wildwood*: Roger Deakin, *Wildwood: A Journey through Trees* (London, 2007), ix.

CHAPTER 7: TEMPERATE RAINFOREST

94 **I fervently devoured:** Especially Rackham, *Woodlands* and *George Peterken, Natural Woodland: Ecology and Conservation in Northern Temperate Regions* (Cambridge, 1996).

94 **Soon I was moving on:** For example: Wilson, *The Future of Life*; Michael Soulé and John Terborgh (eds), *Continental Conservation: Scientific Foundations of Regional Reserve Networks* (Washington, 1999); Aldo Leopold, *A Sand County Almanac, and Sketches Here and There* (New York, 1949); William Allen, *Green Phoenix: Restoring the Tropical Forests of Guanacaste, Costa Rica* (Oxford, 2001).

94 **an entirely separate biome:** A biome is a loose category of ecological community that occurs on a global scale in particular, especially climatic, conditions; other examples are savannah, dry desert, and tundra.

94 *temperate* **rainforest:** Dominick DellaSala (ed.), *Temperate and Boreal Rainforests of the World: Ecology and Conservation* (Washington, 2011), 160–5.

95 **the number of 'wet days':** Frank Mitchell and Michael Ryan, *Reading the Irish Landscape* (Dublin, 2003), 101; Cornelius J. Murphy, *The Prehistoric Archaeology of the Beara Peninsula* (Galway, 1997), 10.

96 **rainforests of New Zealand:** Wilson, *The Future of Life*, 20.

96 **Knysna-Tsitsikamma forests:** DellaSala (ed.), *Temperate and Boreal Rainforests*, 234–42.

100 **wiped out by hunting:** Winifred Tapson, *Timber and Tides: The Story of Knysna and Plettenberg Bay* (Johannesburg, 1961), 129–34.

100 **more open *fynbos*:** Pronounced 'fain-boss', fynbos is a shrubby, heathy habitat found only in South Africa's Cape Provinces. It is one of the most botanically rich on the planet, with over 9,000 plant species, of which an extraordinary almost 6,000 are endemic.

100 **complex in southern Africa:** Izak Van der Merwe, *The Knysna and Tsitsikamma Forests: Their History, Ecology and Management* (Knysna, 2002), 58.

100 **with about 90 different trees:** *ibid.*, 82.

100 **elephants, or other mega-beasts:** The definition of megafauna varies, with some people using the term for animals weighing more than 44kg, while others prefer 100kg.

105 **highly beneficial to the overall ecosystem**: Most of these considerations apply equally to woodbine, otherwise known as honeysuckle.

105 ***Ferns of Southern Africa***: Neil Crouch et al., *Ferns of Southern Africa: A Comprehensive Guide* (Cape Town, 2011).

106 **among the most haunting**: I have no real explanation for such trusting behaviour, other than to speculate that the duiker may have become habituated to humans through being fed.

CHAPTER 8: THE DYNAMISM OF AN IRISH RAINFOREST

109 **very same species in Knysna**: Crouch et al., *Ferns of Southern Africa*, 160–5.

110 **identical to the wood sanicle**: The Irish version is Sanicula europaea, while the one I saw in South Africa was almost certainly Sanicula elata.

110 **predatory Knysna velvet worm**: René Gordon, 'The Tsitsikamma Forest National Park', in *The National Parks of South Africa* (Cape Town, 1992), 73.

112 **Woodland-associated species**: A good overview of the most up-to-date thinking on these subjects can be found in Sleeman *et al.*, 'Mind the Gap II'.

115 **a raised 'ditch'**: In Beara, the word 'ditch' means a stone or sod wall/bank, which rises up, for example around a field, rather than the trench-like hollow it refers to in the Pale (the Dublin region), and most other places.

119 **acid taste**: Milner, *The Tree Book*, 61.

119 **largest component species**: Anette Overland and Michael O'Connell, 'Palaeoecological Investigations in the Barrees Valley', in O'Brien, *Early Settlement Landscapes*, 314–15.

120 **'witch's broom'**: Witch's broom is an outgrowth deformity that at first sight resembles a bird's nest, usually occurring in birch and caused by fungal activity, but sometimes also viruses, bacteria, or insects.

120 **'ancient woodland indicator'**: See, for example, Philip Perrin and Orla Daly, *A Provisional Inventory of Ancient and Long-Established Woodland in Ireland*, Irish Wildlife Manuals No. 46, National Parks and Wildlife Service document (2010), 36–44.

120 **anemone is a clonal plant**: Jörg Brunet and Goddert Von Oheimb, 'Colonization of Secondary Woodlands by Anemone Nemorosa', *Nordic Journal of Botany* (25 March 2008). Another dispersal mechanism used by wood anemone is through ants carrying its seeds.

122 **as seventeenth century**: According to Dr Robert Bohan, a woodland historian trained by Oliver Rackham (personal communication).

123 **'Daad O'Huologhan'**: Dive Downes, quoted in Penelope Durell and Cornelius Kelly, *The Grand Tour of Beara* (Allihies, 2000), 18.

Endnotes

123 *corbezzolo*: 'Corbezzolo!' is also sometimes used as a polite substitute for a certain swearword in Italian.

124 **an archaeophyte:** Milner, *The Tree Book*, 48; Micheline Sheehy Skeffington and Nick Scott, 'Is the Strawberry Tree, Arbutus Unedo (Ericaceae), Native to Ireland, or Was it Brought by the First Copper Miners?', *British and Irish Botany* (30 December 2021).

124 **'Mediterranean-Atlantic':** Neil Lockhart *et al.*, *Rare and Threatened Bryophytes of Ireland* (Holywood, 2012), 10.

125 **comprised around 10 per cent:** Overland and O'Connell, 'Palaeoecological Investigations', 314.

125 **unbroken continuity of presence:** Jennifer Roche, 'The Vegetation Ecology and Native Status of Scots Pine (Pinus sylvestris L.) in Ireland', PhD thesis, Trinity College Dublin (2010).

CHAPTER 9: RECESS OF THE WILD WOOD

126 **Bofickil derives from:** Bruno O'Donoghue, *Parish Histories and Place Names of West Cork* (Tralee, 1983), 314–15.

126 **'fixed [by] the eighth century':** Eileen McCracken, *The Irish Woods since Tudor Times: Their Distribution and Exploitation* (Newton Abbot, 1971), 22.

126 **local historian Cornelius Murphy:** Murphy, *The Prehistoric Archaeology*, 13.

127 **blur the distinction with actual farming:** Graeme Warren et al., 'The Potential Role of Humans in Structuring the Wooded Landscapes of Mesolithic Ireland: A Review of Data and Discussion of Approaches', *Vegetation History and Archaeobotany* (September 2014).

127 **disturbance from around 6400 BC:** Timothy Mighall et al., 'Vegetation Change during the Mesolithic and Neolithic on the Mizen Peninsula, Co. Cork, South-West Ireland', *Vegetation History and Archaeobotany* (November 2007).

127 **significant site at Cashelkeelty:** Murphy, *The Prehistoric Archaeology*, 12.

127 **cleared patches of land:** Mitchell and Ryan, *Reading the Irish Landscape*, 160.

127 **slash-and-burn:** Slash-and-burn is a form of agriculture in which patches of wild forest are cut down and, once dried, burnt. It creates space for cultivation and fertilises the ground with ash at the same time. Ring-barking is a method of killing trees, by peeling a section of bark away right around the trunk.

127 **until the Bronze Age:** Murphy, *The Prehistoric Archaeology*, 12–14, 125–32; Annette Overland *et al.*, 'Beara, SW Ireland: A Liminal Cultural Landscape', in *Cultural Landscapes of Europe: Fields of Demeter, Haunts of Pan* (Bremen, 2009), 164–5.

127 **collapse in tree cover:** O'Brien, *Early Settlement Landscapes*, 313, 325–7.

128 **all three filmy ferns:** Anette Overland and Michael O'Connell, 'Fine-Spatial Paleoecological Investigations towards Reconstructing Late Holocene Environmental Change, Landscape Evolution, and Farming Activity in Barrees, Beara Peninsula, Southwestern Ireland', *Journal of the North Atlantic* (July 2008), 65–6; Tunbridge filmy fern and Killarney fern are more shade-tolerant than Wilson's filmy fern, and so are more likely to be especially associated with forest.

128 **dating to between 2000:** Power et al, *Archaeological Inventory of County Cork*, 13, 15.

128 **active around 1650–1450 BC:** O'Brien, *Early Settlement Landscapes*, 171–81.

128 *fionnán*: The Irish names are still commonly used in Beara for many wild plants, and quickly picked up from neighbours.

129 **echoes other parts:** Mitchell and Ryan, *Reading the Irish Landscape*, 199–202, 246, 248; see also, for example, Anette Overland and Michael O'Connell, 'New Insights into Late Holocene Farming and Woodland Dynamics in Western Ireland with Particular Reference to the Early Medieval Horizontal Watermill at Kilbegly, Co. Roscommon', *Review of Palaeobotany and Palynology* (January 2011), 210–26; Beatrice Ghilardi and Michael O'Connell, 'Fine-Resolution Pollen-Analytical Study of Holocene Woodland Dynamics and Land Use in North Sligo, Ireland', *Boreas* (21 November 2012), 629–49.

129 **trend has been a downward:** Overland and O'Connell, 'Fine-Spatial Paleoecological Investigations', 37–73; in particular the BAR-L1 peat core pollen analysis in fig. 13 (p. 60), and 'Woodland cover', fig. 14 (p. 64).

129 **the spreading of seaweed:** Mitchell and Ryan, *Reading the Irish Landscape*, 103; O'Brien, *Early Settlement Landscapes*, 340; Peter Wohlleben, *The Secret Network of Life: The Delicate Balance of All Living Things* (London, 2017), 43–6.

129 **followed by human abandonment:** Murphy, *The Prehistoric Archaeology*, 12–14, 125–32; O'Brien, *Early Settlement Landscapes*, 340–1.

129 **intensify their forest clearing:** *ibid.*, 356.

130 **and elsewhere in Europe:** Wohlleben, *The Secret Network of Life*, 37–8; see also M.G.L. Baillie and D.M. Brown, 'Some Deductions on Ancient Irish Trees from Dendrochronology', in Jon Pilcher and Seán Mac an tSaoir (eds), *Wood, Trees and Forests in Ireland* (Dublin, 1995), 37–40, and Nicholls, 'Woodland Cover', 202.

130 **Three times Ireland:** *ibid.*, 182.

130 **Giraldus Cambrensis:** Herbert Francis Hore, 'Woods and Fastnesses in Ancient Ireland', *Ulster Journal of Archaeology*, (1858), 147.

130 **The Norman invasion:** Nicholls, 'Woodland Cover', 181.

131 **right back to the Mesolithic:** Mitchell and Ryan, *Reading the Irish Landscape*, 198–202; Warren *et al.*, 'The Potential Role of Humans'; Mighall *et al.*, 'Vegetation Change during the Mesolithic and Neolithic'.

131 **palaeoecological evidence from Barrees:** Overland and O'Connell, 'Palaeoecological Investigations', 310–22.

131 **first maps of the peninsula:** See the frontispiece in Colin Breen, *The Gaelic Lordship of the O'Sullivan Beare: A Landscape Cultural History* (Dublin, 2005). The Glengarriff reference is in Hore, 'Woods and Fastnesses', 155.

132 **Republic the year 1660:** Perrin and Daly, *A Provisional Inventory*, 6.

132 **123 ancient:** *ibid.*, 45.

132 **'the making of ships':** Nicholls, 'Woodland Cover', 186–7.

132 **later 1st earl:** McCracken, *The Irish Woods*, 45, 94; Nicholls, 'Woodland Cover', 191.

133 **all the three kingdoms:** David Heffernan, 'Reconstructing the Estate of Richard Boyle, First Earl of Cork, c.1602–43', *History Ireland* (March/April 2015); Nigel Everett, *The Woods of Ireland: A History, 700–1800* (Dublin, 2014), 144.

133 **Eileen McCracken estimated:** McCracken, *The Irish Woods*, 15.

134 **minuscule 0.2 per cent:** Oliver Rackham, 'Looking for Ancient Woodland in Ireland', in Pilcher and Mac an tSaoir, *Wood, Trees and Forests in Ireland*, 2–3.

134 **joining their own former tenants:** Padraig Lenihan, *Consolidating Conquest: Ireland 1603–1727* (Harlow, 2008), 142.

135 **the Down Survey:** The Down Survey maps are the reason why 1660, rather than 1600, is used as a threshold for determining ancient woodland in Ireland: if it featured on those maps and still exists, it's almost certain to be ancient.

135 **a family named White:** 'UCC Gets Bantry House Archive', *The Irish Times* (20 May 1997).

135 **made themselves extremely wealthy:** McCracken, *The Irish Woods*, 45.

135 **forests had been exhausted:** *ibid.*, 54–5.

135 **with the exception of:** There were active charcoal-burning ironworks in that period at Glengarriff, Adrigole, Dunboy, and Tuosist. McCracken, *The Irish Woods*, 166–7.

136 **missing native woodland fauna:** Regarding wild boar, see William Thompson, *The Natural History of Ireland, Vol. IV* (London, 1856), 36.

136 **agent orange:** Agent orange is a chemical herbicide, widely used by American forces during their 1964–75 war in Vietnam to kill vast areas of forest as a military tactic against opposing Viet Cong guerrillas.

136 'as civil a plantation': McCracken, *The Irish Woods*, 46–7.

137 'extirpation': David Edwards, 'Tudor Ireland', in *The Routledge History of Genocide* (Abingdon-on-Thames, 2015), 30.

137 an estimated 20–33 per cent: Sir William Petty (he was knighted in 1661) estimated the deaths at 40 per cent, but modern historians now put the figure lower, at around 20–33 per cent; Pádraig Lenihan, 'War and Population, 1649–52', *Irish Economic and Social History* (1 September 1997).

137 'between 1546 and 1603': Edwards, 'Tudor Ireland', 23.

137 all 'Irishry': *ibid.*, 23–4, 26, 30–3; Nicholas Canny, 'The Ideology of English Colonisation: From Ireland to America', *The William and Mary Quarterly* (October 1973), 582.

137 'everye corner of the woode': Edmund Spenser, *A View of the Present State of Ireland* (1596), reproduced in *The Corpus of Electronic Texts*, University College Cork, https://celt.ucc.ie//published/E500000-001/

138 a mere 621: Murphy, *The Prehistoric Archaeology*, 14.

138 'a pleasant hunt': McCracken, *The Irish Woods*, 28–9.

138 the European conquest: Eileen Crist, *Abundant Earth: Toward an Ecological Civilization* (Chicago, 2019), 91; Jeremy Lent, *The Patterning Instinct: A Cultural History of Humanity's Search for Meaning* (New York, 2017), 306–15.

138 'West Country Men': Canny, 'The Ideology of English Colonisation', 578.

138 transferred to the New World: *ibid.*, 595–8.

138 translations of Spanish texts: *ibid.*, 593–5.

139 with no signs of slowing: Nicholls, 'Woodland Cover', 203–4, 206.

139 'his diaries [Richard] Boyle': McCracken, *The Irish Woods*, 100.

139 Pure wastage: Nicholls, 'Woodland Cover', 198–201.

140 'Land surveyors': *ibid.*, 186.

140 'pastures of rock': Trans. by Frank O'Connor. McCracken, *The Irish Woods*, 14.

141 'spared in the general havoc': James Anthony Froude, *Short Studies on Great Subjects, Vol. II* (London, 1893), 223–4. Many thanks to Bill Quirke for bringing this to my attention.

142 Gaelic Brehon: David Hickie, *Native Trees & Forests of Ireland* (Dublin, 2002), 32–6.

142 ancient 'fairy trees': Ó hÓgáin, 'Trees in Irish Lore', 46–60; *Milner, The Tree Book*, 137, 139–41.

142 grazing by domestic animals: See, for example, Overland and O'Connell, 'Palaeoecological Investigations, 319.

143 **centred around creachta:** Liam O'Dwyer, *Beara in Irish History* (New York, 1977), 45, 51–2.

143 **slaughtered en masse:** *ibid.*, 55–7.

143 **practice of 'booleying':** Canny, 'The Ideology of English Colonisation', 587–8.

143 **'amount of cultivation':** Kenneth Nicholls, *Gaelic and Gaelicized Ireland in the Middle Ages* (Dublin, 2003), 135–8, and Nicholls, 'Woodland Cover', 203.

144 **including Rackham:** Rackham, *The History of the Countryside*, 116.

144 **ruling that out:** Nicholls, 'Woodland Cover', 205.

145 **'rolling Tuscan landscape':** Lent, *The Patterning Instinct*, 296.

145 **ancient overgrown monuments:** Fred Pearce, *Deep Jungle* (London, 2005), 150–80.

145 **more 'advanced' society:** Cory Rogers, 'Investing in Indigenous Communities is Most Efficient Way to Protect Forests, Report Finds', *Mongabay* (2 July 2018).

146 **most ground-breaking biologist:** Although first and foremost an entomologist (insect biologist) specialising in the eusocial species (ants, bees and termites, for example), Wilson, who passed away in the last days of 2021, was responsible for numerous revolutionary scientific theories in ecology and other related fields. These include (together with Robert MacArthur) in 1967 likely the most important ecological theory of the twentieth century: island biogeography.

146 **'ersatz savanna':** Wilson, *The Future of Life*, 134–43. Professor Gordon Orians expressed the same idea separately: Richard Leakey and Roger Lewin, *The Sixth Extinction: Biodiversity and Its Survival* (London, 1995), 143.

147 **Neanderthals cleared forests:** Wil Roebroeks *et al.*, 'Landscape Modification by Last Interglacial Neanderthals', *Science Advances* (15 December 2021).

147 **'prehistory makes no sense':** Edward O. Wilson, *Half-Earth: Our Planet's Fight for Life* (New York, 2016), 157.

148 **hunger-induced disease:** Christine Kinealy, *This Great Calamity: The Irish Famine 1845–52* (Dublin, 1994), 351–7; Christine Kinealy, 'Food Exports from Ireland 1846–47', *History Ireland* (Spring 1997).

148 **catastrophic crash:** Verling, 'The Decline of Irish', 162.

148 **numbers only stabilising:** Murphy, *The Prehistoric Archaeology*, 14.

149 **'crawl from where they landed':** Williams, *The Berehaven Copper Mines*, 127–8.

150 **the last time they were cultivated:** This is Michael Caupey's opinion also. He told me that no potatoes or any other crop had ever been grown there within the living memory of the older people he had known as a boy, and nor was there any orally passed memory of such.

151 **vacated by people:** For example: Tom Allan, 'Chernobyl: The Wildlife Haven
Created When People Left', *Guardian* (28 May 2019); Lisa Brady, 'How
Wildlife is Thriving in the Korean Peninsula's Demilitarised Zone', *Guardian*
(13 April 2012).

CHAPTER 10: AN UNLIKELY SHEEP FARMER

152 **as the Land War:** For accounts of the fierce resistance of local communities to
evictions and other abuses in Beara, see Fachtna O'Donovan, *Beara: History
and Stories from the Peninsula* (Castletownbere, 2005), 241–4.

154 **steel cattle crush:** A cattle crush is basically a pen in which an animal can be
held safely and securely for veterinary inspections and other purposes.

156 **trying to coordinate dog and sheep:** After the first few years, I was assisted
whenever the sheep needed bringing down off the mountain by a local man
who had a dog better trained for sheep. (Or, more truthfully, I assisted him.)

160 **prevailing wind:** Actually, to say trees are bent into this shape by the wind
is not quite correct. Those shoots and leaves growing on the leeward, i.e.
more sheltered, side of the tree do better than those bearing the full brunt of
the wind. Hence, over time, the tree develops in the direction away from the
wind, and takes on that distinctive windswept shape known in Irish as *leath-
ceann*.

161 **altitudinal limit for rowan:** John Cross, 'The Potential Natural Vegetation of
Ireland', *Biology and Environment, Proceedings of the Royal Irish Academy*
(August 2006), 67.

162 **Costa Rican cloud forest:** Robin Wall Kimmerer, *Gathering Moss: A Natural
and Cultural History of Mosses* (Corvallis, 2003), 143.

163 **around 990 vascular plants:** Peterken, *Natural Woodland*, 209.

163 **Irish and British Atlantic rainforests:** G.P. Rothero, 'Oceanic Bryophytes in
Atlantic Oakwoods', *Botanical Journal of Scotland* (22 April 2009).

163 **the less species diversity:** Wilson, *The Future of Life*, 58–9.

163 *three-quarters of all terrestrial biodiversity*: According to the World Wildlife
Fund; https://www.worldwildlife.org/habitats/forest-habitat

164 **settled in the Neolithic:** Miriam Cubas, 'Latitudinal Gradient in Dairy
Production with the Introduction of Farming in Atlantic Europe', *Nature
Communications* (27 April 2020).

164 **last 150 years:** Costello, 'Hill Farmers, Habitats and Time'.

165 **an extremely tough life:** The National Farm Survey for 2018 produced by
Teagasc (the state Agriculture and Food Development Authority) showed that
the average income of sheep farmers fell by a fifth in just one year, dropping
from €17,357 in 2017 to €13,769 in 2018. It should be understood that most
of this income comes from farm subsidies.

165 **climate change is predicted:** Muhammad Naveed Arshad and Mariecia Fraser, 'Climate Change Could Wreck Traditional Sheep Farming in Wales', *The Conversation* (4 May 2020).

165 **apart from Iceland:** Oisín Sweeney *et al.*, 'Woodlands, Forest and Scrub', in Richard Nairn and John O'Halloran (eds), *Bird Habitats in Ireland* (Cork, 2012), 105.

166 **average of just 3 per cent:** *ibid.*, 107.

166 **pushing out the people:** Kevin O'Sullivan, 'Afforestation: A Source of Environmental Damage and Depopulation', *The Irish Times* (31 January 2019). Despite the damage they cause on so many levels, no environmental impact assessments (EIAs) are required for new plantations initially under 125 acres (so if they are later expanded it is still unnecessary), meaning that practically no EIAs are ever carried out. Caroline O'Doherty, 'Fears Forestry Plantations May Increase Carbon Emissions', *Irish Independent* (26 November 2019).

166 **even more people off the land:** Residents of Leitrim, so far the county worst affected by plantations, formed a 'Save Leitrim Campaign' in early 2018 to oppose what is happening; their lead is now being followed by several other counties, including Kerry.

162 **more appropriately, called:** The term 'climate change' makes an issue that is already becoming catastrophic sound positively benign, akin to normal changing weather. 'Climate breakdown' more accurately reflects the true nature of the challenge, and therefore the seriousness of our situation. Using commensurate language to describe what is happening is imperative, if we are to have any hope of escaping far worse disaster.

169 **Pickering in Yorkshire:** Geoffrey Lean, 'UK Flooding: How a Yorkshire Town Worked with Nature to Stay Dry', *Independent* (3 January 2016).

169 **Ireland became the second country:** Michelle Devane, 'Ireland Declares Climate Emergency: "Things Will Deteriorate Rapidly Unless We Move Very Swiftly"', *Irish Independent* (10 May 2019).

CHAPTER 11: THE RED PILL

172 **'does not want to be told otherwise':** Aldo Leopold, 'The Round River: A Parable', in *Round River* (Oxford, 1966), 165.

172 **the red pill:** When I first wrote this, I thought my analogy was original. However, I later realised that it had already been used by Eileen Crist in a text I had read many years before, and had probably remained in my subconscious ever since. I hope she won't mind my borrowing it. Eileen Crist, 'Ptolemaic Environmentalism', in George Wuerthner et al. (eds), *Keeping the Wild: Against the Domestication of Earth* (Washington, 2014), 23.

173 a *relatively* intact ecosystem: Please note the emphasis on the word 'relatively'. There should be no illusions regarding the fact that, as a fairly tiny fragment, cut in two by a regional road, there are very definite limits as to how ecologically balanced or functional my patch can ever be.

174 'shifting baseline syndrome': The phenomenon was first conceived by marine biologist Daniel Pauly in relation to marine ecosystems, but was found to be equally useful for understanding our perceptions of their terrestrial equivalents, and indeed the social systems we ourselves construct. MacKinnon, *The Once and Future World*, 17–19; Lent, *The Patterning Instinct*, 419–20, 429.

174 Yangtse River dolphin: Crist, *Abundant Earth*, 62.

175 everywhere across the globe: For example: Jonathan Watts, 'Human Society under Urgent Threat from Loss of Earth's Natural Life: Scientists Reveal 1 Million Species at Risk of Extinction in Damning UN Report', *Guardian* (6 May 2019).

175 sliding towards extinction: Kevin O'Sullivan, 'Report Confirms Acceleration of Species Loss and Habitat Deterioration', *The Irish Times* (15 May 2019).

175 'knees in dead canaries': For one example of many showing how seriously natural heritage is taken in Ireland, see Caroline O'Doherty, 'EU Takes Ireland to Court over Wildlife Habitats Neglect', *Irish Independent* (3 July 2020).

175 ecologically trashed: Ciaran Moran, 'Irish Agriculture's "Green" Reputation Not Supported by Evidence – EPA Chief', *Farming Independent* (6 October 2020).

176 only a pale reflection: See, for example, Crist, *Abundant Earth*, 12–13; George Monbiot, *Feral: Searching for Enchantment on the Frontiers of Rewilding* (London, 2013), 231–44.

176 overfishing on an industrial level: Pádraic Fogarty, *Whittled Away: Ireland's Vanishing Nature* (Cork, 2017), Chapter 2.

176 in 63 *nature reserves*: Damian Carrington, 'Warning of "Ecological Armageddon" after Dramatic Plunge in Insect Numbers', *Guardian* (18 October 2017).

176 in 2021 from England: Damian Carrington, 'Flying Insect Numbers Have Plunged by 60% since 2004, GB Survey Finds', *Guardian* (5 May 2022).

177 'Human memory is imprecise': Dave Goulson, *Insect Declines and Why they Matter*, report commissioned by UK Wildlife Trusts (November 2019), 23.

177 car windscreens: Michael McCarthy, *The Moth Snowstorm: Nature and Joy* (London, 2015), 102–5.

177 increasingly, climate: For example, over 100 tons of veterinary antibiotics annually in the Rep. of Ireland alone. 'Report on Consumption of Veterinary Antibiotics in 2016', a report commissioned by the Health Products Regulatory Authority (2016).

177 **innocuous extinction drivers:** Damian Carrington, 'Light Pollution Is Key "Bringer Of Insect Apocalypse"', *Guardian* (22 November 2019).

182 **high-productivity perennial ryegrass:** Even on the rare occasions where multi-species grass (MSG) mixes are sown (PRG accounts for 95 per cent of forage grass seed sold in Ireland), the result is still green sterility in comparison with a true wildflower meadow, native forest, or other natural habitat.

185 **playing out across Ireland:** See, for example, John Devaney *et al.*, *21st Century Deforestation in Ireland, Ecological Protection Agency* (EPA) Report no. 221 (October 2017), 31.

185 **6,000 kilometres of hedgerow:** Kevin O'Sullivan, 'State's Plan for Sustainable Farming "Lacks Ambition" on Biodiversity', *The Irish Times* (9 February 2022).

186 **30 per cent of a farm:** Hannah Quinn-Mulligan, 'Scrubland To Be a Thorny Issue', *Irish Farmers Journal* (21 July 2021).

188 **marginal, disadvantaged:** In areas like Beara, the average income from sheep farming is likely to be significantly less than Teagasc's average figure of €13,769 for 2018. My own income from farming sheep on about 50 acres for that year was in the region of €6,500, but when expenditure on fencing and other costs is factored in, I actually made a slight loss. Other years there was some profit, but not much. I don't know of any sheep farmers who don't have other work to provide off-farm income.

190 **rewetting *all* their bogs:** Bord na Móna has at least begun taking steps in this direction, with plans to rewet 80,000 acres of bog: Mark Hilliard, 'Major Peatland Restoration Initiative Is Anything But Bog-Standard', *The Irish Times* (24 November 2020).

191 **selling up and moving away:** Ciaran Moran, 'Proportion of Farmers in the Workforce Down 85% in Last 50 years – CSO', *Farming Independent* (15 June 2017).

191 **rather than purely for money:** Kate Raworth, *Doughnut Economics: Seven Ways to Think Like a 21st-Century Economist* (London, 2017), 120–3.

192 **both nature and people:** Thelma Gómez Durán, 'Community Forest Enterprises Provide Win for Forest and People: Study', *Mongabay* (21 May 2020).

CHAPTER 12: REWILDING THE LAND

193 **biologists Michael Soulé:** Caroline Fraser, *Rewilding the World: Dispatches from the Conservation Revolution* (New York, 2009), 9.

194 **missing vital species:** See, for example, Michael Soulé, *Collected Papers of Michael Soulé: Early Years in Modern Conservation Biology* (Washington, 2014).

194 **missing keystone species:** Like the keystone of an arch, keystone species
are those that have a central role in the functioning and stability of healthy
ecosystems, to a degree that is far out of proportion to their numbers. In
addition, that role cannot usually be performed by other species within the
ecosystem – only beavers make dams, for example.

195 **'self-willed':** Tom Butler, 'Protected Areas and the Long Arc towards Justice',
in George Wuerthner, Eileen Crist and Tom Butler (eds), *Protecting the Wild:
Parks and Wilderness, the Foundation for Conservation* (Washington, 2015),
xxi.

195 **risks becoming meaningless:** A very welcome advance in this respect is
the publication of Steve Carver et al., 'Guiding Principles for Rewilding',
Conservation Biology (15 March 2021), representing the work of the IUCN
Rewilding Thematic Group.

196 **food and other goods:** See Lent, *The Patterning Instinct*, 109–10.

196 **'not controlled by man':** *Collins English Dictionary* (2004 edition), 1082.

197 **relax the pressure on nature:** The hugely inspiring story of Knepp can be
found in Isabella Tree, *Wilding: The Return of Nature to a British Farm*
(London, 2018).

197 **two very different things:** Any misanthropic or other similarly suspect
interpretations of rewilding should be strongly rejected. To be clear, however,
recognising the destructive effects human exploitative activities have on the
natural world, and the consequent need for areas in which those activities
are curtailed or excluded altogether, is not misanthropic. It is merely being
objective (and honest).

199 **scrub:** The word 'scrub' is very commonly used in a derogatory manner,
amazingly enough even by many conservationists, hiding the reality of what it
really is: naturally regenerating wild native forest, which is usually extremely
wildlife-rich and will develop into old-growth forest, given enough time.

200 **impressive tree lungwort:** Paul Whelan, *Lichens of Ireland: An Illustrated
Introduction to Over 250 Species* (Cork, 2011), 111–14.

200 ***whole ecosystem has to work:*** Jason Gilchrist, 'Giant Panda Conservation is
Failing to Revive the Wider Ecosystem – New Study', *The Conversation* (3
August 2020). See also Soulé and Terborgh, *Continental Conservation*, 39–58.

200 **long-term strategy:** Edward Grumbine, *Ghost Bears: Exploring the
Biodiversity Crisis* (Washington, 1992), 26–8.

201 **'confusing to the public':** Imagine if UK Conservation Managed the Jungle,
blog post on 'godneymarshes' (20 February 2020), https://godneymarshes.
com/2020/02/20/imagine-if-uk-conservation-managed-the-jungle/

203 ***land sparing on the other:*** Fred Pearce, 'Sparing vs Sharing: The Great
Debate over How to Protect Nature', *YaleEnvironment360* (3 December
2018).

203   **presently farmed organically**: Seán McCárthaigh, 'Irish Authorities Failing to Fully Implement EU Directive on Pesticides, Audit Finds', *Irish Examiner* (20 August 2019).

203   **majority of wild**: Benjamin Phalan, 'What Have We Learned from the Land Sparing–Sharing Model?', *Sustainability* (28 May 2018); Ben Balmford *et al.*, 'How Imperfect Can Land Sparing Be Before Land Sharing is More Favourable for Wild Species?', *Journal of Applied Ecology* (5 October 2018).

204   **highly problematic and questionable**: George Monbiot, 'The UK Government Wants To Put a Price on Nature – But That Will Destroy It', *Guardian* (15 May 2018).

205   **conference on that very issue**: While chairing a public session on the first day, Pádraic Fogarty of the Irish Wildlife Trust attempted to get the panel to discuss rewilding, without much success. That was the sole mention I (or anyone else I spoke to) heard any of the official speakers make of anything relating to that side of it in two whole days of talks.

205   **right up to the whole biosphere**: Christof Schenck, 'Rewilding Europe', in Wuerthner *et al.*, *Protecting the Wild*, 100; Grumbine, *Ghost Bears*, 21.

205   **the be-all-and-end-all**: J.B. MacKinnon, 'Tragedy of the Common: The Extinction Crisis Extends Far Beyond Rare and Endangered Species', *Pacific Standard* (17 October 2017).

207   **'mesopredator release'**: Soulé, *Collected Papers*, 119–21.

207   **as many natural ecological**: Justin Yeakel *et al.*, 'Diverse Interactions and Ecosystem Engineering Can Stabilize Community Assembly', *Nature Communications* (3 July 2020).

207   **'The essence of nature'**: Susan Wright *et al.*, *Scotland: A Rewilding Journey* (Ballintean, 2018), 28. A special thanks to Pádraic Fogarty for gifting me this lovely book.

209   **and other native wildlife**: For example, a 2012 study estimated that in the US alone, cats kill 1.3 to 3.7 billion birds and 6.3 to 22.3 billion mammals every single year. The same is true of other continents. Scott Loss *et al.*, 'The Impact of Free-Ranging Domestic Cats on Wildlife of the United States', *Nature Communications* (29 January 2013). Fitting bells to pet cats' collars can reduce, but not prevent, the onslaught; keeping pet cats indoors, and the removal of feral cats, are the only truly effective solutions.

209   **another form of human impact**: Soulé, *Collected Papers*, 99–140.

210   **during the warmer months**: *Bats and Their Habitats, Countryside Management Series 6* (Bat Conservation Ireland).

CHAPTER 13: THREE REVOLUTIONS, THREE EXTINCTION WAVES

213   **lack of nesting sites**: Allan Mee *et al.*, 'Reintroduction of White-tailed Eagles Haliaeetus albicilla to Ireland', *Irish Birds* (January 2016), 301.

213 **extinct as a breeding species:** *ibid.*, 302.

213 **goshawk, marsh harrier:** *ibid.*, 302.

214 **donated to Ireland by Norway:** *ibid.*, 301.

214 **settled in Beara:** Golden eagles have also been reintroduced to County Donegal and red kites to County Wicklow, while buzzards recolonised naturally into the northeast from Scotland in the 1930s, and have been spreading south ever since. There is a tiny goshawk population in Northern Ireland, and in 2020 wild marsh harriers bred in the Republic for the first time in a century. Our raptors are slowly returning.

214 **fractious and confrontational:** Majella O'Sullivan, 'From Protests to Partnerships: How Farmers Are Supporting the Reintroduction of the White-tailed Eagle', *Farming Independent* (9 December 2017).

215 **collision with wind turbines:** Mee *et al.*, 'Reintroduction of White-tailed Eagles', 307–8.

215 **even warm enthusiasm:** Kathleen O'Sullivan, 'Reintroduction of Eagles: Farmer Worries over Threat to Livestock "Have Changed"', *AgriLand* (1 July 2020).

215 **Glengarriff Woods Nature Reserve:** The Glengarriff Woods Nature Reserve is a breath of fresh air for anyone familiar with the ecological devastation at Killarney National Park and other state-run reserves. While rhododendron and other invasive plant species are an issue in Glengarriff too, they are much more under control. In addition, the natural regeneration of native trees is evident throughout, and overall the woodland appears to be in a relatively healthy state.

217 **result of Storm Hannah:** Anne Lucey, 'Eddie the Eagle – First Wild Eagle to Fledge in Cork for 100 Years – Found Dead', *Irish Examiner* (30 July 2018).

217 **contributes more than £4.8 billion:** *Wellbeing through Wildlife* (RSPB document), 8.

217 **island economy:** Emily Beament, 'First White-tailed Eagles Released on Isle of Wight in Reintroduction Project', *Belfast Telegraph* (22 August 2019).

217 **over 3 per cent every year:** John Scanlon, 'The World Needs Wildlife Tourism. But that Won't Work Without Wildlife', *Guardian* (22 June 2017).

220 **biological colonisation of Ireland:** Sleeman *et al.*, 'Mind the Gap II', 3, 108.

220 **connection to Ireland:** Ian Montgomery, 'Origin of the Holocene Mammals of "These Islands"', in Sleeman *et al.*, 'Mind the Gap II', 138.

220 **finds from East Anglia:** Ian Sample, 'First Humans Arrived in Britain 250,000 Years Earlier than Thought', *Guardian* (7 July 2010).

220 **33,000 years ago:** Alan O'Keefe, 'First Humans Came Here 33,000 Years Ago, Reindeer Bones Reveal', *Irish Independent* (18 April 2021).

221 **evolved no defence:** *Diamond, Guns, Germs and Steel*, 39.

221 *progressively working our way*: The disappearance of megafauna may even have pushed our ancestors into developing agriculture. Nick Longrich, 'How the Extinction of Ice Age Mammals May Have Forced Us To Invent Civilisation', *The Conversation* (3 January 2020).

221 **driven into global extinction**: Yadvinder Malhi *et al.*, 'Megafauna and Ecosystem Function from the Pleistocene to the Anthropocene', *Proceedings of the National Academy of Sciences of the United States of America* (26 January 2016).

222 **argument is now essentially over**: Christopher Sandom *et al.*, 'Global Late Quaternary Megafauna Extinctions Linked to Humans, Not Climate Change', *Proceedings of the Royal Society B: Biological Sciences* (22 July 2014); Lewis Bartlett *et al.*, 'Robustness Despite Uncertainty: Regional Climate Data Reveal the Dominant Role of Humans in Explaining Global Extinctions of Late Quaternary Megafauna', *Ecography* (6 August 2015); Felisa Smith *et al.*, 'Body Size Downgrading of Mammals over the Late Quaternary', *Science* (20 April 2018).

222 **megafaunas had survived perfectly intact**: For example, Lee Drake, 'The Extraordinary Mediocrity of the Holocene', *EarthArXiv* (15 March 2018).

222 **humid climates no less than cold**: Todd Surovell *et al.*, 'Global Archaeological Evidence for Proboscidean Overkill', *Proceedings of the National Academy of Sciences of the United States of America* (26 April 2005).

222 **all megafaunal species were extinct**: Wohlleben, *The Secret Network of Life*, 206–7; Fraser, *Rewilding the World*, 322.

222 **In New Zealand**: Yuval Noah Harari, *Sapiens: A Brief History of Humankind* (London, 2011), 74.

223 **human colonists (the Maoris)**: Wilson, *The Future of Life*, 91–4.

223 **quickly brought a wipeout**: Elizabeth Kolbert, *The Sixth Extinction: An Unnatural History* (London, 2014), 229–35.

223 **replacement through the birth**: Ed Yong, 'In a Few Centuries, Cows Could Be the Largest Land Animals Left', *The Atlantic* (19 April 2018).

223 **throughout their life cycles**: Soulé and Terborgh, *Continental Conservation*, 52–3.

223 **as their prey disappeared**: Lent, *The Patterning Instinct*, 97–9.

224 **lion kills into quite recent times**: MacKinnon, *The Once and Future World*, 209.

224 **large-scale 'fire agriculture'**: Harari, *Sapiens*, 13, 95.

225 **entire ecosystems in many parts**: Edward O. Wilson, *The Social Conquest of Earth* (New York, 2012), 93; Harari, *Sapiens*, 75–6.

225 **included southern Europe**: Jed Kaplan *et al.*, 'Large Scale Anthropogenic Reduction of Forest Cover in Last Glacial Maximum Europe', *Plos One* (30 November, 2016).

225 **'genera of large mammals'**: A genus is a taxonomic subdivision that often comprises several closely related species. A familiar example is Panthera, which includes Panthera leo (lion), tigris (tiger), onca (jaguar), pardus (leopard), and uncia (snow leopard). So even many of the genera that weren't completely wiped out would still have lost species.

225 **Others say 37 and 51 genera**: Drake, 'The Extraordinary Mediocrity', 2.

226 **'even insects and parasites'**: Harari, *Sapiens*, 79.

226 **like the Amazon rainforest**: Dalya Alberge, '"Sistine Chapel of the Ancients" Rock Art Discovered in Remote Amazon Forest', *Guardian* (29 November 2020).

226 **wary of pre-*sapiens***: Drake, 'The Extraordinary Mediocrity', 2; George Monbiot, 'Is This All Humans Are? Diminutive Monsters of Death and Destruction?', *Guardian* (24 March 2014).

226 **cascading effect**: Mauro Galetti *et al.*, 'Ecological and Evolutionary Legacy of Megafauna Extinctions', *Biological Reviews of the Cambridge Philosophical Society* (9 October 2017).

226 **the 'planetary killer'**: Wilson, *The Future of Life*, Chapter 4.

227 **puny-looking, largely hairless**: *ibid.*, 94–8.

227 **29 genera were made extinct**: Drake, 'The Extraordinary Mediocrity', 2.

227 **a more meat-based diet**: Monbiot, 'Is This All Humans Are?'

227 **complex and abstract**: Wilson, *The Social Conquest*, 85–7, Harari, *Sapiens*, 23–4.

227 **human-engineered landscapes**: Harari, *Sapiens*, 111. Lent, *The Patterning Instinct*, 109–16, 295–7.

227 **seriously affect marine ecosystems**: Harari, *Sapiens*, 82–3.

228 **lasting from the Pleistocene**: Todd Braje and Jon Erlandson, 'Human Acceleration of Plant and Animal Extinctions: A Late Pleistocene, Holocene, and Anthropocene Continuum', *Anthropocene* (December 2013).

228 **wild terrestrial vegetation worldwide**: Yinon Bar-On *et al.*, 'The Biomass Distribution on Earth', *Proceedings of the National Academy of Sciences of the United States of America* (19 June 2018).

228 **average body mass**: Jacob Dembitzer *et al.*, 'Levantine Overkill: 1.5 Million Years of Hunting Down the Body Size Distribution', *Quaternary Science Reviews* (15 December 2021).

230 **'pristine' rivers in Ireland**: Tim O'Brien, 'Just 20 of Ireland's Rivers Are "Pristine", Down from 500 in 1980s', *The Irish Times* (10 December 2019).

230 **as climate breakdown worsens**: For a fascinating and hugely entertaining account of the reintroduction of beavers to Britain, see Derek Gow, *Bringing Back the Beaver: The Story of One Man's Quest to Rewild Britain's Waterways* (London, 2020).

231 **hedgehog, pygmy shrew and wolf**: Sleeman *et al.*, 'Mind the Gap II', 12–13, 32–4. One paper suggests that most of what we consider to be Ireland's native fauna was likely introduced by human agency in prehistory: Ian Montgomery *et al.*, 'Origin of British and Irish Mammals: Disparate Post-Glacial Colonisation and Species Introductions', *Quaternary Science Reviews* (August 2014).

231 **mountain hare, stoat and otter**: Montgomery, 'Origin of the Holocene Mammals', 139.

CHAPTER 14: BEARA RAINFOREST

241 **futuristic cityscape**: A handy trick for getting a macro view of lichens, mosses, and other smaller growths when up close is to invert a pair of binoculars, i.e. looking through the objective lens, which then works like a hand lens.

242 **the Crowleys called Gloun**: Gloun almost certainly derives from gleann (valley), given the nearby sheer banks of rock that rise steeply up the sides of 'Crowley's Currachán' (a currachán is a small rocky knob or hill).

245 **Anthropocene**: Although the designation of the Anthropocene, and thus the end of the 12,000-year Holocene, hasn't yet been officially approved by the relevant scientific bodies, ratification is in progress. The year 1950 is likely to be chosen as the starting point, since it roughly marks the start of what has been termed the 'Great Acceleration': the period in which the rate of human impact on the biosphere has skyrocketed. Raworth, *Doughnut Economics*, 46, 253–4.

245 **decaying wood**: Milner, *The Tree Book*, 110, 173; Grumbine, *Ghost Bears*, 51.

245 **billhook slung from my belt**: A billhook is a hand tool of similar size and shape to a machete, except the blade curves forward into a hook at the end.

246 **fifth of all species**: cited in Deakin, *Wildwood*, 135–6.

247 **spores of fungi**: Sam Wong, 'Woodpeckers Carry Wood-Eating Fungi That May Help Them Dig Holes', *New Scientist* (23 March 2016).

249 **the lone acacias**: Wilson, *The Future of Life*, 135.

CHAPTER 15: FLEETING SHADOWS

252 **'canyon coyotes and the chaparral birds'**: Biologist Michael Soulé found that in the canyons near his home in California, those in which coyotes had been exterminated had a very low diversity and abundance of wild birds, while those in which the coyotes were still present were the opposite. He realised that the coyotes were controlling the numbers and behaviour of domestic cats and other medium-sized predators (mesopredators). Once the coyotes were gone, there was nothing to stop the cats from wiping out the birds. This understanding led to his theory of mesopredator release, which has already been mentioned.

253 **'grind to a halt'**: Fraser, *Rewilding the World*, 5.

254 **a dramatic turnaround**: Colin Lawton *et al.*, *Irish Squirrel Survey 2012*, *Irish Wildlife Manual No. 89*, prepared for the National Parks and Wildlife Service (2015).

254 **in alien conifer plantations**: Joshua Twining *et al.*, 'Habitat Mediates Coevolved But Not Novel Species Interactions', *Proceedings of the Royal Society B* (12 January 2022).

254 **returning in their wake**: Colin Lawton *et al.*, 'All-Ireland Squirrel and Pine Marten Survey 2019' (National Parks and Wildlife Service report, 2020).

255 **effect on grey squirrels**: Emma Sheehy *et al.*, 'The Enemy of My Enemy Is My Friend: Native Pine Marten Recovery Reverses the Decline of the Red Squirrel by Suppressing Grey Squirrel Populations', *Proceedings of the Royal Society B* (7 March 2018).

255 **goshawk**: A very few goshawk are present in Northern Ireland, but not in numbers that are considered to constitute a viable population. A planned reintroduction would probably be necessary for the species to take off properly (no pun intended). What are we waiting for?

257 **solution to invasive species**: Adrian Wallach *et al.*, 'Predator Control Promotes Invasive Dominated Ecological States', *Ecology Letters* (14 July 2010).

258 **a 'trophic cascade'**: Soulé and Terborgh, *Continental Conservation*, 39–58.

258 **spectacular recovery**: MacKinnon, *The Once and Future World*, 143–4.

259 **Contraception is impractical**: George Monbiot, 'I Shot a Deer – And Still Believe It Was the Ethical Thing To Do', *Guardian* (11 February 2020).

260 **'target-rich'**: Anne Lucey, '"Significant" Cull of Deer Taking Place in Killarney National Park Branded as "Mass Slaughter"', *Farming Independent* (24 September 2018).

260 **shooting does nothing**: Soulé and Terborgh, *Continental Conservation*, 56.

261 **big stags**: Shooting males does little to reduce a population.

261 ***Whittled Away***: Fogarty, *Whittled Away*, 298–301.

261 **gone by about 1710**: McCracken, *The Irish Woods*, 30.

262 **'cost-effective biological control'**: Jennifer Raynor *et al.*, *Quantifying Economic Benefits of Apex Predators: Effects of Wolves on Deer-Vehicle Collisions*, joint study by Wesleyan University and the University of Wisconsin-Madison (October 2019).

262 **wild prey species**: John Platt, 'How to Protect both Wolves and Livestock', *The Revelator* (14 May 2020).

263 **hasn't been generally accepted**: Peter Woodman *et al.*, 'The Irish Quaternary Fauna Project', *Quaternary Science Reviews* (December 1997), 141.

263 **lynx's native status:** Fogarty, *Whittled Away*, 301.

264 **ease the mesopredator release:** Marianne Pasanen-Mortensen *et al.*, 'Where Lynx Prevail, Foxes Will Fail – Limitation of a Mesopredator in Eurasia', *Global Ecology and Biogeography* (19 February 2013).

264 **reintroduction in Ireland too:** Patrick Barkham, 'Dam Fine: Estate Owners Across UK Queue Up To Reintroduce Beavers', *Guardian* (1 February 2020).

CHAPTER 16: MORE COMPLEX THAN WE CAN THINK

268 **healthy local population:** I subsequently found from the invaluable Biodiversity Ireland database that pine martens had been in the locality for at least some years before.

268 **brown trout, eels:** Although I have yet to see fish in the streams, freshwater ecologist Bill Quirke, who visited the woods in 2021, told me their presence was not unlikely. The otters' visits reinforce that possibility.

270 **16,000 species in Ireland:** Eileen Reilly, 'An Ever Closing Gap? Modern Ecological and Palaeoecological Contributions towards Understanding the Irish Post-Glacial Insect Fauna', *Irish Naturalists' Journal* (July 2008), 65.

270 **same goes for the bryophytes:** Lockhart *et al.*, *Rare and Threatened Bryophytes*, 2; Whelan, *Lichens of Ireland*, 1.

272 **'free game for inquiry':** Lent, *The Patterning Instinct*, 235–8.

272 **and are mutually reinforcing:** *ibid.*, 357–73.

278 **static equilibrium thereafter:** Grumbine, *Ghost Bears*, 32–6, 58–63.

278 **'shifting-mosaic steady state':** *ibid.*, 55.

278 **Heraclitus's observation:** Heraclitus further encapsulated this philosophy with the observation that 'No man ever steps into the same river twice, for it is not the same river, and he is not the same man.'

279 **known as Dexters:** Bought from a possible local descendant of Randolph O'Lynchigh, the pre-Cromwellian landowner in the area, if the surname is anything to go by.

280 **harsh Atlantic weather:** Katie Manning *et al.*, 'Size Reduction in Early European Domestic Cattle Relates to Intensification of Neolithic Herding Strategies', *Plos One* (2 December 2015).

281 **survived in folk memory:** Verling, *Beara Woman Talking*, 23.

284 **well established as scientific fact:** Many of these revelations have recently been very neatly distilled by Peter Wohlleben in his brilliant book *The Hidden Life of Trees: What They Feel, How They Communicate: Discoveries from a Secret World* (London, 2017).

285 **fungi can't photosynthesise:** Long thought of as plants, fungi now form their own scientific kingdom, distinct from plants or animals; indeed, molecular evidence has shown them to actually be more closely related to the latter.

286 **chances of survival** *fourfold*: Suzanne Simard, *How Trees Talk to Each Other* (TEDSummit talk, June 2016).

287 **pheromones that convey**: Wohlleben, *The Hidden Life of Trees*, Chapter 2.

287 **community self-help group**: Michael Pollan, 'The Intelligent Plant: Scientists Debate a New Way of Understanding Flora', *The New Yorker* (23 December 2013).

288 **alone or in hedgerows**: Kelly, 'Trees and Woodlands', 62–3.

288 **symbiosis, rather than competition**: Charles Mann, 'Lynn Margulis: Science's Unruly Earth Mother', *Science* (19 April 1991).

288 **'Life did not take over'**: quoted in Capra, *The Web of Life*, 232

289 **'They have the behaviors'**: Brandon Keim, 'Never Underestimate the Intelligence of Trees: Plants Communicate, Nurture Their Seedlings, and Have Emotional Responses', *Nautilus* (31 October 2019).

CHAPTER 17: THE NARROW STRIP OF EARTH/AIR/WATER

293 **TD Neasa Hourigan**: TD stands for Teachta Dála: member of the Dáil, the Irish parliament; Uragh was discussed in the Dáil on 7 October 2021. I was later privately informed that, earlier that year, a funding application for a new fence around Uragh had been turned down by decision-makers in the NPWS.

294 **causing to ecosystems**: Stephan Harding, *Animate Earth: Science, Intuition and Gaia* (Cambridge, 2009), 58.

295 **Lovelock was also the first**: Though one of the greatest scientists and thinkers of the last hundred years, like all of us Lovelock gets it very seriously wrong sometimes too, as demonstrated by his enthusiastic support for highly polluting, climate-wrecking and dangerous fracking (hydraulic fracturing). Leo Hickman, 'Interview with James Lovelock: The UK Should Be Going Mad for Fracking', *Guardian* (15 June 2012).

295 **working for NASA**: Harding, *Animate Earth*, 60.

296 **writer William Golding**: Lovelock, *The Vanishing Face of Gaia*, 128–9.

297 **'but not as a scientist'**: James Lovelock, *Homage to Gaia: The Life of an Independent Scientist* (Oxford, 2000), 291–2.

298 **'and she regulates herself'**: *ibid.*, 292.

298 **so is our biosphere**: Capra, *The Web of Life*, 104.

299 **how our home planet works**: *ibid.*, 213–16; Harding, *Animate Earth*, 72–91.

299 **'which in turn is part of Gaia'**: Lent, *The Patterning Instinct*, 371.

300 **Gaia seems to resonate**: Harding, *Animate Earth*, 264.

300 **'no pre-determined end point'**: Wright *et al.*, *Scotland: A Rewilding Journey*, 34.

300 **a total of 440 million:** Brian Hutton, 'Climate Change: Ireland Plans To Plant 440m Trees by 2040', *The Irish Times* (31 August 2019).

301 **the last *15 million years*:** Jonathan Watts, 'CO₂ in Earth's Atmosphere Nearing Levels of 15m Years Ago', *Guardian* (9 July 2020).

301 **loaded into the atmosphere in 2021:** 'Global CO₂ Emissions Rebounded to their Highest Level in History in 2021', International Energy Agency press release (8 March 2022).

302 **mostly non-native conifers:** Patrick Monahan, 'Europe's Trees Have Been Warming the Planet', *Science* (5 February 2016).

302 **reflect solar radiation:** Milner, *The Tree Book*, 110–11.

302 **The Amazon alone:** Fraser, *Rewilding the World*, 8.

303 **carbon is actually *emitted*:** Kevin O'Sullivan and Seán McCárthaigh, 'Irish Forestry "Net Emitter of Greenhouse Gases"', *The Irish Times* (29 October 2020).

303 ***40 times* more carbon:** Simon Lewis *et al.*, 'Restoring Natural Forests is the Best Way to Remove Atmospheric Carbon', *Nature* (2 April 2019).

303 **'any other forest ecosystem':** Sara Oldfield, *Rainforest* (London, 2002), 143; Paul Koberstein and Jessica Applegate, 'Tall and Old or Dense and Young: Which Kind of Forest is Better for the Climate?', *Mongabay* (23 May 2019).

303 **block up the drains:** Paddy Woodworth, *Our Once and Future Planet: Restoring the World in the Climate Change Century* (Chicago, 2013), Chapter 13.

304 **from elephants and lions:** The numbers of African lions in the wild, for example, have dropped by a full half since the animated film *The Lion King* was released in 1994. Poaching, habitat loss (due to the expansion of farmland), and lack of prey (due to hunting for bushmeat) are the main drivers of their rapid disappearance. Olivia Prentzel, 'Where Lions Once Ruled, They Are Now Quietly Disappearing', *National Geographic* (July 2019).

304 **even more pressing issue:** John Vidal, 'The Rapid Decline of the Natural World is a Crisis even Bigger than Climate Change', *Huffington Post* (15 March 2019).

304 **defies all logic:** Bibi Van der Zee, 'Planting Trees is only a Good News Story if it's Done Right', *Guardian* (25 December 2019).

304 **So why do governments:** Lewis *et al.*, 'Restoring Natural Forests'.

305 **'bulldozer run on hydrogen':** Paul and Anne Ehrlich, *The Dominant Animal: Human Evolution and the Environment* (Washington, 2008), 308.

306 **'either a madman':** Mark Riley Cardwell, 'David Attenborough: Someone Who Believes in Infinite Growth is "Either a Madman or an Economist"', *Mongabay* (16 October 2013).

Endnotes

307 **a complete fallacy:** Jason Hickel and Giorgios Kallis, 'Is Green Growth Possible?', *New Political Economy* (17 April 2019); James Ward *et al.*, 'The Decoupling Delusion: Rethinking Growth and Sustainability', *The Conversation* (12 March 2017).

308 **'improving human well-being':** William Ripple *et al.*, 'World Scientists Warning of a Climate Emergency', *Bio Science* (5 November 2019).

308 **more balanced model:** David Hall, 'NZ has Dethroned GDP as a Measure of Success, but will Ardern's Government be Transformational?', *The Conversation* (7 June 2019).

308 **change in direction *is* possible:** Kate Raworth's *Doughnut Economics* is a 'must read' for anyone interested in creating a decent society for everyone, but within planetary limits.

309 **'the major factor':** Jared Diamond, *Collapse: How Societies Choose to Fail or Survive* (New York, 2005), 487.

CHAPTER 18: SHARING OUR EARTH WITH OTHER CREATURES

310 **But it pales utterly:** David George Haskell, *The Songs of Trees: Stories from Nature's Great Connectors* (New York, 2017), 5.

310 **off-the-scale levels:** *ibid.*, 14.

310 **one in nine:** Kolbert, *The Sixth Extinction*, 149.

310 **86 per cent or more:** Traci Watson, '86 Percent of Earth's Species Still Unknown? Millions of Organisms Unnamed as Extinction Accelerates, Study Says', *National Geographic* (25 August 2011).

311 **antiquity is primary:** Kolbert, *The Sixth Extinction*, 153.

311 **a two-way street:** Capra, *The Web of Life*, 226–7.

312 **'empty forest syndrome':** Overfishing by foreign – including Irish – mega-trawlers off the coast of Africa is one of the main reasons why people on that continent are being driven to consume bushmeat for protein. Justin Brashares *et al.*, 'Bushmeat Hunting, Wildlife Declines, and Fish Supply in West Africa', *Science* (12 November 2004).

312 **'save biological diversity':** Wilson, *The Future of Life*, 171.

312 **year to July 2021:** 'Deforestation in Brazil's Amazon at Highest Level since 2006', *Guardian* (19 November 2021). Much of the deforested land is also used to produce soy, more than 90 per cent of which is then fed to livestock, including in Ireland, which annually imports 3.42 million tons of animal feed. Make no mistake: tropical rainforests are being cut down wholesale to produce 'Irish' meat too.

312 **slashing restrictions ever since:** Rhett Butler, '14 straight Months of Rising Amazon Deforestation in Brazil', *Mongabay* (12 June 2020).

313 **grave consequences for all life:** Shanna Hanbury, '"The Tipping Point is Here, it is Now," Top Amazon Scientists Warn', *Mongabay* (20 December 2019).

314 **somehow a natural phenomenon:** Tzeporah Berman, 'Canada's Most Shameful Environmental Secret Must not Remain Hidden', *Guardian* (14 November 2017).

314 **mass extinction event:** Gerardo Ceballos *et al.*, 'Vertebrates on the Brink as Indicators of Biological Annihilation and the Sixth Mass Extinction', *Proceedings of the National Academy of Sciences of the United States of America* (1 June 2020); Leakey and Lewin, *The Sixth Extinction*; Kolbert, *The Sixth Extinction*.

315 **average of 68 per cent:** *Living Planet Report. 2020: Bending the Curve of Biodiversity Loss*, report commissioned by the World Wildlife Fund (September 2020); Vaclav Smil, 'Harvesting the Biosphere: The Human Impact', *Population and Development Review* (13 December 2011).

315 **supercharged impacts:** Patrick Greenfield and Phoebe Weston, 'Banks Lent $2.6tn Linked to Ecosystem and Wildlife Destruction in 2019 – Report', *Guardian* (27 October 2020).

315 **far from straightforward:** Among those environmentalists less aligned with the 'people are part of nature' view is Bill McKibben, for whom nature is 'the separate and wild province, the world apart from man'. Bill McKibben, *The End of Nature* (New York, 1989), 41.

316 **eventual domination:** Harari, *Sapiens*, 41–2.

317 **so presciently wrote:** Leopold, *A Sand County Almanac*, 204.

317 **a chance to recover:** For example: Rebecca Ratcliffe, 'India's Wild Tiger Population Rises 33 Per Cent in Four Years', *Guardian* (29 July 2019).

318 **make 3.1 billion hectares:** J. Poore and T. Nemecek, 'Reducing Food's Environmental Impacts through Producers and Consumers', *Science* (1 June 2018).

319 **climate solutions:** Bronson Griscom *et al.*, 'Natural Climate Solutions', *Proceedings of the National Academy of Sciences of the United States of America* (16 October 2017).

319 **4 per cent of current human:** Jacob Dykes, 'The Carbon Storage Potential of the Great Whales Mean they are Worth Millions to Humanity', *Geographical* (17 November 2020).

320 **at least 1.3 billion people:** Sabira Alkira *et al.*, *Charting Pathways out of Multidimensional Poverty: Achieving the SDGs*, document prepared for the United Nations Development Programme (2020), 3.

321 **setting aside at least half:** Wilson, *Half-Earth*.

321 **High Nature Value farming replacing:** Harvey Locke, 'Nature Needs (at least) Half: A Necessary New Agenda for Protected Areas', in Wuerthner *et al.*, *Protecting the Wild*, 11.

322 **Aichi (Japan) in 2010:** Patrick Greenfield, 'UN Draft Plan Sets 2030 Target to Avert Earth's Sixth Mass Extinction', *Guardian* (13 January 2020).

322 **continues to disappear:** Wuerthner *et al.*, *Protecting the Wild*, 270–1.

322 **'often the best protectors':** Jeremy Hance, 'Could We Set Aside Half the Earth for Nature?', *Guardian* (15 June 2016).

323 **social, as well as ecological:** Helen Kopnina, 'Toward an Equitable Future for All Species', *Springer Nature* (17 January 2020).

323 **fair for all:** Sara Bellan, 'Costa Rica: Paving the Way for Rights of Nature?', *Earth Law Center* (28 January 2019).

323 **'sharing our earth':** quoted in Kolbert, *The Sixth Extinction*, 261.

324 **shape and counterbalance:** Christopher Sandom *et al.*, 'High Herbivore Density Associated with Vegetation Diversity in Interglacial Systems', *Proceedings of the National Academy of Sciences of the United States of America* (18 March 2014).

325 **the predominant vegetation:** Jens-Christian Svenning, 'A Review of Natural Vegetation Openness in North-Western Europe', *Biological Conservation* (2 April 2002).

325 **however 'sustainably':** Few words have been so misused as 'sustainable', to the point where it has almost completely lost any meaning.

326 **actually start doing it:** For example, William Ripple *et al.*, 'World Scientists' Warning of a Climate Emergency', *BioScience* (5 November 2019).

327 **Robert Macfarlane:** Macfarlane, *Landmarks*, 79.

328 **'we belong to it':** Wilson, *Half-Earth*, 16.

Index

Index

Acknowledgements

A great number of people contributed to this book, some of them through comments on the text, others through participation in the story told here, and in some cases both. However, none of those mentioned below or in the text are likely to agree with everything in the book, which is based purely on my own experiences, observations, and thoughts. All errors, and there are no doubt many, are solely mine. Some of what is written will likely also quickly become out of date: throughout the couple of years I spent working on the book, there was a constant need to revise sections as facts shifted or new data came to light. Ours is a time of rapid, exciting, but frankly also terrifying, change.

A first word of thanks has to go to both my parents, who passed on to me a desire to always try to see what lies 'beyond the curtain', rather than passively accepting things as they are, or appear to be. It is to them I also owe a deep belief that we are each responsible for being true to ourselves, and actively doing everything we can to make the world a better, kinder, more equal place for everyone, and for all the non-human life on our wonderful planet.

I am very grateful to all the Harrington (Caupey) family – especially Michael and Finbarr, and to all our other neighbours and the wider Eyeries community for their openness, acceptance, and goodness. I hope they will see that, despite my being 'only an effing Dublin jackeen', this book was borne of a love of the land every bit as deep as their own, and of a desire to seek new ways of relating to it that improve things for struggling nature *and* rural communities.

A big thank you to Carol Coulter and Harry Vince, Owen Kelly, Brian Adams, Andy Grenfell, Jason Ellis and Rachel Moss, Clare Heardman, Robert Bohan, Hattie Thesen, Gill Murphy, Conor McMahon, Peter Murphy, Jonathan Williams (literary agent), Ciara Considine, Ciara Doorley and Elaine Egan (all of Hachette Ireland), Neil Belton (Head of Zeus), Jo Kennedy, Grace Van Sprang, William O'Brien (University College Cork), Dorothy Brophy (Castletownbere Library), Fiona Lynch, Jo Cartmell and Paul Tubb. I am also grateful to the many thinkers and writers – both living and passed – whom I have never met, but who have influenced my own thinking, expanding my universe in diverse directions. Many of them are mentioned in the text or cited in the endnotes.

Last, but absolutely not least, I am indebted to the Bofickil rainforest and all its wild inhabitants. My days brim with profound beauty, astonishment, connection and meaning, far and away beyond the realms of anything I could ever even have dreamt of.